LEARNING
MATHEMATICS
THROUGH
INQUIRY

LEARNING MATHEMATICS THROUGH INQUIRY

Raffaella Borasi

University of Rochester

HEINEMANN
Portsmouth, NH

Heinemann Educational Books, Inc.
361 Hanover Street   Portsmouth, NH 03801-3959
Offices and agents throughout the world

The teaching experience reported in this book was made possible by a grant from the National Science Foundation (award number MDR-8651582). The opinions and conclusions, however, are solely the author's.

We would like to thank the students who have given their permission to include material in this book. Every effort has been made to contact copyright holders for permission to reprint borrowed material where necessary, but if any oversights have occurred, we would be happy to rectify them in future printings of this work.

Library of Congress Cataloging-in-Publication Data

Borasi, Raffaella.
    Learning mathematics through inquiry / Raffaella Borasi.
      p. cm.
    Includes bibliographical references.
    ISBN 0-435-08324-4
    1. Mathematics—Study and teaching (Secondary) I. Title.
QA11.B638 1991
510' .71'273–dc20   91-25704
                                        CIP

Design by Jenny Jensen Greenleaf
Printed in the United States of America
92 93 94 95 96   10 9 8 7 6 5 4 3 2 1

Contents

Acknowledgments

My sincere gratitude is due to many people who have participated, at various stages and in various roles, in the comprehensive project that has culminated in this book. I would like to take this opportunity to mention their contributions, which have supported and encouraged the development of my thinking and writing.

When I began my college education, the stories Frédérique Papy wrote about her innovative teaching experiences with elementary school students made me realize that teaching mathematics could be a creative and exciting enterprise. This realization had a great impact on my decision to enter the field of mathematics education. Years later, the memory of these stories influenced my decision to report one of my most rewarding teaching experiences as a "story."

Stephen I. Brown has been another source of continuous inspiration and support in this as in my other works in mathematics education. In the past ten years, I have greatly benefited from his interdisciplinary scholarship, philosophical perspectives, and creative thinking, as well as his willingness to listen to my ideas and help me develop them. His assistance in this work has been invaluable in many ways, from our early discussions on the experience described in this book to his thought-provoking feedback on various drafts of the manuscript.

A special thanks goes to all those who participated in making the teaching experience narrated in this book a success. First, to all the faculty and students of the School Without Walls in Rochester, New York, who have contributed through the years in creating a lively academic environment conducive to instructional innovation and inquiry. More specifically, I would like to mention Lew Marks, one of the founders of the school and its director when I began my association with it, who immediately encouraged my interest in conducting experimental mathematics classes, and Judi Fonzi, one of the most talented and innovative mathematics teachers I have ever met, who worked with me when I began to teach in the School Without Walls and proved to me, through her own teaching, that regular classes can successfully engage in the kind of mathematical inquiry described here. Marilu Raman's assistance was also very valuable as the nonparticipant observer.

Most of all, I want to acknowledge the unique contribution of Katya McElfresh and Mary Israel, the two students who participated with me in this experience. Their inquisitiveness, their willingness to engage in novel experiences, and their rich sense of humor made our instructional sessions especially stimulating and rewarding. I also greatly appreciated their willingness, years later, to review the manuscript of this book and the trust they implicitly showed in my work by allowing me to use their real names.

As I engaged in "telling the story" of our experience and used it as a specific example to draw larger implications for mathematics education, a number of colleagues and students reacted to various stages and versions of the manuscript, each providing insightful comments. I would like to mention especially David Bleich, Sharon Carver, Jim Connell, Randy Curren, Dale Dannafer, Richard Fasse, Lucia French, Maria Gajary, Madeleine Grumet, Bruce Kimball, Edith Kort, Marilu Raman, Gerald Rising, Barbara Rose, Donna Rose, Alan Schoenfeld, Ellen Skinner, Constance Smith, Joan Stone, Richard Thorley, Philip Wexler, and Warren Wollman.

Marjorie Siegel played a very special role in the final stages of the book. Our collaboration over the past two years on a new synthesis of reading and mathematics instruction from a critical-thinking perspective has brought us together into a close intellectual partnership that has been extremely beneficial and inspiring to my work in other areas as well. As a result of sharing our ideas I have gained a new perspective on my current as well as my earlier work in mathematics education and a better understanding of its wider implications for the field of education. Furthermore, Margie's reading and critique of the manuscript have been thorough and thought-provoking, inspiring and supportive at the same time. The book would not have been the same without her.

Finally, I cannot forget the support my extended family has provided me, especially in the final stages of the work. A special thanks goes to my mother-in-law, Felicia, my aunt-in-law, Poppy, my father, Vincenzo, my mother, Maria Teresa, and my husband, Ashok, for their emotional and practical help. The book, however, can only be dedicated to Luca, who was born almost at the same time as the book itself.

LEARNING
MATHEMATICS
THROUGH
INQUIRY

Introduction | 1

Scope and content of the book

The recent recommendations put forth by the National Council of Teachers of Mathematics and the National Research Council (NCTM, 1989a, 1991; NRC, 1989) call for radical innovations in school mathematics. The emphasis is no longer on transmitting an established body of knowledge but rather on making students good problem solvers and critical thinkers, confident in their mathematical ability and able to apply what they know in novel situations and learn new content on their own. More specifically, the NCTM, in its influential document, *Curriculum and Evaluation Standards for School Mathematics*, has proposed the following guidelines for reshaping the future of mathematics education:

> The K–12 standards articulate five general goals for all students: (1) that they learn to value mathematics, (2) that they become confident in their ability to do mathematics, (3) that they become mathematical problem solvers, (4) that they learn to communicate mathematically, and (5) that they learn to reason mathematically. These goals imply that students should be exposed to numerous and varied interrelated experiences that encourage them to value the mathematical enterprise, to develop mathematical habits of mind, and to understand and appreciate the role of mathematics in human affairs; that they should be encouraged to explore, to guess, and even to make and correct errors so that they gain confidence in their ability to solve complex problems; that they should read, write, and discuss mathematics; and that they should conjecture, test, and build arguments about a conjecture's validity. (NCTM, 1989a, p. 5)

These recommendations present a great challenge for mathematics teachers, since they cannot be implemented without a radical rethinking of current teaching practices and their pedagogical assumptions. If we consider the characteristic sequence of most mathematics classes today—a brief teacher explanation of new content, student practice on routine exercises, and, finally, review or evaluation by the teacher—it is clear that this teaching approach fails to offer students the opportunity to make conjectures and discuss them, to experience genuine problem solving, or to come to understand the nature of mathematics. Yet, it is unrealistic to expect mathematics teachers to abandon this widely accepted routine unless we simultaneously challenge the view of mathematics teaching that dictates it. This model is in fact a direct consequence of a particular view of mathematics teaching, which regards it as the *direct transmission of established results*. This view, in turn, is justified by the identification of mathematics with a body of context-free, value-free, and immutable facts and rules on the one hand, and by the interpretation of learning as the successive accumulation of bits of information and skills, acquired mainly by memorizing and practicing, on the other. Thus, a necessary (though by no means sufficient) condition for changing the current situation is to show that these views are outdated and that they work against students' success in mathematics. At the same time, we need to develop alternative views of mathematics learning and teaching and understand their significance in everyday practice.

What I am suggesting is that making the called-for reform of school mathematics a reality will require a *paradigmatic shift* involving both the development of novel instructional practices and a reconceived view of mathematics, learning, and teaching. In the past few years, along with other members of the mathematics education community, I have explored what such a paradigmatic shift would mean in practice. This has translated into the development and in-depth study of a number of innovative teaching experiences (Borasi, 1986a, 1991; Borasi and Siegel, 1989b), all characterized by the following pedagogical assumptions:

- A view of *mathematics* as a *humanistic*[1] discipline—the realization that mathematical results are not absolutely true and immutable but, like any other product of human activity, are socially constructed and fallible, informed by the purposes and contexts that motivate their development and use, and shaped by cultural as well as personal values (see, for example, Brown, 1982; Lakatos, 1978; Schoenfeld, in press).
- A view of *knowledge* more generally not as a stable body of established results but as a dynamic process of inquiry, where uncertainty, conflict, and doubt provide the motivation for the continuous search for a more refined understanding of the world (see, for example, Dewey, 1933).

- A view of *learning* as a generative process of meaning-making that is personally constructed, informed by the context and purpose of the learning activity itself, and enhanced by social interactions (see, for example, Resnick, 1988; Lave, 1988).
- A view of *teaching* as providing necessary support to students' own search for understanding by creating a rich learning environment that can stimulate student inquiry and by organizing the mathematics classroom as a community of learners engaged in the creation of mathematical knowledge (see, for example, Barnes, 1985; Lampert, 1990; Schoenfeld, in press).

Because of the insights I gained in analyzing examples of innovative practice that were informed by these assumptions, I have identified *humanistic inquiry* as a valuable metaphor for rethinking mathematics education. Rather than attempting to define this notion, I have chosen to let its meaning unfold as I narrate the story of a specific instructional experience in which students engaged in this kind of inquiry within the context of school mathematics. In the final chapters of the book, I will discuss more explicitly the essence of a humanistic inquiry approach to mathematics instruction and its implications for school mathematics reform.

The experience I have chosen to describe consisted of a ten-lesson "mini-course" on mathematical definitions. It was conducted with two sixteen-year-old female students who perceived mathematics as a cut-and-dried, deterministic discipline and consequently disliked it. The course was designed to engage the students in a personal inquiry into the nature of mathematical definitions. A series of thought-provoking mathematical activities was organized to help the students appreciate some of the special characteristics of mathematical definitions, to recognize their various roles and uses within mathematics, and at the same time to become aware that mathematical definitions are not as "perfect" as one might expect.

Learning about mathematical definitions, however worthwhile in itself, was not my only objective in this mini-course. I had chosen to focus on this topic because I believed it could provide a good context for the students to engage in genuine mathematical inquiry and thus act as "real" mathematicians. By using the notion of mathematical definition as a case study, I also hoped that the students would come to appreciate the humanistic dimensions of mathematics—in particular, that even in this discipline there are issues about which no agreement can be reached and for which alternative solutions are possible; that there are mathematical results that are not always absolutely right or wrong but depend to a certain extent on context; and that there are places in mathematics where personal judgment and creativity can be exercised.

In a teaching situation such as this—conducted with only two students outside a regular mathematics course—very close interaction is possible. Although this does not replicate the student-teacher relationship typical of regular classroom instruction, it does provide useful insights and even has some important advantages over research conducted in a large classroom setting. The small number of participants, in fact, makes it possible to monitor the experience carefully, and thus to report in detail on students' mathematical activities, learning, and growth. The results can thus highlight important aspects of the learning and teaching of mathematics that also operate in the regular classroom, although they may be more difficult to study in this larger, more complex setting.

To best capture the richness and complexity of this instructional experience as well as its larger implications for mathematics education, my report will take the form of a story (Connelly and Clandinin, 1990; Rosen, 1984). I will describe the students' activities in a series of eight "instructional episodes," each dealing with a specific aspect of the notion of mathematical definition and marking an important step in the students' inquiry. My narrative, however, will not be confined to the description of "what happened" in the course of our instructional sessions. Rather, I will try to make explicit the rationale behind the design of each episode and other important instructional decisions. I will report and comment on both the students' and the teacher's reflections on the experience and attempt to highlight mathematical and educational issues worthy of discussion. In this way, the development of the students' inquiry will remain in the foreground, although more general themes regarding the teaching and learning of mathematics will be played out throughout, to be addressed more explicitly in the final chapters.

In the last two chapters of the book, I will move beyond the specifics of the mini-course to discuss the approach to mathematics instruction this experience exemplified. In Chapter 11, building on the results of research in mathematics education and relevant literature in a number of other fields, I will discuss the fundamental assumptions briefly stated here and address issues of equity in school mathematics. In light of this theoretical framework, I will, in Chapter 12, identify what it means in practice to conceive of mathematics education as humanistic inquiry, building on the specific instructional experience reported in the first part of the book and on other examples of instructional innovation. More specifically, I will propose a number of ways in which mathematics teachers can support their students' mathematical inquiries, focusing especially on instructional strategies that exploit uncertainty and ambiguity in mathematics and help students appreciate the full significance of their investigations. I will then consider the major consequences of an emphasis on students' inquiry in mathematics instruction in terms of curriculum choice, evaluation, classroom organization, and students' and teachers' expectations.

In choosing to have the story precede instead of follow a more theoretical discussion of a humanistic inquiry approach to mathematics education I was motivated by both logistical and theoretical considerations. Undoubtedly, I found it easier to write about abstract issues such as what mathematics is and what the goals for school mathematics should be once I could refer to examples in the story. My decision to present the story first, however, was also based on the belief that an alternative pedagogical paradigm gains meaning and credibility only after it is observed "in action," so that its implications for curriculum choices and teaching practices are clear. Readers who prefer to examine the theoretical framework up front should refer to Chapter 11 for a discussion of pedagogical assumptions and to the Appendix for a discussion of research methodology.

In the remaining part of this chapter, I will provide a brief overview of the mini-course on mathematical definitions, in order to help the reader follow the detailed report of the students' inquiry unfolding in the story.

Overview of the instructional experience

After a brief introductory and "diagnostic" activity (Episode 1), our mini-course on mathematical definitions began with some concrete tasks aimed at helping students recognize and appreciate the "standard" requirements for mathematical definitions, such as *isolation of the concept, precision of terminology,* and *essentiality*. Focusing on the familiar concept of *circle*, the students first analyzed a list of incorrect definitions and tried to criticize and improve them to fit their own intuitive image; they then used the "correct" definitions of circle they had produced to solve a few problems involving circles (Episode 2). Both activities helped them identify what characteristics "good" mathematical definitions should or should not have, and why, in the context of some typical school mathematics activities.

The criteria for evaluating mathematical definitions that the students had established were then partially challenged as they tried to create a "good" definition of *polygon*, a concept with which they were unfamiliar (Episode 3). This experience raised questions about how definitions for novel notions are created in mathematics and provided an opportunity to introduce the students to the process of "proofs and refutations" which Lakatos (1976) considers a major tool in constructing mathematical knowledge (see Chapter 4 for a description of this approach). As a result of this activity, the students started to recognize the dynamic nature of mathematical definitions and of mathematical knowledge more generally.

A further challenge to the students' initial expectation that mathematical definitions should be perfectly precise and correct was presented by the activity of extending the operation of *exponentiation* to numbers other than whole numbers (Episode 4). As the students realized the possibility of assigning values to negative and fractional exponents, they also had to accept the fact that they would have to abandon the original intuitive meaning (and definition) of the operation of exponentiation as "repeated multiplication." Furthermore, they encountered unavoidable limitations— such as the impossibility of defining 0^0—that made them seriously question the validity of the results they had reached thus far in their extension of exponentiation. By experiencing these dilemmas and uncertainties, they were able to identify with mathematicians engaged in the creation of new mathematical knowledge, and their view of mathematics as a deterministic discipline began to change.

Their realization that the meaning of a mathematical definition depends essentially on *context* became even clearer when they were asked to interpret the familiar definition of circle in a new mathematical context—*taxicab geometry* (Krause, 1986; Papy and Papy, 1973), which involves the idealization of the regular street pattern of a modern urban area such as Manhattan (Episode 5). (For a description of its basic elements, see Chapter 6.) Encouraged by the novel experience of working in this kind of "nonstandard" mathematical situation, the students showed remarkable creativity and engaged in genuine mathematical debate. As a result, they spontaneously began to question the nature of mathematical definitions in particular and the "truth" of mathematical results in general.

Toward the end of the mini-course, the students were encouraged to examine further evidence of the fact that mathematics too is a product of human activity by noticing the many similarities between mathematical definitions and definitions in other fields. This they did, first of all, by considering mathematical concepts, such as *variable*, that do not necessarily require a formal definition to be used in school mathematics (Episode 6). They also wrote definitions for a number of nonmathematical notions in order to make a more explicit comparison between the characteristics and uses of definitions in various fields (Episode 7).

The formal evaluation of the students' learning in the unit was conducted by means of an individual take-home project assigned at the end of our ten instructional sessions (Episode 8). Both the genesis and the results of this project provided valuable data on the students' growth as a result of the teaching experience. In fact, the active role that the students assumed in defining the final project demonstrated their increased confidence in their own mathematical ability and the degree of ownership they were beginning to take in their learning.

At the end of the instructional sessions, the students' reactions to the experience were solicited in a series of interviews. The results of these interviews, together with some informal remarks made by the students during the instructional sessions, shed further light on the effects of the experience and complement my own analysis.

Setting the Stage | 2

How the experience came about

Several elements contributed to the design and implementation of the mini-course that forms the core of this book. First, there was my underlying interest in creating alternatives to traditional mathematics instruction that would illustrate how students can successfully engage in mathematical inquiry to begin to understand the true nature of mathematics as an intellectual discipline and become proficient problem solvers and critical thinkers.

I had already developed a specific interest in mathematical definitions, which a series of instructional experiences with both students and teachers had suggested are often not well understood. This, in turn, prompted me to look more closely at the notion of mathematical definition itself and at its treatment in the mathematics curriculum. An analysis of the most popular syllabi and textbooks, as well as conversations with several mathematics teachers, soon made it clear that despite its importance, the notion of mathematical definition is rarely, if ever, explicitly examined in precollege mathematics instruction. At the same time, as I started to explore the characteristics, requirements, and uses of definitions in mathematics, I soon became aware of the complexity of this fundamental notion and of the fact that it presents a beautiful example of the more humanistic and contextualized aspects of mathematics. My inquiry also suggested that such an exploration would be accessible to secondary school students and that it could help them examine, and perhaps reconceive, their conception of mathematics and their attitudes toward it.

An ideal opportunity to put my hunches to the test soon presented itself. As part of an ongoing research project in mathematics education, I had just completed teaching a semester-long experimental course for eleventh-grade students in a local high school. Two of my students—Katya and Mary—came to me and asked if they could make up the coursework they had missed due to many absences and thus earn academic credit for my course. In response to this request, I suggested a "mini-course" on the topic of mathematical definitions, and they readily agreed with this proposal.

This setup was particularly attractive to me because it presented many of the advantages of extracurricular activities (such as extreme flexibility in terms of curriculum content and classroom organization). At the same time, because it offered academic credit, it had the credibility and weight of a legitimate curricular activity—a crucial element in ensuring the participation of students who did not really like mathematics and would never have volunteered for "extra" mathematical instruction. In addition, as a result of the course the two students had just taken with me, I knew that I could count on an already established and positive student-teacher relationship and benefit from my prior knowledge of the students. The students and I agreed that the mini-course on definitions should correspond to two to three weeks of regular instruction. With this time constraint and the two students' specific backgrounds and interests in mind, I began to plan the instructional unit.

As a result of my own prior inquiry into this topic, at this initial stage my overall goals for the unit were to make the students at least aware of the complexity of the notion of mathematical definition, of the diverse uses made of definitions in mathematics, of the dynamic nature of mathematical definitions, and of the role played by context in the interpretation of a specific definition. At the same time, I wanted to use the students' specific inquiry into mathematical definitions as a way to encourage them to reflect on the nature of mathematics, to invite them to challenge and reconceive their view of mathematics, to become more confident in their ability to do mathematics, and to take a more active stance as mathematics learners.

I was aware that secondary school students needed appropriate learning experiences to achieve these goals, so I planned a series of activities centered around the analysis of a few specific definitions, which I hoped would provide a concrete context for the students to raise and explore some fundamental questions. My initial plan, however, was meant only as a guideline for the actual development of the instructional sessions, since I was expecting these ideas to go through a considerable amount of elaboration and change in response to the students' input and reactions. The design and rationale of each instructional episode thus form part of the story. Further details on the planning process and the specific agenda for each instructional session can be found in the Appendix. This chapter provides information about the context in which the teaching experience took place—about me as the researcher/instructor who designed and led the instructional experience, about the school the students attended and where the meetings were held, and finally, about the two students themselves.

The researcher/instructor

To correctly interpret any instructional experience, it is important to know about the beliefs, goals, attitudes, and personality of the teacher. In this case, the reader will be able to gather most of these elements as my own character as well as the students' unfold along with the story of our inquiry on mathematical definitions. Furthermore, my mathematical and pedagogical assumptions will be explicitly stated in Chapter 11. At this point, however, I would like to provide some information about myself as a "high school mathematics teacher" and about the roles I played in the teaching experience.

The students were aware that I was not a regular teacher in their school but a university researcher in mathematics education—although Mary admitted to me later that, when I started coming to their school, she believed for a while that I was a student teacher because of my appearance. Yet my credibility and legitimacy as a mathematics teacher were already firmly established when the mini-course took place, because of the regular semester-long mathematics course I had already taught, during which I had been treated as a peer by their mathematics teacher. As I started the mini-course, my experience as a high school teacher was limited to that course and a few other isolated experimental lessons. Having completed most of my education in Europe, I was also somewhat new to the climate and traditions of American high schools. While this lack of familiarity with secondary school teaching occasionally caused some blunders, I also believe it contributed some positive elements. Since I did not have to break free of past practices that had proved successful in the context of the regular classroom, it was often easier for me to conceive and adopt unconventional teaching approaches and roles than it would have been for an experienced mathematics teacher.

My double role of researcher and instructor provided considerable advantages. Since I was designing the very unit I was teaching, I had many opportunities to adapt the curriculum to fit both my research goals and the specific needs and personalities of the students. In order to be most effective, I found that it was important for me to be able to modify some of the planned activities "on the spot," in response to the students' reactions and immediate feedback. I also took advantage of my dual role to review my rationale as a teacher for all the instructional decisions I made while teaching the unit, as well as to probe the students about their own thinking processes and decisions whenever I felt the need. Both my teaching and my research benefitted as a result.

The school

It is important at this point to briefly describe the unusual philosophy, character, and organization of the school attended by the two students and where the teaching experience took place. Even if no constraints or influence on the content and structure of the mini-course came from the school itself, the environment and culture it provided had a considerable impact on the experience.

The School Without Walls in Rochester, New York, is one of the oldest alternative high schools in the country. As its name suggests, it has attempted to reconceive schooling in order to break down the barriers that currently exist between school and community, students and teachers, and the various subjects into which the curriculum is traditionally subdivided. A characteristic feature of this school is its "extended classes," which run for two and a half hours four mornings a week and integrate instruction in basic skills, humanities, and social sciences around some unifying theme, such as "The Human Mind" or "Living in the Twentieth Century." Students are encouraged to use resources outside the school for at least some of their assignments. They are also expected to perform some form of community service as one of their graduation requirements, in order to take advantage of the kind of informal education provided by participating in "real-life" activities.

The ultimate goal of the School Without Walls is that of enabling its students to learn how to learn. Thus, in all courses explicit attention is devoted to the processes and methods employed in learning. Students are expected to become highly independent learners responsible for their own learning. This translates most of the time into an emphasis on individual projects that allow students to choose what to focus on and how and to demonstrate their ability to carry on learning on their own. Some teachers also try to involve the students to some extent in planning the content and organization of their courses. Consistent with these principles, evaluation in the school is also conducted in an alternative way: grades have been replaced by detailed individual reports on how each student is progressing in the course. These reports are prepared jointly with the student after periodic teacher-student conferences.

The educational goals informing the School Without Walls were compatible with those motivating my own attempts at instructional innovation. I knew this would provide invaluable support for my own efforts, and this realization weighed heavily in my decision to conduct my teaching within this setting. It is important, however, to dispel the notion that the School Without Walls provided an ideal "out-of-this world" haven for implementing instructional innovation in mathematics. Despite its emphasis on academic integration, at the time the mini-course took place both mathematics and science played a minor role in the school. Mathematics instruction took the form of separate subject matter courses offered in the afternoon and was not a part of any of the extended classes. The students themselves, and some of the faculty as well, often favored humanities and social studies over scientific topics. Furthermore, the School Without Walls is far from being an elitist institution. As part of the Rochester City School District, a large inner-city school district, it enrolls a varied student population. Although students and parents must consciously choose this school over other "regular" high schools in the same district, this does not automatically eliminate problems of misbehavior or irresponsibility among its student population. It is not unusual for a student to misuse the high degree of freedom and initiative allowed by the school's structure, especially as a freshman. Drug problems, difficult family situations, personal problems, and the like affect the student population of the School Without Walls as they do the students in most other inner-city schools, although faculty, staff, and students may approach these situations rather differently here than in more traditional institutions. In terms of my research, the School Without Walls provided a supportive, stimulating, and open-minded environment even as it presented a number of difficulties and challenges that made the experience itself close to the everyday reality most teachers face in their classes.

The two students

Katya and Mary, the students who elected to participate in the mini-course, were in many respects "typical" of the students at the School Without Walls: capable of considerable initiative and independence, very conscious of and concerned about social problems, fond of the arts and humanities (for which both had shown considerable talent), and quite unconventional in their appearance and style of living. Unfortunately, they also shared with most of the students in the school a strong dislike for mathematics, as they expressed quite openly in the autobiographical essays I had assigned for an experimental math course I taught the semester before. (Here and throughout the rest of the text, the initials R, M, or K indicate whether the person speaking or writing is Raffaella (the researcher/instructor), Mary, or Katya, respectively. The excerpts are verbatim from the dialogue and/or the students' written work, with occasional minor editing.)

> **M:** *Mathematics has always been a sore area for me. Actually, when I was in my first years of elementary school, math was fun. It was simple and precise and I have to (painfully) admit that I liked it. In sixth grade things changed. . . . I failed the class, and every math class since has been a trial for me. I consider myself logical, and I can understand things, but I'd rather avoid ever trying to get math.*
>
> **K:** I don't like math much. It does not stimulate me. Numbers just don't seem very significant in retrospect to everything else that my life involves. Math skills are mandatory in dealing with money. Statistics are interesting. . . . Still I have a hard time doing my math homework, probably because it all seems so silly and pointless. Mathematics just isn't as amusing as talking on the phone, isn't as interesting as reading a book. . . . The prospect of sitting down for two hours, trying to figure out the probability of picking one red chip if there are 2 red chips, 7 black chips, and 1,098 yellow chips in a bag seems ridiculous. . . . Doing mathematics makes me feel frustrated, annoyed, repulsed, [but] confident and competent when I understand. My good tests go on the frig. . . . The problem with mathematics is it is too impersonal, useless, I often don't understand how it will help me or relate to my life. Basic math is necessary but I do not understand why I continued in it.

Despite their shared "rebellion" toward the discipline, the two students reported quite different experiences with school mathematics. While both had encountered some failure in the past, Katya could rely on several positive experiences. Some of these were even quite recent—she proudly mentioned a score of 96/100 on the standardized statewide exam taken at the end of a formal geometry course the previous year. Mary, on the contrary, had met with no success in mathematics after her elementary school years and retained quite unhappy memories of her mathematics classes and teachers.

> **M:** *Starting in sixth grade, I had a horrible, horrible math teacher, who at the time I didn't like, but everybody else liked because he was funny. . . . I wouldn't do well on a test and so I'd stay after, and he would sit and yell "Knucklehead, blockhead, Don't you get this? Don't you get this?" And I: "No, I'm sorry" and I'm in sixth grade! And I tried and I tried and I tried! I really put forth an effort, and my mom was helping me, and I would mess up time after time, and I failed that year. And the next year teacher had heard from that teacher that I was really bad in math, so . . . And when I got into school X I was stuck in an accelerated honors class with the strictest math teacher that was at school. . . . She was really strict and tough and no questions asked: here it is, study it, test in three days. I wasn't ready for that after failing three years of math. And then I gave up. By that time I decided I wasn't meant for the subject.*

More recently, Mary had failed the same standardized state geometry exam Katya did well on, with a score of 39/100. Yet she was not ashamed of this result, which she volunteered with no qualms. Rather, she justified it as the result of her refusal to comply with what she felt was an unreasonable demand on the part of her former teacher—memorizing meaningless properties and proofs.

Their different past histories with school mathematics and their different attitudes toward the traditional approach to mathematics instruction and learning come through in the following conversation between the two students, which Katya herself initiated in one of the interviews:

> *K:* Did you do okay in regular math, math like at school X?
>
> *M: No, I never cared much about it.*
>
> *K:* I'm kind of different in this. . . . I started algebra—I guess it was eighth grade—and I did really well with that and AP geometry. And I started doing bad only when I went to Y high school to take trigonometry and I had class like at 6:30 in the morning. . . . And I really hated it, and I lasted one semester there. And I dropped it. . . . I did so bad. I was so bad. . . . I guess I can work systematically at math. I mean, I remember in eighth grade my algebra teacher would write the expression on the board, and she told exactly what step to do, and how to do it, and what the outcome would be, and we were doing the lesson. . . .
>
> *M: The only thing wrong with that, though, for me is . . . then I don't really get into it. But if I'm using my own hands on it, and then clean it, then I remember it.*

It will be clear as the story unfolds how these differences brought forth from each student somewhat different approaches, attitudes, and responses to the activities developed in the course of the unit.

To add to this portrait of the two students, it is also important to mention that most of their teachers recognized great ability and potential in both Katya and Mary but also reported being disappointed by their occasional lack of commitment and responsibility in their academic work, which in turn caused them to perform below their potential. Our experience was not free from this problem, especially since the two students went through some difficult personal times as the mini-course developed. This resulted in many absences and the consequent need to reschedule many of our meetings (so that the mini-course, originally planned for a period of about three weeks, ended up dragging on for almost two months), and produced uneven commitment to tasks assigned outside of class. It will be useful to keep these elements in mind in evaluating the results.

The report of the first instructional episode, which concludes this chapter, provides some additional data about the students' mathematical background and, more specifically, about their notions about mathematical definitions at the beginning of the unit.

Episode 1: A "diagnostic" activity

Our first instructional meeting was devoted to gathering additional information about the students, in particular their current conception of mathematical definitions. After briefly discussing some organizational details, I tried to prompt them to express their views and reveal what they already knew.

R: Why did you use definitions in geometry?

M: So that we bring unity, to make things uniform. So that when we see a certain figure we know what it is.

K: So that you know what you're working with. Geometry is like "real" math, like working with houses, shapes. When you have definitions, that's on top of being visual.

M: In algebra there are things you cannot really define, it's so varied.

R: For example?

M: Something you couldn't write down; in geometry, it's more regular and more structured; it works different from algebra. You have more universal definitions.

This brief discussion allowed me to introduce the task I had planned for this first lesson—asking the students to write down definitions for a few specific concepts in order to collect indirect data about their knowledge of mathematical definitions and at the same time to generate concrete examples that we could discuss later on in the unit. I encouraged them to contribute concepts to be defined from geometry and algebra and from outside mathematics. We came up with the following list of nine items (those proposed by the students are marked with an asterisk): circle, square*, polygon, variable*, exponent*, equation, cat*, purple*, crazy*.

While Katya and Mary were writing a definition for each of these concepts, they frequently interrupted their work with interesting questions and comments.

K: Could I write examples?

R: Go ahead. [Meanwhile Mary sounds critical of her own work, so R tries to reassure her] *This is only our first effort. Don't be too concerned . . .*

M: When things are more in your imagination . . . when things are more of a concept, it's more in your head, rather than writing a definition . . . how do we call that?

R: Maybe some things cannot be defined.

M: [Continuing her train of thought] *For example, something that you can't picture. You can picture a circle but not an exponent. . . .*

M: Cat, purple, crazy . . . you can't have a universal definition for this [crazy], *so put a ∞ sign for it. What is it called again?*

R: It's the sign for infinity. . . . What do you mean by "universal"?

M: That's the only, the most universal definition. That's a definition that will work.

Notice that besides revealing uncertainties in the students' working knowledge of mathematical definitions, these observations also contained the seeds of several of the issues I eventually wanted to discuss. Consider, for example, Mary's last comment. It shows sensitivity toward the fact that in "real life" there are concepts for which we cannot reach a definition everybody would agree on (what she called a universal definition) and raises the question of whether mathematical definitions can and always should respond to such a demanding standard.

The following is the list of definitions the two students finally produced:

Circle:

M: All the possible series of points equidistant from a single point (A).

K: πr^2, circumference formula, = radius, an exact center, 360°.

Square:

M: A geometric figure that consists of four lines of equal length joining at the ends to form four right angles.

K: Length of all sides equal, all angles are equal, geometric figure all angles are right angles.

Polygon:

M: A geometric figure of straight lines that has no sides of equal length.

K: (Quadrilateral): four-sided geometric figure, angles add up to be 360°.

Variable:

M: A symbol or letter that represents an unknown element of an equation.

K: Used in algebra. What you are looking to solve for. The solution usually referred to as x. W + 1 = 3 in this equation, W is the variable.

Exponent:

M: A # that signifies a power greater than one (power meaning the value of the # ((#'s)) as in the power of x^2. (Harder to explain things when they become less imaginable [sic].)

K: Represents the amount of times to multiply a number by itself. Example: $4^2 = 4*4$; $4^5 = 4*4*4*4*4$.

Equation:

M: A statement that presents a relationship of equality or inequality between/among elements (values).

K: Shows the relationship between numbers or representatives of #'s by setting them equal to equation. Example: 2 + 2 = 4.

Domestic cat:

M: A naturally furry, naturally four-legged animal with whiskers and claws and fuzzy ears that meows and eats cat food.

K: Furry, four legs that it walks on, eats, sleeps, purrs. Oppressed by society and often shaved by ruthless punk Satan worshippers.

Crazy:

M: A state of mind considered beyond the normal scale of mentality (of a given society).

K: A state of mental health in which a person is unable to function in a way acceptable to the majority of society.

Purple:

M: A color that is the equal blend of amount of blue and red.

K: You can create it by mixing blue and red or by looking into my eyes.

Let me comment briefly on the content of this list, since it suggests some interesting differences in Katya's and Mary's conceptions of definitions (at least in mathematics) at this initial stage. Mary seemed to have internalized at least the characteristic form of formal definitions as used in a mathematics textbook or a dictionary, since in each case she tried to describe some key properties of the concept in question. When the concepts were sufficiently simple and familiar (as in the case of circle and square) she produced definitions close to those found in mathematics textbooks. But whenever the concept itself presented some complexity or she could not easily picture it (as, for example, in the case of exponent), the result was a rather superficial description.

In contrast, Katya's mathematical definitions seemed written with a greater concern for communicating the meaning of the particular concept in question than for adhering to conventional formats or styles. Once again, this approach produced unequal results. Some of her definitions comprise a list of unrelated and not necessarily essential properties (as in the case of circle and square), while in other cases (see, for example, her definitions of variable and exponent), Katya managed to create a good characterization of the concept by providing useful information about what the concept is supposed to *do* or *serve for*, rather than by reporting superficial attributes.

It is also worthwhile to note the level of sophistication demonstrated in both students' definitions of complex real-life concepts such as crazy and purple, and to contrast it with the poor results they achieved with most of the mathematical definitions in the list, despite the rather elementary nature of the concepts chosen.

While this activity was certainly worthwhile in gathering information about the two students' mathematical backgrounds, it was limited as a means of determining deficiencies in their understanding of mathematical definitions, a fact I became aware of only later in reexamining the experience. Indeed, writing a definition for a given concept "in a vacuum"—that is, without a *purpose* or a *context*—suggests that a "correct" definition should be retrieved from one's previous knowledge. Thus, it is not a "fair" test of one's ability to deal with definitions, which will become even more clear as we proceed.

It seems amazing to me now that I did not realize these important limitations at the time, despite the conscious emphasis on *process, context,* and *purpose* in my initial planning. It was actually a comment from Mary in a later session, when she was expressing her dislike for this activity and her uneasiness about it, that started me thinking about the appropriateness of this task as a "diagnostic" tool. She said, "I was afraid that, when writing definitions, we were going to be right or wrong, according to a book. You didn't make us feel that way, but I felt that way myself. I felt I was going to be right or wrong, according to what the classic idea was." This was one of many occasions that caused me to look at myself as a teacher and reexamine my own beliefs and practices.

Becoming Aware of the Standard Requirements for Mathematical Definitions

3

Episode 2: Working with the definition of the familiar notion of circle

The activity described in Episode 1, however faulty in design, revealed that neither Katya nor Mary felt very secure or comfortable thinking about what the requirements for "good" mathematical definitions should be. Thus, before we could challenge the limitations of established requirements and consider more humanistic and contextualized aspects, it seemed important to examine the established criteria for evaluating definitions in formal mathematics.

In an earlier inquiry on definitions, which was part of a graduate course at the State University of New York at Buffalo (see Borasi, 1986a), the following points emerged as commonly accepted requirements for mathematical definitions:

- *Precision in terminology.* All the terms employed in the definition should have been previously defined, unless they are one of the few *undefined terms* assumed as a starting point in the axiomatic system one is working with.
- *Isolation of the concept.* All instances of a concept must meet all the requirements stated in its definition, while a noninstance will not satisfy at least one of them.
- *Essentiality.* Only terms and properties that are strictly necessary to distinguish the concept in question from others should be explicitly mentioned in the definition.
- *Noncontradiction.* All the properties stated in a definition should be able to coexist.

- *Noncircularity.* The definition should not use the term it is trying to define.[1]

These criteria seem quite reasonable if, given a specific mathematical concept,[2] we want its definition to

1. Allow us to discriminate between instances and noninstances of the concept with certainty, consistency, and efficiency (by simply checking whether a potential candidate satisfies *all* the properties stated in the definition).
2. "Capture" and synthesize the mathematical essence of the concept (*all* the properties belonging to the concept should be logically derivable from those included in its definition).

The rationale behind each of these requirements can be made even more obvious if we try to understand what is "wrong" with incorrect definitions of a well-known concept. This is why I decided to start Episode 2 by asking Katya and Mary to examine a list of "incorrect" definitions for *circle*.

Since both students could easily distinguish between instances and noninstances of circle, I expected that they would be able to evaluate whether each of these definitions described circles precisely, discuss what was wrong with each definition, and abstract some of the general characteristics that good mathematical definitions should or should not have (Episode 2.1). At the same time, I hoped that this activity would naturally suggest how to refine the most promising definitions on the list and thus produce a good definition of circle which we could then use to solve specific mathematical problems.

The following collection of definitions of circle was proposed to the students:

1. *All the possible series of points equidistant from a single point (A).*
2. *πr^2 circumference formula, = radius, an exact center, 360°.*
3. *Round—3.14—shape of an orange, coin, earth—Pi.*
4. *Circle = something whose area is = to πr^2.*
5. *Circle: $(x)^2 + (y)^2 = r^2$. Round.*
6. *A circle is a geometric figure that lies in a two dimensional plane. It contains 360° and there is a point called the center that lies precisely in the middle. A line passing through the center is called the diameter. One-half of the diameter is the radius. I don't like circles too much any more because they look like big fat zeros but they can be fun because you can make cute little smiley faces with mohawks out of them.*
7. *A closed, continuous, rounded line.*
8. *I sometimes find myself going around in them . . .*

The first two definitions were those produced in Episode 1 by Mary and Katya, respectively. I selected the remaining six items from more than fifty definitions of circle produced by high school students, college students, and mathematics teachers. My goal was to create a list of definitions of circle that differed substantially in terms of the following elements: the properties of circle they identified and focused upon, the notion of definition their authors assumed, and the possibility of "fixing them up" in order to create a definition of circle acceptable to the mathematics community. While other definitions would probably turn out to be equally satisfactory, this specific selection served its intended purposes and even went beyond them. In fact, the examination and critique of these definitions not only led the students to recognize important characteristics of good mathematical definitions and to create two acceptable definitions of circle (the usual *metric*[3] definition focusing on the property that all points in a circle are equidistant from the center and an *analytic* definition making use of the equation of circle in analytic geometry), it also stimulated other unplanned but worthwhile mathematical activities.

Verifying whether a definition is good enough to allow us to discriminate satisfactorily between instances and noninstances of a concept, however, only partially illustrates the purpose of some of the standard requirements usually imposed on mathematical definitions. It does not really justify, for example, the need or value of the criteria of *essentiality*. To complement the previous activity, therefore, I also wanted the students to reflect on the use made of definitions in some typical mathematical applications, such as problems and proofs.

To this end, I asked the students to participate in three mathematical tasks, each requiring the use of a definition and/or different properties of circle and a few other familiar mathematical notions. These tasks were:

- "Finding the circle passing through three given points" (Episode 2.2). This problem was selected because it requires a "good" mathematical definition of circle in order to show that the figure produced as a solution, besides containing the three given points, *is* indeed a circle; furthermore, while both the metric and the analytic definitions of circle could be used successfully to solve this problem, the process of solution is very different depending on which of the two definitions is chosen, a fact that can invite reflection on the values and implications of having alternative definitions for the same mathematical concept.
- "Finding the measure of the interior angle of a regular pentagon" (Episode 2.3). To solve this problem, one needs to use several properties of circles, including some that are not explicitly mentioned in

either the metric or the analytic definition; the definition and properties of another familiar figure, the isosceles triangle, also play an
important role in the solution.

- "Debugging an incorrect proof for the well-known theorem, *Any triangle inscribed in a semicircle is a right triangle*" (Episode 2.4). This
  problem was selected first of all because the theorem in question
  involves the formal derivation of a nonintuitive property of circle
  from its definition; second, the proposed proof (which follows later
  in this chapter) was based on the unjustified assumption that a right
  triangle can be defined as "a triangle whose sides a, b, and c satisfy
  the Pythagorean relation $a^2 + b^2 = c^2$," and thus would invite a discussion of the distinction between *properties* and *definitions* of a given
  mathematical concept.

Because these tasks involved using the properties and definitions of well-
known concepts (*circle, isosceles triangle*, and *right triangle*) I hoped that they
would provide the students with the criteria and the procedures necessary
to create and evaluate the definition of a familiar mathematical notion and
to use it appropriately in a variety of mathematical contexts.

Episode 2 developed during most of our second, third, and fourth meetings, for a total instructional time of a little less than two hours. The
following sections describe in detail what happened when each of the
components of this instructional episode was implemented.

Episode 2.1: Analyzing incorrect definitions of circle

A comment Mary made during Episode 1 allowed me to introduce in a
natural way the task of analyzing the list of "incorrect" definitions of circle:
"Since Mary was saying that probably people would all agree about what a
circle is, I would like to give you a collection of definitions of circle that I got
from various people—including you. I would like you to read them and to
comment on them."

In their first pass at the eight definitions presented to them, the students focused on rather obvious shortcomings (remarking that definition
8 was unacceptable, for example, because it was "so vague") or on the
inability of specific definitions to distinguish circles from other figures. As
Mary remarked about definitions 7 and 4,

> *M:* "Closed, continuous, rounded line": that could just be a spiral . . . a closed one.
>   [Mary draws Figure 3–1 as she talks] . . .
> *M:* Whose area is πr^2! Improper English . . .
> *R:* Would that be a definition of circle?
> *M:* No, it's an element of the circle . . .

FIGURE 3–1

R: *Why would you exclude this definition then? Can you show a figure that satisfies this definition and is not a circle?*

[In response, Mary once again suggests her "closed" spiral (Figure 3–1) and observes that it would have the same area as the outer circle.]

An awareness of the requirement of isolation, especially by Mary, was further confirmed by her ability to correct her original definition (definition 1) when I pointed out that a ball would also satisfy it. This produced the first acceptable definition of circle: "All the points *in the plane* equidistant from a single point." In what follows, I will refer to this definition as the metric definition of circle (since it employs only a metric property to characterize this geometric figure). Throughout our mini-course on definitions, I assumed that, despite its unconventional and less precise wording, this definition was essentially equivalent to the definition of circle reported in most geometry textbooks: "the set of all points at a given distance from a given point in a plane." In reality, the use of the term "equidistant" instead of "at a given distance" could be considered a little more ambiguous and difficult to interpret. This did not seem to create any problem in our instructional experience, however, since both the students and the instructor implicitly attributed the same meaning to the two expressions.

Soon the task of analyzing a list of incorrect definitions of circle brought the students new insights about what constitutes a good mathematical definition. The following conversation illustrates how the activity stimulated them to question the distinction between a *definition* and a *comprehensive list of properties* of a given concept, and also to begin to appreciate the value of the requirement of essentiality.

R: *Is there any other definition that you would like to eliminate?*

K: Yes, mine. [The response comes very quickly and forcefully.]

R: *Why?* [laughing]

K: Because I just put anything I could possibly think of . . . and I was wrong: πr^2 is not the circumference, it's the area. I put 360° but I didn't know . . . I don't know what I am talking about!

Even when she had corrected these most obvious mistakes, however, Katya remained dissatisfied with her definition:

> *R:* *All the things you wrote down are correct, right?*
>
> *K:* Yes. But I was not able to put down a round answer, I just put what came to my mind . . .
>
> *R:* *That's also what definition 6 does. Why do you think we may not want to have a long list of properties in a definition?*
>
> *K:* I am not saying that it would not be good, but . . .
>
> *R:* *Oh, you would like to have put even more?*
>
> *K:* I just did not remember . . .
>
> *M:* *But for a definition, it should be stated as simply as possible.*
>
> *R:* *So, we want a definition to be able to identify only circles. And a longer list of properties would probably do that even better. Then why don't you like it?*
>
> *M:* *Why? Because a definition is something you have to remember . . . you don't want to remember all the little things . . . the whole list . . .*

The criterion of essentiality and the distinction between *definition* and *set of properties* of a given concept raised in this exchange are very complex issues. Rather than trying to resolve them, I pointed out their importance and suggested that we leave them aside for the moment, since we would come back to them in later lessons.

At this point, instead, the consideration of definition 5 (Circle: $(x)^2 + (y)^2 = r^2$. Round.) moved us into a mathematically worthwhile digression, which I had not planned or foreseen as possible. It all started because neither Katya nor Mary was able to recognize this formula as the analytic geometry equation for a circle with center in the origin, despite the fact that we had spent quite some time deriving such an equation in my course just the previous semester. This shortcoming, however, proved beneficial, since it allowed them to interpret this definition with more naive eyes than I had done and thus to point out some elements that were left implicit:

> *K:* I don't know what x and y are . . .
>
> *R:* *You are right, we have to say what x and y are, or it does not make any sense. Let's say we were using graph paper . . .*
>
> *K:* Oh, that makes sense! . . .
>
> *M:* *But this is not the full sense of what a circle is, because you do not always have graph paper.*
>
> *R:* *That's a good point. But we can say . . . if you have a circle, you can put on it graph paper.*
>
> *M:* *With some work. . . . This is a good definition, though, because it will only give circles . . .*
>
> *R:* *But, how can you check if it really does?*

Both Katya and Mary raised some good points. I would like to remark especially on Mary's realization that a good definition is one that enables you to isolate instances of the concept and also on her concern for making sure that a definition of circle that relies on "graph paper" is really general enough to include *all* circles. It would have been worthwhile to follow up on this last point to help the students gain a better understanding of the fact that a coordinate system is indeed just a heuristic device and not a "real" grid, and that it can be generated and applied in any geometrical situation as a tool for describing relationships and solving problems. Unfortunately, I did not fully appreciate this opportunity at the time.

Instead, since the students still seemed a bit shaky about analytic geometry, I suggested that they choose a specific value—5—for the radius and then try to verify that the equation $x^2 + y^2 = 25$ indeed identified a circle by creating an x-y chart of values satisfying the equation and plotting those coordinates on graph paper. The students successfully performed the task and seemed convinced of the appropriateness and value of describing a circle by means of its equation in Cartesian coordinates. But this activity also inspired a new question from Mary:

> M: *How would you figure out if something is a circle, if there is no measurement for the radius?*
> R: **Ah! This is a good point!**
> M: *What if they just say "draw a circle" and you are . . . what's its "r"?*

This question at first took me by surprise. Indeed, it is tempting to think that a mathematical definition should allow you to produce automatically an instance of the object it characterizes. Yet we also have to realize that a concept is always an abstraction of a family of objects, which share some common characteristics but also present some differences. In the specific case of circle, although all its instances share the same *shape* they may have different *dimensions* (that is, different radii) and occupy different *positions* in the space (an aspect we often tend to disregard, but one that may be crucial in some circumstances, for example when writing the equation associated with a specific circle in a given system of Cartesian coordinates). At the time I was not able to articulate the argument so clearly for myself and even less to take advantage of the opportunity offered by Mary's observation for leading the students in a discussion of *what a concept is*. The best I could do on the spot was to offer the following response:

> M: *So it doesn't work, because you don't know a circle if you don't know its radius.*
> R: **Do you think you also need to know where a circle is placed, where its center is?**
> M: *No . . .*

I doubt that Mary was able to see through my rather cryptic question. This was one more occasion when (as I would realize later) I missed a valuable opportunity for learning and inquiry. At the time, I was more concerned that Katya and Mary would recognize the equivalence of the metric and analytic definitions of circle and understand the process followed in establishing this result. This is why I decided at this point to engage them in the derivation of the equation of a circle with center in the origin with the help of Figure 3–2. With some help from me, Katya and Mary managed the task successfully and even tried to generalize the formula thus derived ($x^2 + y^2 = r^2$) to cases where the center of the circle was not placed in the origin of the coordinate system. It was clear to them that it was indeed possible to define circle rigorously by means of its analytic geometry equation. Though we never formally wrote down the analytic definition of circle, this did not impede the use of such a definition to solve problems and derive proofs during the following lessons. In each of those cases, we simply used the equation $(x - h)^2 + (y - k)^2 = r^2$ to characterize a generic circle, while at the same time *assuming* all the analytic geometry apparatus. The students had no problem accepting the existence of two different, yet equally acceptable, definitions of circle, as Mary remarked, "They are just two different ways of looking at it. That's a very healthy attitude!"

As our second instructional session was drawing to an end, we had to leave aside our analysis of the list of definitions of circle temporarily. In order to have Katya and Mary start to consider how a definition of circle could be used to solve mathematical problems, for homework I assigned them the task of "finding the circle passing through three given points."

FIGURE 3–2

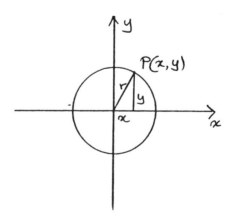

Episode 2.2: Finding the circle passing through three given points

The homework assignment had been given to the students on the hand-out reproduced in Figure 3–3. The accompanying picture was meant to give the students a hint that the problem could be approached in two alternative ways:

- *Synthetically*, by using ruler and compass to draw the perpendicular bisectors of two pairs of the given points and by recognizing that the intersection of these lines is a point equidistant from all the three given points and is thus the center of the circle to be drawn.
- *Analytically*, by finding the values of the coordinates of the center of the circle (h, k) and the measure of its radius (r) by solving the system of equations

$$\begin{cases} (7 - h)^2 + (0 - k)^2 = r^2 \\ (5 - h)^2 + (4 - k)^2 = r^2 \\ (6 - h)^2 + (-3 - k)^2 = r^2. \end{cases}$$

FIGURE 3–3

Find the circle passing through the following points:

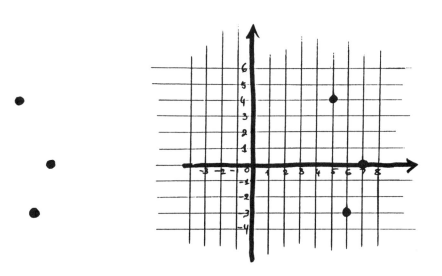

Interestingly, however, in doing their homework neither student even considered the possibility of a synthetic approach. Rather, both of them had attempted to solve the problem using the tools of analytic geometry, and with little success at that! First, they had tried to use $x^2 + y^2 = r^2$ as the equation for a generic circle, and this, obviously, did not work. As a second attempt, Katya had tried to use the more general equation of circle ($(x - h)^2 + (y - k)^2 = r^2$), but she had not been able to handle the algebraic manipulations necessary to solve the problem.

Though the students felt considerably frustrated because of their lack of success in this task, I did not want to spend much time discussing the solution of this problem per se, since it was not crucial to my instructional plan. Thus, I decided to present my own solution using the analytic approach and then to help each student solve the problem by using the synthetic approach so that we could quickly come to what I thought was the most interesting point of the activity: the comparison between the two approaches and their use of alternative definitions of circle.

In a handout I had previously prepared, I had sketched all the steps necessary to solve the system of three equations in h, k, and r and thus find the location of the center and the radius of the solution circle. I asked the students to follow each step in the procedure with me, asking questions whenever they wanted clarification. Both students seemed quite interested in and surprised by the "neat" solution that this procedure offered, though Katya stated, "I would never have thought of that!"

I then suggested that it was possible to solve the problem in a different way by using purely synthetic considerations. With some prompts on my part, and working collaboratively, Katya and Mary were able to construct the perpendicular bisectors for two pairs of the given points (as reconstructed in Figure 3–4) successfully and to recognize that their intersection point would provide the center of the circle they were looking for. Throughout this activity, the two students displayed remarkable enthusiasm, initiative, and creativity, as the following exchange illustrates:

K: It [pointing to the intersection of the two perpendicular bisectors] is the point in common with all three of them . . . equidistant!

R: Okay. So?

K: So it is the center.

M: How do you prove it? Oh, you can make triangles [and proceeds to draw the necessary elements for the proof].

K: Oh, wow!

R: So now you have the center.

M: So now you can use your compass and you are done!

I would like to remark that it was Mary, not the instructor, who questioned Katya's conclusion that the intersection of the perpendicular bisectors is the

FIGURE 3–4

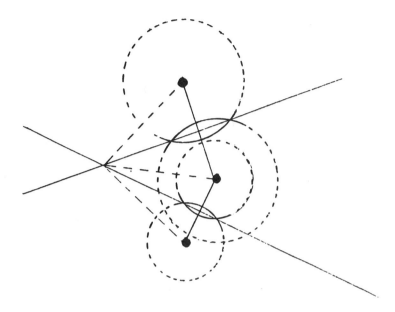

center of the solution circle and asked for a "proof" of such a result. And Mary herself was able to provide such a proof soon afterwards.

To summarize the results of this activity and make its relevance for our inquiry into the nature of mathematical definitions more explicit to the students, I then concluded by observing that we had succeeded in solving our original problem in two very different ways, depending on which definition of circle we used. In each case, however, it had been essential to use a correct definition. To emphasize this point, I suggested that we go back to the list of definitions we had analyzed in Episode 2.1 and check to see whether any of them could have been used to solve this problem. Both Katya and Mary were quick to point out that most of those definitions were too vague or imprecise to be of any help. In particular, the length and detail of definition 6 made them start to appreciate the criterion of essentiality, since it would have been very cumbersome to try to verify such a long list of statements every time we had to decide whether a proposed solution was a circle or not. These considerations brought us to revisit once again the distinction and relationship between the *definition* and the *set of properties* of a given concept:

> *R:* *If we put something like "the area is* πr²*" in the definition of circle, then it means we have to check whether the area of our figure is indeed* πr² *before we can conclude that it is a circle.*

M: *So with the other properties, can we use them to double-check our definition?*

R: **Those other properties may be helpful in other kinds of problems . . . but a definition is what allows you to make sure, once I give you something, whether it is a circle or not.**

M: *So, when we get to polygon our definition will be the same . . . it will allow us to decide what is a polygon?*

The end of our third meeting forced us to interrupt our conversation at this point, but this instructional episode actually did not conclude here. In a later session, in fact, Katya asked us to look at her first unsuccessful attempts to solve the problem in order to help her understand "where she went wrong." The analysis of some of the errors she had made was very interesting and revealed some previously unrealized parallels between the synthetic and analytic approaches used to solve the problem of "finding the circle passing through three given points." It also reconfirmed the potential for surprise and new discoveries even within elementary mathematics problems, provided that students and teachers are ready to take advantage of unexpected instructional opportunities. This activity may not have added to the students' understanding of mathematical definitions directly, but it contributed to their growing confidence in their mathematical ability and demonstrated how easily an inquiry into mathematical definitions can be integrated into other worthwhile activities in the mathematics curriculum.

At Katya's request, we started our fourth meeting by going over her homework attempts to solve the problem of "finding the circle passing through three given points." After trying unsuccessfully to "fit" the coordinates of the three given points in the equation $x^2 + y^2 = r^2$, Katya had actually considered the use of the more general equation of a circle with the center in a generic point (h, k). Since she felt uncomfortable working with more than two equations at a time, however, she had set up a system of two equations making use of the coordinates of only two of the three given points and had then proceeded to solve it, obtaining the following results:

$$\begin{cases} (7 - h)^2 + (0 - k)^2 = r^2 \\ (5 - h)^2 + (4 - k)^2 = r^2 \end{cases}$$

$$\begin{cases} (7 - h)^2 + k^2 = r^2 \\ (5 - h)^2 + (4 - k)^2 = r^2 \end{cases}$$

$$(7 - h)^2 + k^2 = (5 - h)^2 + (4 - k)^2$$

$$49 + h^2 - 14h + k^2 = 25 + h^2 - 10h + 16 + k^2 - 8k$$

$$24 - 4h = 16 - 8k$$

$$8 - 4h = -8k$$

$$\frac{8 - 4h}{-8} = k$$

$$\frac{-2 + h}{2} = k$$

$$k = h - 2.$$

After correcting the numerical mistake in the last step (so that the final result read $2k = h - 2$), I tried to point out to Katya that she had really been on the right track. Since she used only part of the given information (the coordinates of only two of the three given points), however, she had not been able to reach a final numerical result; hence her initial feeling that all her work had led nowhere.

As I talked to Katya, it suddenly hit me that her system of equations had inadvertently led her to solve (and to *pose*) a different problem from the one I had assigned. Her "solution" $2k = 2 - h$ actually represented *the locus of points equidistant from the two given points (7, 0) and (5, 4)*. In other words, it was the equation of the *perpendicular bisector* of those two points! Once I realized this, Katya's incomplete solution also suggested an alternative approach for solving the original problem analytically. This approach, sketched out below, represents the exact analogue of the procedure followed to solve the problem synthetically: first find the perpendicular bisectors of two pairs of the given points and then find their intersection in order to locate the center of the solution circle:

- Set up and solve a system of two equations to find the equation representing the locus of points equidistant from two of the given points (just as Katya did); for example:

$$\begin{cases} (7 - h)^2 + (0 - k)^2 = r^2 \\ (5 - h)^2 + (4 - k)^2 = r^2 \end{cases}$$

solution: $2k = h - 2$ (equation of the perpendicular bisector of a pair of points).

- Do the same, but with another pair of points; for example:

$$\begin{cases} (7 - h)^2 + (0 - k)^2 = r^2 \\ (6 - h)^2 + (-3 - k)^2 = r^2 \end{cases}$$

solution: $k = 2 - h$ (equation of the perpendicular bisector of another pair of points).

- Now set up and solve a system with the two equations thus found to find the intersection of the two perpendicular bisectors; following our example:

$$\begin{cases} 2k = h - 2 \\ k = 2 - h \end{cases}$$

solution: $h = 2$, $k = 0$ (intersection of two perpendicular bisectors and center of the "solution" circle).

- The radius of the solution circle can then be found by substituting the values of h and k just found in any of the previous equations; for example:

$$(7 - 2)^2 + (0 - 0)^2 = r^2$$

solution: $r = 5$ (radius of the "solution" circle).

This alternative method is not only perfectly acceptable and accurate, it also presents some advantages over my original approach (which is the one generally found in mathematics textbooks) of setting up a system of three equations with three unknowns. In addition to allowing us to better appreciate how the same approach can be translated first in analytic and then in synthetic terms, this alternative analytic approach provides a number of interesting mathematical results along with the solution circle: the equation characterizing the *locus of points equidistant from two given points in the plane*; the realization that this locus is a line; the fact that, while there is only *one* circle passing through *three* given points, *infinitely* many circles pass through *two* given points; and the fact that the centers of all the circles passing through two given points lie on the same line.

I attempted to communicate these new insights to Katya and Mary by engaging them in the verification of my "hunches." This turned out to be quite successful, as the following excerpts from the conversation illustrate:

R: *If you use only the information from two points, what this* [pointing to the equation $2k = h - 2$] *tells you is that there are really infinitely many circles that pass through those two points. Do you understand what I am saying?*

M: *Many circles are passing through those two points just because they can change all the time?*

R: *Right, many values of h and k satisfy this equation.*

M: *k and h are the coordinates of the center, right?*

R: *Yes. . . .*

M: *Wait, wait! No!*

R: *I might be wrong.*

M: *It can't be a bigger circle . . . because when you draw it, it goes like that* [she shows on the figure that this circle would not pass through the third point] *. . . the way Katya got this . . . did she use two of these points?*

> **R:** *Yes, she used only two of them . . . these two.*
>
> **M:** *If she pulled in the third point, then it would make it definite, because . . . there is no other circle than that one that would pass through all three.*
>
> **R:** *So if we have three points, only one circle passes. If we have two—which is what Katya started to do—then we find many circles that pass through those points. But only one of those will also pass through C* [the third point]. . . . *Can you notice anything special about these circles?*

[A few values for the coordinates of the center of those circles are computed once again and plotted on the graph.]

> **M:** *It's going to be a straight line! Because I remember when we were doing the line equations it always ended up like that* [pointing to the equation $2k = h - 2$].
>
> **R:** *Could you have known it beforehand?*
>
> **M:** *No.*

Once again, our open-ended inquiry into mathematical definitions produced some new learning not only for the students, but for the teacher as well!

Episode 2.3: The problem of finding the angle of a regular pentagon and the definition of an isosceles triangle

My major objective in presenting the problem of "finding the measure of the interior angle of a regular pentagon," as I have said, was to initiate a discussion on the nature and role of the *definition* versus the *set of properties* of a given concept. The implementation of my original idea, however, took an unexpected and rewarding direction that turned out to be even more valuable.

I presented the problem in question by drawing a (somewhat) regular pentagon inscribed in a circle and asking the question, "How can we determine the measure of the angles in a regular pentagon?" I also suggested that the students look back at Katya's definition of circle (which, with the corrections we had made in Episode 2.1, now read "$2\pi r$ circumference formula, equal radius, 360°").

With these hints, the solution to the problem itself did not take much time. Katya's first impulsive answer was that the interior angle would be 72°, a result she had obtained by dividing 360° by 5. But she immediately realized her error when confronted with Figure 3–5, and with Mary's help she was able to correct it and to suggest 108° as the final solution.

Mary, however, did not feel satisfied by having produced what *appeared to be* a reasonable solution to the original problem. With no prompting on my part, she reexamined the procedure they had followed in order to convince herself of its soundness, remarkable evidence of a critical stance unfortunately rare among precollege mathematics students. Her inquiry led us to analyze the use made of the properties and/or definitions of circle in solving the problem, much as I had hoped would happen:

FIGURE 3–5

M: *So you divide . . . 180 minus 72 . . . wait a minute . . . Why 72°?*

R: **Because Katya used the fact that the angle in the center is 360°, and there are five equal triangles . . .**

M: *But if we are using this as a property, why are we assuming that?*

R: **Yes, we are using it as a property. We know that this is a circle . . .**

M: *Oh, okay, so we are using it to prove that it is a circle . . .*

R: **No, no! We know that this is a circle—even if I drew it awfully. That's exactly the difference I was trying to point out between definitions and properties. Once we already have the circle, and are instead trying to figure out something else, for example the value of this angle . . .**

M: *Then we use the properties that we know . . .*

As this exchange reveals, Mary was still struggling to sort out the distinction between *definition* and *properties* she had begun to question in Episode 2.1, an issue she never fully resolved although a continuous progress and increasing sophistication in her analysis of it can be observed throughout the teaching experience.

We also unexpectedly revisited the issue of what constitutes a good mathematical definition during this episode, since Mary's inquisitiveness caused us to consider the definition of *isosceles triangle* and the crucial role it plays in the solution of the problem in question. In the following dialogue, this issue was raised in an attempt to justify some of the steps of the procedure used to determine the angle of a regular pentagon:

M: *. . . all these five triangles are the same . . .*

R: **Then this angle** [indicates angle y in the picture reproduced in Figure 3–5] **will be 72. But this is not enough, because it is this other angle (x) that we wanted to know. So Katya was saying, these two angles** [indicates angles x and z in the same picture] **are the same . . .**

M: [To Katya] *How do you know that?*

K: Because all radius are equal and so . . . those angles are equal.

M: *Are you saying "the sides are equal, therefore the angles are equal?"* [In a wondering tone] *This looks like a geometric rule!*

> *K:* It does make sense to me: the sides are equal, so the angles are equal.
>
> *R:* **Okay. How can you show that if these two sides are equal, then these two angles are equal?**
>
> *K:* [A little annoyed] But it is a rule!
>
> *R:* **Well, probably we are again using this business of definitions and properties. What is the definition of isosceles triangle?**
>
> *K:* It either has two angles equal, or two sides equal.

This exchange shows Katya's knowledge of the fact that in an isosceles triangle the property of "having two equal angles" can be deduced from the definition: "an isosceles triangle is a triangle with two equal sides." Furthermore, it seems as though Katya was well aware of the possibility of defining *isosceles triangle* in two alternative ways as "a triangle with two equal sides" or "a triangle with two equal angles."

Her response to my direct question "What is the definition of isosceles triangle?" however, shows a creative departure from what Katya had been taught in previous mathematics classes and led me to perceive for the first time the possibility and value of using disjunctive properties in a mathematical definition.

The definition proposed by Katya—"an isosceles triangle is a triangle with two equal sides *or* two equal angles"—is in my opinion very elegant, albeit unorthodox. It manages to capture the two most fundamental and useful properties of isosceles triangles. At the same time, it does not present the problem most common to redundant definitions: that is, requiring more than what is strictly necessary to identify the concept and consequently imposing unnecessary constraints whenever we need to verify whether a given object is an instance of the concept or not. The use of the disjunction *or*, in fact, makes it sufficiently clear that in order to determine whether a triangle is isosceles it is sufficient to verify only one of the two conditions, whether it has two equal angles or whether it has two equal sides. Since an "or" definition of this kind could turn out to be quite helpful in the solution of problems and since it may come closer to matching the mental image a student may have of the mathematical notion in question, we might well wonder why we never see such definitions reported in mathematical texts or used in mathematics instruction.

All these considerations about the interest and value of "or" definitions in mathematics caught my attention only when I was analyzing the protocol of this lesson later on, so I missed the opportunity to share these observations and questions with the students. At the time, we simply continued to focus on Mary's current overwhelming concern—verifying whether the condition of having two equal sides would actually be sufficient to derive the result that a given triangle also has two equal angles—a concern I also wished to exploit in order to continue our discussion of alternative definitions for the same mathematical concept.

M: *If you have two sides equal, then the two angles are equal . . .* [She seems a bit puzzled].

K: Right, one is going to imply the other . . .

R: *So, if you wanted to give the definition of isosceles triangle, what would you say?*

M: *Two equal angles and two equal sides.*

R: *Is it necessary to say all that?*

M: [Almost whispering] *Not really . . .*

K: [Puzzled] Well, either, but . . . if it's either . . . then . . .

R: *This is really a good example, so let's go back . . .* [writes on a piece of paper while talking]:

Isosceles triangle:
Properties: two sides are equal, two angles are equal

These are properties, but if we want to come up with a definition of an isosceles triangle, do we need to put both of these properties?

K + M: *No!*

R: *No, because in the definition we are trying to write the least we can to decide whether a given triangle is isosceles or not. So what would a definition of isosceles triangle be?*

M: *A triangle with two equal sides.* [R writes this down as "definition."]

R: *Is this the only possible definition?*

K: Well, also "a triangle with two equal angles." [R writes this down as a definition, too.]

M: [After a moment of silence] *Yes, but, but . . . does it really guarantee that if a triangle has two equal angles then it is isosceles?*

R: *Well, let's try, let's check!*

K: Yeah [and she draws a triangle and marks equal sides and angles].

M: [Half joking] *I'm not convinced, Katya!*

With Katya taking the lead in this exercise, the two students worked for a while at proving that the two definitions they had suggested were really equivalent and ended up producing a convincing proof.

As we were approaching the end of the allotted time, I tried to conclude the lesson by highlighting and summarizing the major results of our activity, since it is often the case that students can overlook and easily forget valuable achievements and discoveries if they are not put in the right perspective, especially when they occur as the result of nonstandard learning activities. I pointed out that the activity we had engaged in while discussing the definition of isosceles triangle had put us in the exact position of a mathematician working at creating a definition. Our efforts had not only established the acceptability and equivalence of two definitions of isosceles triangle, but also recognized fundamental properties of isosceles triangles that could be useful in mathematical applications of this concept. Finally, I suggested that the students try to use the definition "an isosceles triangle is a triangle with two equal sides *and* two equal angles" to solve our original problem of "determining the measure of the interior angle of a regular pentagon." Katya and Mary were quick to realize the shortcomings of such a definition in this specific case, since we could easily verify that each of the five triangles making up the pentagon had two equal sides (since they were the radii of the same circle), but we had no immediate way of showing that angles *x* and *y* (see Figure 3–5) were equal. We had finally encountered a powerful reason to justify the mathematicians' requirement of essentiality for mathematical definitions.

Episode 2.4: Analyzing a wrong proof for the theorem, *All angles inscribed in a semicircle are right*

For homework I had given the students a handout reporting a non-traditional proof for the well-known theorem, *Any triangle inscribed in a semicircle is a right triangle* (see Figure 3–6), and asked them to find out what was wrong with it. As I mentioned in the chapter overview, the proposed proof can be considered faulty since it assumes, without justification, that the *property* of satisfying the Pythagorean relationship is a *definition* of a right triangle.

When I asked the students what they found out as a result of their homework assignment, however, both Katya and Mary declared that they had found no fault with the proof. From their reports, it was obvious that they had checked the logic (especially the computations) at each step but had never even thought of challenging the basic idea behind the proof itself. In fact, they were much taken aback when I suggested that they do so in class. Unfortunately, this should not come as too much of a surprise when we consider what is usually required of students in "proving theorems" in high school geometry in the United States—reproducing with accuracy the individual steps of a proof previously presented to them by the teacher or the textbook.

It thus seemed important to spend some time addressing the important issue of how mathematicians approach the construction of a proof to produce a result that nobody has verified before, and the importance of having a "plan" before even getting into a step-by-step derivation of the thesis from the given hypotheses.

Then we approached the original task of finding the "error" contained in the given proof:

FIGURE 3–6

Theorem: Any triangle inscribed in a semicircle is a right triangle.

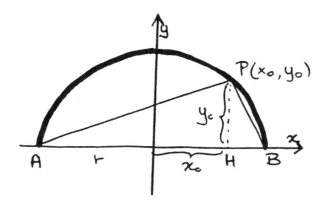

Proposed Proof:
I want to prove the theorem by showing that the triangle is right because it satisfies the Pythagorean Theorem, i.e.: $AP^2 + PB^2 = AB^2$.
We can compute:

$$AB^2 = (2r)^2 = 4r^2$$
$$AP^2 = PH^2 + AH^2 = y_0{}^2 + (r + x_0)^2 = y_0{}^2 + r^2 + 2rx_0 + x_0{}^2$$
$$PB^2 = PH^2 + HB^2 = y_0{}^2 + (r - x_0)^2 = y_0{}^2 + r^2 - 2rx_0 + x_0{}^2$$

Thus:

$$AP^2 + PB^2 = 2y_0{}^2 + 2r^2 + 2x_0{}^2 = 2(y_0{}^2 + x_0{}^2) + 2r^2$$

Since P is on the circle of radius r, its coordinates must satisfy the equation of the circle ($x^2 + y^2 = r^2$), thus $x_0{}^2 + y_0{}^2 = r^2$. Substituting this result in the previous expression, we get:

$$AP^2 + PB^2 = 2r^2 + 2r^2 = 4r^2 = AB^2$$

So the theorem is proved.

> **R:** *Do you think that this is an acceptable way to prove that something is a right triangle? What is a definition of right triangle?*
>
> **K+M:** *A triangle with a 90° angle.*
>
> **R:** *So what would be a reasonable way to prove if something is a right triangle or not? Do you remember what we said about definitions? A definition should allow you to decide if something is, or is not, that object . . . So, if we have a triangle and we ask, "Is it right?" . . .*
>
> **M:** *We have to know the definition.*
>
> **R:** *And we have just said that a definition—it may not be the only one—is "a triangle with a 90° angle." What am I using here?*

K: You are using it to prove it . . .

M: *No, she is not using it to prove it . . . you are using one of the . . . isn't it a theorem, not a definition but . . .*

R: ***A property?***

M: *A property!*

R: ***That's surely a property, because the Pythagorean theorem tells you that if you have a right triangle , then $a^2 + b^2 = c^2$ is true.***

M: *Yes, so . . . you used a property when you should have been using a definition.*

Mary correctly diagnosed the problem with the proposed proof. Now that this point was settled, we briefly discussed how the proof could be "fixed up." Mary's original suggestion was to try to prove that if a triangle satisfies the property $a^2 + b^2 = c^2$, then it must have a 90° angle. She correctly reasoned that this would establish the equivalence of the two "definitions" of right triangle and allow us to maintain all the rest of my proof. I was delighted by this response, since it showed further evidence of Mary's understanding of the role and value of equivalent definitions, but I felt uneasy with the idea of actually trying out Mary's suggestion. My reservations originated mainly in the fact that I had not previously tried to solve this problem myself and that I expected it to be very difficult, perhaps even inaccessible to these students. Therefore, I suggested that they think about the approach suggested by Mary at home, while in class we could try to come up with a different proof of the theorem based on the generally accepted definition of right triangle as "a triangle with a 90° angle."

This decision seemed reasonable at the time and produced some positive results, since the students were able to perform the required task with considerable success. I felt that such experience made them feel more confident in their mathematical ability and more eager to engage in other novel tasks. But my hesitation about following Mary's hunch gave me much to think about later on.

Despite my belief in the value of engaging students in problems for which even the teacher does not know the solution beforehand, when I was presented with an opportunity to do so I clearly got cold feet and opted for a "safer" alternative. Why? Partly, there was my own hunch that the problem was not solvable with only the limited knowledge and experience these students had and my tendency to avoid too much frustration and failure. Furthermore, since I had not tried the problem myself, I had no confidence that I could offer valuable support to the students in their own search for a proof. While these reasons may seem well founded and reasonable, they actually rely on pedagogical assumptions that may be worth challenging. Perhaps it is really only when the teacher herself has no prior knowledge of the problem under study that she can genuinely *participate with* the students in a real problem-solving activity. In this way she can share with them her expertise as a mathematical problem solver by modeling and reflecting upon the heuristic techniques that can be used to approach the novel problem, the decisions about when to follow one possible approach over another, and the procedures for checking the work done and using mistakes constructively. Even more important, the experience of shared failure could be very powerful, inviting students and teacher to reflect upon and reconceive their conceptions of mathematics, knowledge, learning, and teaching.

The students' responses to a review sheet

As the teaching experiment progressed and began to stretch over a longer period of time than I had initially planned, I realized that the students needed some reminder of what we had done in previous sessions. We had no textbook to refer to, and the highly interactive and open-ended nature of our meetings was not conducive to note taking during class. Furthermore, I knew that students in a nontraditional learning experience needed the opportunity to look back at what they had accomplished and be helped to identify, synthesize, and value what they had learned as a result of their activities.

My first idea was to give the students some "notes" summarizing the major results of our learning activities and highlighting their relevance for our ongoing inquiry into mathematical definitions. These notes could then be read and discussed in class. This solution, however, did not fully satisfy me, because it assigned a rather passive role to the students and because it would not allow me to tap into what they had made of their learning experience.

In the end, I decided to try a format I called a "review sheet." I provided the students with a very brief summary of the major activities we had participated in together (to remind them of what we had done in class and why) but then complemented this teacher-generated text with a series of open-ended and thought-provoking questions, which I hoped would lead the students themselves to synthesize and elaborate on what they had learned.

What follows is the section of the first review sheet that deals with the activities involving the definition of circle described in this chapter (for the complete text, see Chapter 10). It provides a good illustration of the spirit and content of the review sheets and contributes valuable information about what the students learned as a result of Episode 2. The original page breaks are indicated by asterisks.

We started our unit on "mathematical definitions" by writing tentative definitions for nine chosen concepts from geometry, algebra, and "real-life" (they were: circle, square, polygon, variable, exponent, equation, cat, purple, crazy). We will come back later to those definitions to discuss the differences and similarities between definitions within mathematics and outside of mathematics.

Then we started to work on definitions of *circle*.

You were presented with eight incorrect definitions of circle (written on index cards), and asked to discuss them.

What were we looking for when trying to find a good definition for "circle"?

M: Something clear, precise, universal, exceptionless.

Do you remember how you decided whether a definition was correct or not?

M: Yes, whether it was universal or not; no exceptions, included enough information to make the def. identifiable.

K: We were looking for a universal definition of circle, facts that were true to a circle and could not be misunderstood as something with the same or similar properties of a circle. I decided by using the trial and error method: basically checking to see if what I understood as the definition could also apply to some other geometric figure. [A few figures are given as an example.] So saying that a circle has 360° would not be a good definition because it also applies to a square.

* * * * *

From this preliminary analysis, we came up with two definitions of *circle* that seemed acceptable to us:

"A circle is the collection of all points on a plane equidistant from a given point."

"A circle is the collection of all points of coordinates (x, y) which satisfy the equation: $(x - h)^2 + (y - k)^2 = r^2$, where (h, k) are the coordinates of the center and r is the length of the radius."

We actually showed why the formula above does describe a circle.

This is not the only case in which we can have more than one correct definition for a concept. We also showed that an isosceles triangle can be defined in two alternative ways:

1: A triangle with two equal sides.
2: A triangle with two equal angles.

Can we have more than one definition for a concept?

M: Yes.

K: Yes.

How can we show that two definitions are equivalent?

M: Yes.

K: Apply them to a proof and see if they both work.

What are the advantages of having more than one definition?

M: A particular def. can be used in problem solving where it is most helpful, or the information obtainable suits it.

K: Well, you can use one definition to construct a figure, then the other to check if they may define the concept in different aspects—one may be a visual description, where the other may simply be a mathematical equation.

* * * * *

In order to explore the role of definitions in mathematics, we discussed some problems involving circles—to see when and how we really had to use a definition of circle.

We solved the following problems:

- How to determine the circle passing through three given points (and we did this in two alternative ways:

  1) by using the formula for circles and setting up a system of equations.
  2) by using the fact that all the points in the circle are equidistant from the center).

- How to determine the angle of a regular polygon inscribed in a circle. (Actually, we solved this problem only in the case of a pentagon, but it should not be difficult to generalize our procedure to regular polygons with a different number of sides.)
- How to prove that all triangles inscribed in a semicircle are right triangles. (A first proof I suggested attempted to prove this by showing that the sides of the triangle satisfy the Pythagorean theorem equation $a^2 + b^2 = c^2$, but we recognized that this was not correct. We then proved this result in a different way, trying to show that the triangle has a 90° angle.)

Can you remember when in these proofs we needed to use definitions and when instead we could simply use properties of a mathematical object? Why?
M: No.

Can you try to distinguish between a definition and a property?
M: Definition → overall identifier. Properties → 2nd opinions, reaffirm.

K: I see them as mostly the same thing. Definitions can be a group of properties or one exact property, but a circle has properties that are also common to other geometric figures, so one property alone would not usually be an accurate definition, but most definitions are made up of properties. I guess I don't understand the difference.

Concluding observations

It is amazing how much learning and thinking went on in this episode, which altogether amounted to less than two hours of instruction. As a result of the various activities involving circles, the students now seemed aware of most of the requirements usually imposed on definitions in formal mathematics and could appreciate their rationale. While they might have recognized and used some of these requirements (such as *isolation* and *precision*) already, their responses on the review sheet and their observations throughout the problem-solving sessions revealed an increasingly sophisticated understanding of the same requirements.

In addition, Katya and Mary had just begun to recognize a distinction between the *definition* and the *set of properties* of a given mathematical concept, even if they were still struggling to understand the relationship between these two notions. Perhaps because of their unclear distinction between the two and their inability at this point to consider the role that context can play in interpreting a definition, they accepted without question the possibility of alternative definitions of the same mathematical concept. It will be interesting to observe them later as they discover the problems and complications equivalent definitions may lead to in their exploration of what happens when the definition of circle is interpreted in the nonstandard context of *taxicab geometry*.

Like the students, in this episode I too discovered some new aspects of mathematical definitions that I had not previously been aware of or fully appreciated. I would like to highlight two instances in particular: first, that in most cases we cannot expect a definition to provide all the necessary instructions for producing an instance of the concept in question automatically, since we have to fill in the value of some parameters, such as the length of the radius and the location of the center in the case of the metric definition of circle (interestingly, this is something that a person could do without even thinking, but it would be difficult for a computer); second, that the pedagogical value of "or" definitions partially challenges the requirement of *essentiality* stated earlier and may suggest modifications to its original description.

Before moving to Episode 3, let me briefly remark on the digressions from the central topic of mathematical definitions that characterized many of these activities, such as the time spent actually solving the three given problems, our derivation of the equation of circle in analytic geometry, and our analysis of Katya's homework assignment and the explorations it invited. I find these "digressions" to be a strength rather than a weakness in the design of this instructional episode, since I believe that mathematical definitions become abstract and meaningless unless we analyze them "in action," as an integral part of regular mathematical activity. Furthermore, I think that this episode in particular provides a good illustration of how reflection and inquiry about mathematical definitions could easily become a theme cutting across the whole mathematics curriculum rather than just a topic in an isolated unit.

4 | *The Challenge of Creating a Definition for an Unfamiliar Concept*

Episode 3: Creating a definition for the unfamiliar concept of polygon

Now that Katya and Mary seemed confident enough with the evaluation and creation of "good" mathematical definitions for mathematical concepts[1] that were clear-cut and previously established, I thought it was time for them to realize the limitations of what they had learned so far. Their experiences with the definitions of circle and isosceles triangle had, in fact, succeeded in providing them with general criteria for evaluating mathematical definitions. They had also become familiar with—and used with success—a concrete process for creating "good" mathematical definitions: Start with a tentative definition and then try to refine it by (a) verifying whether the definition makes it possible to correctly distinguish between known instances and noninstances of the concept in question; (b) making sure all assumptions are made explicit and vague terms avoided; and (c) eliminating any condition or information that is not absolutely necessary for the accurate identification of the concept.

Unfortunately, the very success of this procedure lies in the assumption that we are already familiar with what we are trying to define, at least familiar enough to be able to distinguish between instances and noninstances of the concept without doubt. But what if the concept we are trying to define has not yet been precisely characterized? In other words, if we do not yet know what all the instances and noninstances of the concept are, how can we expect to be able to analyze its tentative definition on the basis of the criteria of isolation? This apparent paradox—having to know a priori

42

all the instances of the concept we are trying to define in order to evaluate its proposed definitions—becomes even more evident as soon as we move away from concepts as intuitive and familiar to us as circle and consider instead what may happen when mathematicians define novel concepts in their exploration of new mathematical domains.

Imre Lakatos has presented a beautiful historical example that can help us appreciate the complexity of this issue and move toward some resolution (Lakatos, 1976). He analyzed how the notion of *polyhedron* and its definition actually developed together with the refinement by "proofs and refutations" of one of the most fundamental theorems of topology, first stated by Leonhard Euler in the following way: "In a polyhedron the relationship among the number of faces (F), sides (S), and vertexes (V) satisfies the relation: $V + F - S = 2$."

Lakatos's historical analysis pointed out how the initial intuitive definition of polyhedron as "a three-dimensional object with polygonal faces" created problems for the mathematicians of the time, since it presented counterexamples to Euler's theorem. According to this definition, in fact, all the shapes in Figure 4–1 satisfy the requirement of having polygonal faces and thus should be considered as examples of polyhedra; at the same time, their *characteristic* (the value of $V + F - S$) is respectively 4 for Figure 4–1a and 3 for Figures 4–1b and 4–1c instead of 2, as stated in Euler's theorem.

At this point, one would expect that Euler's theorem could be relinquished, having been disproved beyond doubt. Yet this is not what happened. The mathematicians of the time decided that in this case it would be more worthwhile to try to salvage Euler's theorem than to stick to the previously assumed definition of polyhedron. This is a good example of how new developments in the discipline occasionally invite mathematicians to modify an established *concept* and, consequently, its *definition*, in

FIGURE 4–1

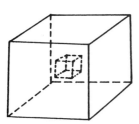
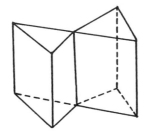

a   b   c

order to make it more interesting and useful mathematically—quite a blow for anyone believing in the absolute truth of mathematical results!

Thus, the task became that of finding a definition of polyhedron that would exclude those "pathological instances" (as Lakatos described an object that satisfies the conditions stated in a tentative definition but does not fit our image of the concept in question) presenting counterexamples to Euler's theorem. The following progressive refinements of the initial intuitive definition of polyhedron were suggested by various mathematicians:

- " *A polyhedron is a surface consisting of a system of polygons*" (Lakatos, 1976, p. 14). This solution, however, is not very satisfactory, since the new definition implies the exclusion of Figure 4–1a as an example of polyhedron but not of Figures 4–1b and 4–1c, which could then still present a counterexample to Euler's theorem.
- " *A polyhedron is a system of polygons arranged in such a way that (1) exactly two polygons meet at every edge and (2) it is possible to get from the inside of any polygon to the inside of any other polygon by a route which never crosses any edge or vertex*" (Lakatos, 1976, p. 15).

It is interesting to notice that even this last and rather detailed definition still might not be sufficient to solve all the problems presented by possible "pathological" counterexamples to the theorem, though it certainly eliminates the threat presented by all the figures in Figure 4–1 (since these could no longer be considered polyhedra). Therefore, even this last definition of polyhedron can at this point be assumed only "tentatively" (for a fuller discussion see Lakatos's reconstruction of this fascinating story in Lakatos, 1976).

This situation is certainly not unique to this historical example and could easily be recreated in the case of many other notions even simpler than polyhedron. Reflecting on this kind of situation could help students appreciate that definitions are really *created by us*, even in mathematics, where everything may seem rigid and predetermined (at least to most students). At the same time, it also shows that mathematical definitions are not totally arbitrary but are created as mathematicians try to shape "useful" concepts to best fit our intuitive images and provide valuable tools for describing and identifying the properties of the mathematical situation they are studying.

At this point in the unit I thought it would be important for Katya and Mary to engage in the creation of a suitable definition for a mathematical concept relatively unfamiliar to them. While trying to apply the procedure for refining tentative definitions to such an unfamiliar concept, they would most likely encounter problems in deciding whether certain "borderline cases" should be considered as instances of the concept and thus realize some shortcomings in the method itself.

For this activity, I decided to focus on the concept of *polygon*. It seemed easy to translate the process described by Lakatos for the definition of polyhedron to this simpler but similar concept. At the same time, although all high school students encounter polygons in the course of their mathematics curriculum, both Katya and Mary had shown considerable uneasiness when asked to come up with a definition of polygon in Episode 1, thus confirming my initial expectation that the concept of polygon is not as familiar to precollege students as we might think.

As a starting point in our search for a "good" definition of polygon I planned to use the two tentative definitions of the concept Katya and Mary had already produced:

> *M:* *Polygon: a geometric figure of straight lines that has no sides of equal length.*
> *K:* Polygon (quadrilateral): four-sided geometric figure, angles add up to be 360°.

As I expected, the analysis and refinement of these two initial definitions did not lead them very far (see Episode 3.1). It was important to me, however, that the students not perceive this failure as simply a result of their own ignorance or shortcomings, as could so easily be the case if they believed that an expert mathematician, or even a good mathematics student, should have known what a polygon really is. Rather, I hoped to encourage Katya and Mary to relate this experience to what happens when novel definitions are created in mathematics—when what characterizes a given concept (and, consequently, its definition) is established even as the concept itself is being shaped—and to make them appreciate that such an activity is truly an important component of the work of research mathematicians and that, in such a context, new criteria and procedures may be needed to evaluate the definitions proposed.

To do so, I thought it would be important to make the students themselves experience the existence of some alternative procedures that make it possible to approach the task of creating a good mathematical definition reasonably, even when the concept in question is not totally familiar or predetermined. To adapt Lakatos's "proofs and refutations" process to the case of polygon I planned to use the following well-known theorem as a starting point: *In an n-sided polygon, the sum of the interior angles measures $(n - 2) \times 180°$.* This theorem was of special interest in our teaching experience, since it could be considered a generalization of the property mentioned by Katya in her definition of polygon-quadrilateral, and its intuitive proof could build on much of what the students had discovered and learned earlier while trying to determine the measure of the angle in a regular pentagon (see Episode 2.3).

In fact, a rather intuitive procedure for deriving this property of polygons is to break the original figure up into triangles—since we know that the sum of the interior angles of a triangle is 180°—as suggested by either of the two figures reported in Figure 4–2. Unfortunately, both this procedure and the statement of the theorem itself may be challenged by the consideration of the "pathological" figures reported in Figure 4–3. Figures 4–3f and 4–3d clearly challenge the statement of the theorem, since the sum of their interior angles is in the first case smaller and in the second bigger than $(n - 2) \times 180°$.[2] In the other four cases, the problem is even greater, since we may not be able to decide without doubt which ones are the interior angles (as in Figures 4–3b and 4–3c), how to measure them (as in the case of Figure 4–3a), or even how many sides the figure in question has (as in Figures 4–3c and 4–3e).

As in the case of Euler's theorem, we would not like to reject this tentative theorem about polygons too lightly. The theorem seems very useful for evaluating the sum of the interior angles of at least the most usual examples of polygons (such as squares, rectangles, pentagons, and so on); it also seems reasonable as a generalization of some known properties of triangles and quadrilaterals; finally, it could be potentially useful in several mathematical applications. Therefore, the best way out of our impasse seems to try to hold on to the theorem and reject instead the geometric figures shown in Figure 4–3 as instances of polygon. To do so, the definition of polygon that may have served well up to this point—say, a modified version of Mary's definition ("A polygon is a geometric figure made of

FIGURE 4–2

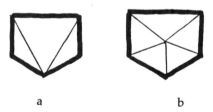

a   b

FIGURE 4–3

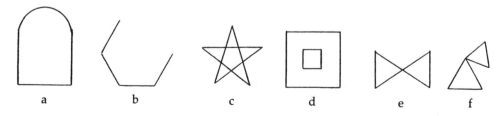

a   b   c   d   e   f

straight lines")—may need to be revised and perhaps modified. A definition of polygon that excludes *all* the counterexamples given in Figure 4–3 may turn out to be quite complex; for example: "A polygon is a simple, closed plane curve, created by the union of line segments only and where no two common segments with a common end point are collinear" (paraphrased from Billstein, Libeskind, and Lott, 1990, p. 372). This is a natural result of the fact that our concept of polygon is taking on a more precise shape and that we are deciding more consciously what properties should be attributed to it. For this reason, we may also be aware that even the definition stated above still may not be the "ultimate answer" because new counterexamples (which we may not even conceive of at this point) could always come up later. Working with a tentative theorem and definitions along with "pathological" examples of polygons, regardless of whether we produce a "correct" definition, has a pedagogical value per se. In this case, it can enable us to gain a better understanding of plane geometric figures and a better sense of which of their properties may be of mathematical interest.

I expected that the decision to assume as an important element of polygons the property stated in the theorem *In an n-sided polygon, the sum of the interior angles measures* $(n - 2) \times 180°$ could provide Katya and Mary with some reasonable criteria for refining their initially vague notion of the concept of polygon itself and suggest a general procedure for the creation of a meaningful (if not ultimate or "perfect") definition for novel or unfamiliar concepts. Even more important I hoped that the experience of critically examining the *creation* of a novel theorem and definition would lead to the consideration of the dynamic nature of mathematical knowledge and of definitions in particular.

The implementation of these ideas in the mini-course certainly confirmed the educational potential of this kind of activity, as revealed by the students' struggle with the concept and definition of polygon that follows. It may also be worth mentioning that the instructional time for this whole experience corresponded to a class period, since Episode 3.1 (the first attempt on the part of the students to refine their initial definitions of polygon as they had previously done with circle) occurred briefly toward the end of lesson 4 and Episode 3.2 (working "à la Lakatos" using a tentative theorem on polygons) did not even require all of lesson 5.

Episode 3.1: Analyzing incorrect definitions of polygon

My suggestion to the students that they apply the procedure used in Episode 2.1 to their two initial definitions of polygon in order to generate a "good" definition did not meet with much enthusiasm. Both students now felt quite dissatisfied with the definitions they had produced in Episode 1, and they were almost a little ashamed to go back to them. Nor did their confusion about the concept of polygon per se make them very hopeful about their ability to improve on the result of their previous efforts. Neither very convinced of nor reassured by my remark that those definitions would only provide us with a starting point and that it did not matter now whether they were correct or not, Mary and Katya nevertheless complied with my request, and we started to examine the two definitions:

> M: *Polygon: a geometric figure of straight lines that has no sides of equal length.*
> K: Polygon (quadrilateral): four-sided geometric figure, angles add up to be 360°.

Little discussion was needed to decide unanimously that Katya's definition was too restrictive, since there were many other figures besides quadrilaterals—pentagons, hexagons, and so on—that we would definitely want to consider as polygons. Therefore, our ensuing discussion focused mainly on refining Mary's definition.

Mary first noticed, with no help from anyone, that her condition that a polygon should not have equal sides was definitely uncalled for and suggested that we eliminate it from the definition. Once this easy correction was taken care of, I presented the students with the "pathological" figure reproduced in Figure 4–4, hoping to focus their attention on the issue of whether the sides should always be straight line segments or not.

> R: *Do we want this to be a polygon?*
> M: *No, let's kick 'em out. Let's be elite!*

Although Mary's intuition serves her well here, her response clearly shows a very shaky basis for her decision. I thought it worthwhile at this point to ask the students to make their own mental image of polygon more explicit:

FIGURE 4–4

FIGURE 4–5

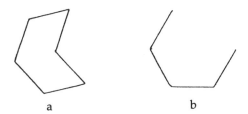

a   b

> *R:* *What do we want to do with polygons . . . so we can decide if certain kinds of figures will or will not be polygons?*
>
> *M:* *I know we have several different kinds of polygons. It doesn't really have a definite shape* [mumbling] . . .
>
> *R:* *Why do you think we may want to have a concept like "polygon"?*
>
> [Silence].

My initiative obviously did not meet with much success. The students preferred to continue to decide almost blindly whether the specific border-line cases (such as those shown in Figure 4–5) I was presenting to them should be considered as instances of polygons or not. They accepted examples of nonconvex polygons (Figure 4–5a) with no problem but refused to consider open figures such as Figure 4–5b as polygons. In order to eliminate the possibility of such "pathological" examples, they decided that a polygon should be a closed figure. Consequently, Mary's definition was further modified to become "Polygon: a closed geometric figure of straight lines." While this final product of our activity was not so far from the definition of polygon usually found in precollege geometry textbooks, neither student was very confident about this result, and they left class quite dissatisfied with what they had accomplished.

Episode 3.2: Working "à la Lakatos" at refining a definition of polygon

In the next class when I proposed that we abandon our "blind" attempts to refine Mary's definition and move on to try to prove a tentative theorem about polygons, the students received the suggestion with considerable relief. The first statement of the theorem I presented to the students contained an unintentional error. It read: *In any polygon the sum of the interior angles is 180° times the number of sides.* This is a case, however, when I do not regret having made an obvious mistake. Because of it, the students were put in the position of judging and modifying the theorem as originally proposed, and the whole activity of "proving" became more meaningful and less contrived than is usually the case in mathematics classes.

The students were invited to try to prove (or disprove) the statement about polygons I had presented, assuming for the moment the tentative definition reached at the end of the previous class: "Polygon: a closed geometric figure of straight lines."

> R: *How do you think we can prove something like this?*
> M: *I don't know. Take a polygon as an example.* [R immediately draws one, a convex pentagon.] *We never really got to the definition of a polygon. We think this is a polygon.*

I want to call attention to Mary's remark here. Not only does it add further evidence to support my belief that the students were still dissatisfied with the definition of polygon produced thus far and critical of it, it also reveals Mary's appreciation of the key role played by the *definition* of polygon in proving the proposed theorem.

Once we clarified that we were assuming "with caution" such a definition of polygon and expected that it would be further modified and improved as a result of this activity, we then proceeded to devise an approach that would somehow allow us to evaluate the sum of the angles in a given polygon. In this process, the students showed considerable creativity and mathematical intuition, hitting very soon on the crucial idea of breaking up the original figure into triangles.

> R: *How could we figure out the sum of the interior angles?*
> M: *Put a circle around it that meets all the points.*
> R: [Drawing a very "skinny" pentagon] *What if the polygon is like this?*
> K: [Has a great insight] Make it into triangles.
> M: *Take a center point. But if it's really weird shaped you can't do it. Oh yes, you could do it. . . .*
> R: *It seems that whenever I have a polygon I can pick a point in the center, more or less. Does it matter which point I pick? Maybe we should ask Katya why it is that you wanted to break it down into triangles like this.*
> K: When you have a triangle, you could work it into two triangles like that, and draw another triangle. Divide it into triangles.

Even if this last comment made me doubt whether Katya had fully appreciated the potential of her initial intuition, I decided to go ahead and apply her idea to my original pentagon and thus obtained five neat triangles, as shown in Figure 4–6.

But Katya obviously had another image in mind, as illustrated by the figure she herself produced while I was drawing mine (see Figure 4–7).

With two figures to support our intuition and our arguments, we were now better equipped to continue our discussion.

FIGURE 4–6

FIGURE 4–7

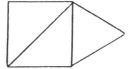

> **R:** *Let me get back to the original idea. Why is it that you thought that dividing the polygon into triangles could be helpful?*
>
> **K:** Because we know more about triangles . . . we know isosceles triangles and how all the angles amount to 180°.
>
> [Some moments of silence.]
>
> **R:** *Let's remember here, the question talks about sum of angles. So one property that seems very promising is that in a triangle the sum of the angles is 180°. And now that we have broken the polygon into triangles, what can we say about the angles of these triangles?*
>
> **M:** *That is 3 × 180° altogether.*
>
> **R:** *Okay. Correct? Then is my theorem correct?*

It was only at this point that I finally realized the mistake in the text of the theorem I had proposed to the students. But all seemed to have been for the best, since the contrast between the result we had just found and the one proposed by authority (my statement of the theorem) stimulated some spontaneous and valuable reflections and suggested that we needed to verify and justify the process that had led to our result.

> **K:** [To Mary] Why do you say this is 3 × 180°?
>
> **M:** [Pointing to the two triangles in the "square" part of the pentagon] *There are two triangles in there.*
>
> **K:** [Still doubting] But you could make this [and she draws another diagonal in the square in Figure 4–7, thus producing five triangles in all—see Figure 4–8].

FIGURE 4–8

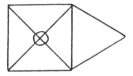

> R: *Okay, interesting. Then you would have five triangles.*
> M: *Good point* [almost believing she has been proven wrong].

In this exchange the students have been suggesting hypotheses and verifying them almost without prompting from me.

As we continued with the analysis of the procedure and were able to justify it satisfactorily, logic soon won over authority:

> R: *Well, the sum of all the angles of these triangles is 5 × 180°. We are sure of that. But is it the sum of the angles of the original polygon? Or do we have something extra here?*
> [Katya immediately points to the four central angles in Figure 4–8].
> R: *So if you want to use this idea, you should take away these extras. How much are these extra angles?*
> M: *All together?*
> K: *. . . okay, these are all 90°.*
> M: *Wow! 90°, these are 180° × [2]* [doubting that such a conclusion can be drawn]. *But you haven't proven that's a square yet.*
> R: *No, that's correct. Can we say this is 360° even without knowing if this is a square?*
> M: *Yes, you can, because it's a circle! All the angles put together make one big angle all the way around! Wow! We are the "discovery channel" today!*
> R: *So we have 360°, which is like 2 × 180°. So the sum of the angles of the polygon is 5 × 180° − 2 × 180°, which is 3 × 180°. So now the two methods have given us the same result. Does it fit with the theorem I stated? How many sides did our polygon have here?*
> M: *Five.*
> R: *So, instead here we have three* [pointing to the result 3 × 180°]. *So do you trust my theorem more, or do you trust this?*
> M: [Without hesitation] *Trust ourselves.*

After correcting the text of the theorem under consideration, I suggested that we repeat the procedure using a different example. I then proceeded to draw a convex hexagon and divide it into triangles according to Katya's approach in order to confirm the result we had previously obtained with a pentagon. This led us to confirm the theorem once again.

M: She's right.
K: I don't want you to be right.
M: It's too neat.

At this point Mary became interested in finding out if there could be any exception to the theorem. Her first candidate for a counterexample was a five-pointed star, which she drew as shown in Figure 4–9, while at the same time asking, "Did we dismiss polygons that look like that? I think we have."

This brought us finally to reexamine explicitly the definition of polygon, as I had hoped the exercise would lead us to do. And this time we had some concrete ways to judge whether a specific figure, such as the star in Figure 4–9, could be considered an instance of polygon. In fact, as we noted, it was impossible to determine without ambiguity which angles in Mary's star were the interior angles; thus it would be impossible even to try to verify whether this figure satisfied the property stated in the theorem. I suggested that this could be a good enough reason to decide that Mary's star should not be considered a polygon.

Yet Mary was still keen on pursuing her original intuition and very creatively suggested a modification to her first star, one which would eliminate the interior lines that were causing all the problems (see her drawing in Figure 4–10), because "then we just count the outside lines!"

On the "modified star" Mary set out to check whether the theorem would still hold and was delighted to discover that it did. Her initiative and

FIGURE 4–9

FIGURE 4–10

her engagement in this activity were indeed remarkable, especially since she was herself able to pose new questions, generate critical cases to be considered, and then proceed to examine them, a good example of "problem posing."

When we went back to the definition of polygon for a moment at the end of this activity, the students were now more confident in their support of their initial decision that open figures and figures with curved sides should not be considered as instances of polygon. Furthermore, working with the two stars had made them aware of yet another requirement worth adding to the definition:

> *R:*   *Can we write down a definition of "polygon" that gives the best description? We had so far "a geometric figure made of straight lines." What else should we add?*
> *M:*   *In which no lines cross over.*
> *K:*   More than three lines.
> *R:*   [Correcting] *At least three straight lines.*
> *K:*   [Surprised] It can be three.
> *R:*   *Yes, a triangle is a special case of polygon.*
> *K:*   Closed.
> *R:*   *Closed, in which lines never cross.*

It is a pity that at the time none of us thought of considering other pathological figures such as the ones reported in Figure 4–11. These figures would have allowed us to apply the procedure of breaking the figure up into triangles to the "pathological polygon" and thus to find out that the sum of the interior angles would not yet satisfy the formula stated by the theorem. Nevertheless, as a result of our labor, we had reached a "better" definition of polygon, which the students felt ready to justify and support: "Polygon: a closed geometric figure with straight edges that do not cross."

FIGURE 4–11

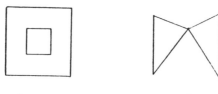

a   b

Concluding observations

Working on polygons "à la Lakatos" undoubtedly provided the context for valuable mathematical thinking and for activities that encouraged Katya and Mary to make use of their considerable mathematical intuition and ability, qualities that the more traditional approach to mathematics learning they had thus far experienced might not have allowed them to recognize or demonstrate. Especially worth noting is the considerable initiative Mary showed in looking for potential "exceptions" to the rule we were trying to establish.

In terms of the quest for a deeper understanding of the nature of mathematical definition, this episode constituted an important turning point. Both students now seemed able to recognize *tentativeness,* at least in some mathematical definitions. Their responses on the first review sheet when asked to comment on the definition of polygon were indicative of this new insight:

> **Are you satisfied with this definition? How could we ever know if it is correct? Explain your answer.**
>
> **M:** *Not quite. Play w/ polygons. Test the theory. Use examples of figures that meet the requirements for the def. but don't meet properties. Or just T&E [use "trial and error"].*
>
> **K:** I am satisfied with this for the time being but I think possibly as I start to use them more and more, I may desire something more exact.
>
> **What is the value, then, of a preliminary, tentative definition?**
>
> **M:** *It's like a theory that hasn't been fully tested yet and therefore is open to modification.*
>
> **K:** Getting acquainted with a new concept—have something to base further defining on. You have to start with something.

Our activities had clearly succeeded in at least making both students more cautious. But their responses also suggest an appreciation for the fact that mathematical definitions have meaning and purpose. Thus the very reasons that motivate the refinement of a currently accepted definition can also suggest what needs to be modified. As a result of Episode 3, both students had begun to move from the deterministic, dualistic view of mathematical definitions they had demonstrated in Episode 1 toward an appreciation of more relativistic and constructivist aspects of this notion.

I am not convinced, however, that the students were able to appreciate the fundamental difference between the approaches used when dealing with the definition of circle (a *familiar* concept they knew already very well) and the definition of polygon (an *unfamiliar* concept yet to be fully understood). This doubt is confirmed by their responses to another question on the first review sheet:

What are the main differences between this case and the definition of concepts such as circle?

M: *We already had a definition and a picture of the figure in our head before testing definitions and exceptions (with the circle).*

K: Circle is just one figure, one concept → [picture inserted]—a polygon is more general and includes many kinds of geometric figures [pictures of a triangle, square, parallelogram, and two more unusual concave polygons are given].

Yet how could the students be expected to make this conceptually sophisticated distinction on the basis of just one encounter with either type of concept and no explicit discussion on the subject? Many more similar experiences are necessary before such a process of abstraction can be reasonably expected to occur.

It may be interesting to focus our attention for a moment on the pedagogical value of the two kinds of activities our search for a good definition of polygon involved, that is, the attempt to refine tentative definitions of polygon by checking them against known instances and noninstances of the concept (Episode 3.1), and our work "à la Lakatos" to refine a tentative definition of polygon while at the same time trying to prove a theorem involving such a concept (Episode 3.2). In light of the students' experience, I believe these activities are truly valuable and necessary and that they complement each other well. But I would also suggest that their effectiveness could be improved by avoiding some of the shortcomings in their implementation in Episode 3.

The first activity was certainly quite frustrating for the students and did not lead them far. I would not consider this a shortcoming to be eliminated per se; on the contrary, the primary scope of this activity was to make the students confront the limitations of a known method by experiencing its failure in some circumstances. Trying to avoid potential causes of student frustration in mathematics teaching is not only unrealistic but also pedagogically unsound. Presenting a mathematical topic and assigning mathematical tasks so that a "good" student (that is, a student who has followed what was explained in class and studied the material) is guaranteed success will make those students who fail interpret that failure as a result of their own shortcomings and something to be ashamed of. In addition, this kind of teaching is untrue to the process by which mathematicians obtained those very results. In other words, such an instructional approach would encourage students in their belief that mathematics is a dualistic and deterministic discipline and discourage them from taking learning risks.

Nevertheless, the activity developed in Episode 3.1 could still be considerably improved. Examining only the two definitions of polygon initially produced by the students constituted a real handicap and forced me to take too much of a leading role in suggesting possible examples and counterexamples to be checked against those definitions. A richer list of incorrect definitions produced by others would have been a more natural stimulus for taking into consideration other properties or geometric figures beyond those they had thought of. It is a pity that at the time I did not think of collecting such a list from other students, as I had done in the case of circle.

In contrast, in considering the implementation of the "à la Lakatos" approach (Episode 3.2), I am satisfied by the amount and quality of mathematical activity the exercise stimulated. At the same time, the connection between proving and refining the theorem on the one hand and defining polygon on the other was not really developed as much as it could have been. Counterexamples like those reported in Figure 4–11 would probably have made the students question the statement of the theorem, the procedure used to derive the sum of the interior angles of a figure, and the definition of polygon more deeply. As a valuable addendum, we could have started to classify geometric figures on the basis of the relation between their sides and the sum of their interior angles, thus providing the opening for an activity in which students could engage in the simultaneous creation of *novel* concepts and their definition.

5 | *Extending a Known Definition*

Episode 4: Extending exponentiation beyond the whole numbers

Their experience with polygon had clearly made both Katya and Mary more aware of the presence and role of *tentativeness* in mathematical definitions. But I was afraid that they would still perceive this tentativeness as only temporary, a necessary step in *their* search for a mythical "ideal definition." To dispel this notion and help them see that the meaning of a definition may need to change as it is *extended* and applied to wider domains, I introduced the activity of extending the operation of *exponentiation* beyond the whole numbers. A weakness in their mathematical background worked to my advantage here. I was aware that, although they had been through eleventh grade mathematics, they had happily forgotten most of what they had learned about exponents except for the intuitive definition of exponentiation as "repeated multiplication." My plan was to lead them to realize that such a definition would be of little help, that in fact they would have to relinquish it as soon as they considered exponents other than whole numbers. At the same time, I wanted them to experience the possibility and mathematical value of finding a meaning for negative and fractional exponents consistent with, though different from, repeated multiplication.

This initial plan, however, required slight modification when I realized that both Katya and Mary were at a total loss when asked to "guess" the value of expressions such as 3^{-2} or $2^{1/2}$ and that they had had no experience in extending a known notion to a more inclusive number system, either by relying on patterns or by using known properties of numbers and operations.

It therefore seemed best to start by first considering the extension of a more familiar operation: *multiplication* (see Episode 4.1). Here, at least, they would already know the end result of the proposed extension, even if they might not realize (or perhaps even question) *why* and *how* such results were reached and justified.

To achieve this intermediate goal, I turned to two of the most famous curricular projects of the 1960s for help—the School Mathematics Study Group (SMSG) and the School Mathematics Project (SMP). In introducing the multiplication of signed numbers in their textbooks, the developers of these projects propose two different yet equally convincing approaches to justify the extension of multiplication beyond the whole numbers.

The SMSG textbook, for example, presents the following "proof" of the result $3 \times (-2) = -6$:

$3 \times 0 = 0$	because of the multiplicative property of zero
$3 \times (2 + (-2)) = 0$	because of the property of additive inverses
$3 \times 2 + 3 \times (-2) = 0$	because of the distributive property of multiplication over addition
$3 \times (-2) = -(3 \times 2)$	because of the property of additive inverses
$3 \times (-2) = -6.$	

This approach assumes that the properties of the four arithmetic operations derived in the case of the whole numbers will be maintained in the wider system of the signed numbers, and it employs these properties to "define" in a reasonable way the result of multiplying 3 by -2—an operation that would have no meaning if interpreted as *adding* "3" "-2" *times*. It is important to note, as Stephen I. Brown points out (Brown, 1969), that this assumption is not always necessarily justified, as our extension of exponentiation, for example, will demonstrate, and that it would therefore be incorrect to conclude that by means of the above derivation we have *proved* beyond doubt that $3 \times (-2) = -6$. Given this clarification, however, the desire to maintain existing properties when an operation is extended to a wider domain can be seen as a powerful heuristic, one that can serve as a guide in the definition of the "extended operation" itself. This approach appears especially suitable in the specific case of exponentiation, as shown by the following derivation (which appears in several current high school textbooks):

$$\text{Since } a^{b-c} = a^b/a^c \text{ and } 3^2/3^4 = {}^9/_{81} = {}^1/_9, \text{ then } 3^{-2} = {}^1/_9,$$

and:

$$\text{Since } a^{bc} = (a^b)^c \text{ and } (\sqrt{3})^2 = 3^1, \text{ then } 3^{1/2} = \sqrt{3}.$$

An alternative approach for deriving the same result ($3 \times (-2) = -6$) is proposed in the SMP textbook. This approach relies on the discovery of *patterns* among already established results and assumes that these patterns will continue to hold in moving into the new expanded system. For example, consider the following multiplication sequence. We can derive the result using the definition of multiplication as "repeated addition" only in the first four cases:

$$3 \times 4 = 12$$
$$3 \times 3 = 9$$
$$3 \times 2 = 6$$
$$3 \times 1 = 3$$
$$3 \times 0 = ?$$
$$3 \times (-1) = ?$$
$$3 \times (-2) = ?$$

In this sequence we can easily see that, when operating with whole numbers, "a decrease by 1" in the factor that multiplies 3 corresponds to "a decrease by 3" in the overall result of the multiplication. This is consistent with the meaning of multiplication as "repeated addition" among whole numbers, since multiplying for "one less" is equivalent to adding "one less 3."

By continuing this pattern even when the second factor is no longer a whole number, we can derive the remaining values in the sequence as follows:

$$3 \times 4 = 12$$
$$3 \times 3 = 9$$
$$3 \times 2 = 6$$
$$3 \times 1 = 3$$
$$3 \times 0 = 3 - 3 = 0$$
$$3 \times (-1) = 0 - 3 = -3$$
$$3 \times (-2) = -3 - 3 = -6$$

While we may all be aware that patterns can occasionally be deceptive, they nevertheless provide another valuable heuristic to guide the extension of a known operation to a wider domain. Once again, the analogy in the case of exponentiation is immediate, as shown in the following sequence:

$$3^4 = 81$$
$$3^3 = 27 \quad (81 \div 3 = 27)$$
$$3^2 = 9 \quad (27 \div 3 = 9)$$
$$3^1 = 3 \quad (9 \div 3 = 3)$$
$$3^0 = ? \quad (3 \div 3 = 1)$$
$$3^{(-1)} = ? \quad (1 \div 3 = 1/3)$$
$$3^{(-2)} = ? \quad ((1/3) \div 3 = 1/9)$$

I was confident that Katya and Mary would be able to generalize the two heuristics—using "patterns" and using the "extension of rules"—once they had seen them operate in the multiplication case, and that they could then use these heuristics to construct rules and meaning for negative and fractional exponents even if they had to relinquish the original definition of exponentiation as "repeated multiplication"—an activity that we pursued in Episodes 4.2 and 4.3. At the same time, I was also eager that the students realize the limitations that such an extension necessarily entails.

In fact, it is not always the case that in mathematics "more is better." While we clearly gain by extending the operation of exponentiation to integers and rational numbers, in the process some of the original properties of exponentiation are lost. The intuitive meaning of the operation as "repeated multiplication" is one of these unavoidable losses. Furthermore, by extending the operation of exponentiation we introduce some potential *contradictions* and thus need to consider some *exceptions*—a fact that may be especially difficult to accept for someone who sees mathematics as a discipline in which results are always predetermined and absolutely right or wrong.

Let me be more specific about this last point. If the heuristic of extending a pattern is applied when we try to evaluate 0^0, a potential contradiction follows, since two alternative patterns seem both possible and reasonable and yet each suggests a different value for the result:

$$5^0 = 1, 4^0 = 1, 3^0 = 1, 2^0 = 1, 1^0 = 1, \text{ hence: } 0^0 = 1;$$
$$0^5 = 0, 0^4 = 0, 0^3 = 0, 0^2 = 0, 0^1 = 0, \text{ hence: } 0^0 = 0.$$

To avoid this apparent contradiction, mathematicians had to conclude that 0^0 must remain *undefined*, an exception to the rule of exponentiation.

Another case in which the extension of exponentiation causes unsuspected problems may seem even more disturbing than the impossibility of defining 0^0. This has to do with the use of negative bases. As long as we are working within the set of integers, a negative base presents no problem, since if m and n are whole numbers:

$$(-m)^n = \underbrace{(-m) \times \ldots \times (-m)}_{n \text{ times}} = (-1)^n m^n$$

and:

$$(-m)^{-n} = \frac{1}{(-m)^n} = \frac{1}{(-1)^n m^n}.$$

When we move to the set of rational numbers, however, negative bases start to create considerable trouble. We can still evaluate expressions such as $(-3)^{1/5}$ or $(-1/2)^{2/3}$ as:

$$(-3)^{1/5} = \sqrt[5]{(-3)} = \sqrt[5]{(-1)(3)} = (\sqrt[5]{(-1)})\,(\sqrt[5]{3}) = -\sqrt[5]{3};$$

and:

$$(-1/2)^{2/3} = \sqrt[3]{(-1/2)^2} = \sqrt[3]{(-1)^2(1/2)^2} = (\sqrt[3]{(-1)^2}\,(\sqrt[3]{(1/2)^2} = \sqrt[3]{(1/2)^2}.$$

For cases such as $(-2)^{1/2}$ or $(-\frac{1}{4})^{3/4}$, however, no solution can be found within the real numbers. One way to overcome this problem would be to accept complex numbers as a possible result of the operation of exponentiation. But this would only partially solve the problem, because trouble may sometimes arise over the interpretation of expressions such as $(-2)^{1.4}$. In fact, depending on whether we interpret 1.4 as $^{14}/_{10}$ or $^{7}/_{5}$, we may conclude that the result is a positive or a negative number, since by applying the extended definition of exponentiation for fractional exponents we obtain respectively:

$$(-2)^{14/10} = \sqrt[10]{(-2)^{14}} = \sqrt[10]{(-1)^{14}(2)^{14}} = (\sqrt[10]{(-1)^{14}}\,(\sqrt[10]{(2)^{14}} = \sqrt[10]{(2)^{14}} = \sqrt[5]{(2)^7}$$

and:

$$(-2)^{7/5} = \sqrt[5]{(-2)^7} = \sqrt[5]{(-1)^7(2)^7} = \sqrt[5]{(-1)^7}\,(\sqrt[5]{(2)^7}) = -\sqrt[5]{(2)^7}.$$

To avoid these complications, mathematicians have chosen to limit the application of the extended operation of exponentiation to *positive bases*.

A discussion of these limitations seemed to me an especially useful way to challenge the students' initial expectation that, in mathematics, definitions can always be perfect (as long as we work hard enough and carefully enough). In addition, I expected that such a discussion would prepare the ground for a comparison of the nature and use of definitions in mathematics and other fields. Thus, we spent almost a full lesson analyzing the problems presented by 0^0 and negative bases (Episode 4.4), a lesson that inspired quite interesting reactions from the two students, Mary in particular.

Because of the numerous components of this episode and the time required to let Katya and Mary explore alternative ways of extending multiplication and exponentiation, the activities described here developed over our lessons 6, 7, 8, and 9, but the total amount of instructional time corresponded to only a little more than two regular class periods.

Episode 4.1: The extension of multiplication to signed numbers revisited

I introduced the activity of looking back at how multiplication has been extended beyond the whole numbers in response to the students' initial difficulties with the homework assignment: "Think about a possible meaning for exponents such as (-2), 1 or 0."

R: *I thought you would have trouble with this homework assignment. Let's start with something easier, something we feel more confident with: multiplication. You know what it means to multiply by 3. If I say 4 × 3, what does it mean?*

[Using the students' own suggestions, R writes: $4 \times 3 = 4 + 4 + 4$. To be precise, using the accepted definition of *multiplier* and *multiplicand* this should have been written: $4 \times 3 = 3 + 3 + 3 + 3$. The commutative property of multiplication and some common misconceptions about it is discussed later in the chapter].

R: *You're adding 4 three times. Do you think that defining multiplication as "repeated addition" would work with all sorts of multiplication?*

Since Katya and Mary did not seem to understand my question, I then suggested that they generate other examples of multiplication, making them as varied as possible. They came up with the following items: $4 \times (-1)$; $\sqrt{3} \times \sqrt{2}$; $(-3) \times (-2)$; $1/2 \times 2^{3}/4$; $\sqrt{2} \times 3$.

R: *If we look at all these examples, are they always "repeated addition"? 4×3 is like taking 4 and adding it 3 times. But what does it mean to take 4 "minus one" times? What about $(-3) \times (-2)$? How can we add -3 "minus two" times? What about $\sqrt{2} \times 3$?*

K: *I'd say we add radicals.*

R: *Yes, we can add the radical three times: $\sqrt{2} \times 3 = \sqrt{2} + \sqrt{2} + \sqrt{2}$. But in the other cases we can't think of adding the first term this [the second term] number of times, because we don't know what it means to add something a "negative number" of times or "a radical number of times."*

It surprised the students that all these years they had been confidently using rules to multiply fractions and negative numbers, never questioning that the meaning of multiplication as "repeated addition" might not hold anymore. This discovery intrigued them and made them curious to know how mathematicians had been able to come up with these new rules in the first place. This led to the discussion of a handout I had previously prepared (reproduced in Figure 5–1), in which the SMSG and SMP approaches to justifying the extension of multiplication to signed numbers were concretely presented.

After their first reading of the handout, I encouraged the students to look for a pattern that would suggest a reasonable value for the missing values in the first column. Except for Mary's observation that all the numbers multiplied by zero would give zero "because of the property of zero," at first they had no other suggestions or reactions. I began reading in a deliberate voice:

R: *Three times four is twelve. Three times three is nine. Three times two is six. Three times one is three. What do you notice?*

M: *Going down by three! Wow!*

R: [Agreeing] *We are going down by three. Why? Because every time we add a "3" less.*

FIGURE 5–1

What does it mean to multiply by a negative number?

$3 \times 4 = 12$	$4 \times 4 = 16$	$(-2) \times 4 =$
$3 \times 3 = 9$	$4 \times 3 = 12$	$(-2) \times 3 =$
$3 \times 2 = 6$	$4 \times 2 = 8$	$(-2) \times 2 =$
$3 \times 1 = 3$	$4 \times 1 = 4$	$(-2) \times 1 =$
$3 \times 0 =$	$4 \times 0 =$	$(-2) \times 0 =$
$3 \times (-1) =$	$4 \times (-1) =$	$(-2) \times (-1) =$
$3 \times (-2) =$	$4 \times (-2) =$	$(-2) \times (-2) =$
$3 \times (-3) =$	$4 \times (-3) =$	$(-2) \times (-3) =$

What do you think of this proof for:

$$3 \times (-2) = 6$$
$$3 \times 0 = 0$$
$$3 \times (2 + (-2)) = 0$$
$$3 \times 2 + 3 \times (-2) = 0$$
$$3 \times (-2) = -(3 \times 2)$$
$$3 \times (-2) = -6$$

If we wanted to do something similar with "negative exponents":
  • What properties of exponents would you like to preserve?
  • What kind of "pattern" would you like to use?

At this point Katya had no hesitation in completing the first column with the values $-3, -6, -9$, which she obtained by subtracting 3 each time from the previous result. She correctly filled in the missing values in the other columns in a similar way in no time. Neither Katya nor Mary, however, were yet ready to commit themselves when I asked whether they were sufficiently "convinced" by this approach.

We then moved to the derivation suggested by the SMSG textbook but again with little reaction from either student. Instead, Mary brought up an alternative derivation that she found simpler and more convincing: she suggested that we look at $(-2) \times 3$ or $3 \times (-2)$ as "three negative twos," i.e., $3 \times (-2) = (-2) + (-2) + (-2) = -6$.

In a sense, Mary's derivation can be interpreted as an analogue of the SMSG approach. The only difference is that here Mary assumes that the *commutative* property of multiplication will continue to hold in the new system of signed numbers, while the SMSG derivation makes this assumption about the *distributive* property of multiplication over addition. It is important to point out, however, that this was *not* the way Mary saw it, since she was unaware that her calculation made use of a property of multiplication, as she reveals in the following dialogue:

> *R: Did you notice what you did in this calculation? You switched the "−2" and the "3". You said that $3 \times (-2) = (-2) \times 3$.*

> M: *Not really, you don't have to switch it. You just do the multiplication.*
> R: *So you are saying that 4 × 3 can be seen as 4 added 3 times or 3 added 4 times . . .*

At this point Katya intervened, observing that she too did not find much difference between 4 × 3 and 3 × 4. Indeed, we are all so used to interchanging the factors in multiplication and so little aware of the original meaning and definition of *multiplier* and *multiplicand*, that we often seem not to appreciate the commutative property of multiplication—as I, too, did in interpreting the meaning of 4 × 3 as 4 + 4 + 4 at the beginning of this lesson.

It might have been interesting at this point to remark on how the equivalence of expressions such as 4 × 3 and 3 × 4 is not so intuitive after all and to digress briefly from the original scope of the lesson to examine the commutative property and how it operates (or does not operate) for different operations and in a variety of domains. At the time, however, it seemed better not to lose the momentum, so I proceeded instead with the extension of the operation of exponentiation to signed numbers using "patterns" and the "extension of rules" as heuristics.

Episode 4.2: Constructing rules and meaning for negative exponents

By implicit agreement, we considered first the possible use of patterns to suggest how to deal with negative integers as exponents:

> R: *Let's start with something you know already.*
>
> [R writes: $2^3 = 2 \times 2 \times 2 = 8$; $2^2 = 2 \times 2 = 4$; $2^1 = 2$; $2^0 = ?$]
>
> M: *Zero, or undefined?*
>
> [Both suggestions are written down with a question mark.]
>
> R: *Any other suggestions? . . . What happened when we went from 2^3 to 2^2? Were we subtracting, dividing, or what?*
>
> K: Yeah! Dividing. We were taking half of it. Just keep taking half of it.
>
> R: *If you take half of 2, what do you get?*
>
> K: One. Oh yeah, I remember, isn't that right?
>
> R: *Instead of 0, or undefined, it makes sense for the moment to say that $2^0 = 1$. What would 2^{-1} be?*
>
> K: One half, isn't that right?
>
> R: *I'm going with your suggestion! And it seems reasonable, so what would 2^{-1} be?*
>
> M: *Maybe we should make those into decimals, like $2^{-1} = .5$*

I acknowledged the possibility of this alternative notation, while trying at the same time not to lose track of the main topic. Using the students' own suggestions, we were soon able to complete the sequence as follows: $2^3 = 2 \times 2 \times 2 = 8$; $2^2 = 4$; $2^1 = 2$; $2^0 = 1$; $2^{-1} = 1/2 = .5$; $2^{-2} = 1/4 = .25$; $2^{-3} = 1/8$.

At this point Mary interrupted the step-by-step procedure to suggest a more general rule: "So if we have 2^{-6}, without going through all that, it would be $1/2^6$. Could we work it that way?"

Since I remained noncommittal and avoided answering her question directly, Mary tried to evaluate the expression $1/2^6$ on her own. In doing so, she made a convenient mistake that led us to consider the value of using the familiar rule $a^b \times a^c = a^{b+c}$ when computing large exponents:

R: *Okay, what would 2^6 be?*

M: *Hold on . . . 64.*

R: *Tell me how you got it. Shall we trust her?*

M: *Wait, one more coming: 128, so it would be negative . . . no $1/128$.*

R: *How did you get 128?*

Mary explained that she had kept on multiplying by 2. As an alternative approach (and to verify Mary's result) I then suggested that she group the twos, so as not to lose count, and wrote: $2^6 = (2 \times 2 \times 2) \times (2 \times 2 \times 2) = 2^3 \times 2^3 = 8 \times 8 = 64$. Mary appreciated my suggestion and used the partial result ($2^6 = 64$) to complete her evaluation of $1/2^6$. "Put it into the denominator of the fraction, as $1/64$. Sounds neat, but I don't know if it is right."

Mary's critical view of this result offered the opportunity to use the other heuristic we had employed in the case of multiplication—assuming that the original properties of the operation in question are maintained in the new domain and drawing consequences from this assumption—as a way to support and confirm her result. I thus suggested that we look at whether some known properties of exponents could help us further justify Mary's hypothesis, and, more specifically, the "definition" $2^{-1} = 1/2$.

R: *Which [properties of exponents] do you remember? For example, what did I use in [computing] 2^6?*

K: $2^3 \times 2^3 = 2^{3+3}$

R: *Do you remember this rule of exponents? And it makes sense: I group things, I just add the exponents. Shall we see if this works? $2^a \times 2^b = 2^{a+b}$. Let's take $2^3 \times 2^{-1}$. If this rule were to hold, how much should that be?*

Thus, while Katya wrote: $2^3 \times 2^{-1} = 2^{3+(-1)} = 2^2 = 4$, I verified that the same result would be reached by using the "definition" $2^{-1} = 1/2$, by computing: $2^3 = 8$; $2^{-1} = 1/2$, and $2^3 \times 2^{-1} = 8 \times 1/2 = 4$.

This result got a "wow, that works really well" out of Mary, who was now convinced of the soundness of her original intuition. Her excitement with these discoveries inspired her to engage in other computations to apply what we had just learned and better understand its power and limitations. Mary suggested, "But you can use that rule only when you're combining exponents where the base numbers are the same! I was thinking, what if you want to compute $3^2 \times (12)^{-1}$?" She then showed us her computation for this case: $3^2 \times (12)^{-1} = 3^2 \times 4 \times (3)^{-1} = 3^{2-1} \times 4 = 3 \times 4 = 12$. I noticed the mistake, and with it the opportunity it could offer to introduce yet another property of exponents: $(ab)^c = a^c \times b^c$. Thus, instead of pointing out her mistake, I suggested that we try to verify Mary's result by using our tentative definition of negative exponent. All three of us separately computed: $3^2 \times (12)^{-1} = 9 \times 1/12 = 3 \times 1/4 = 3/4$.

Mary was really disappointed to discover that her earlier answer of 12 did not match this new result, but she was also quick to look for and find a possible explanation for this discrepancy.

M: *Maybe 4 should keep a -1 too!*

R: *Let's see if that'll work:* [Writes] $3^2 \times (12)^{-1} = 3^2 \times (4)^{-1} \times (3)^{-1} = 3^{2-1} \times 4^{-1} = 3 \times 1/4 = 3/4.$

R: *The result is $3/4$. What are we getting at here?*

M: *You can't separate . . .*

R: *. . . when you distributed the -1 on both* [factors], *you got the right result.*

M: *Wait a minute, it's like the "distributive" property of multiplication, wow! . . . So we have made a new pattern. So it's treated like multiplication. Put it in the definition.*

R: [Writes] $(a \times b)^3 = a^3 \times b^3; (a \times b)^{-2} = a^{-2} \times b^{-2}.$

M: [This means that] *you could do it too with a big number, like $(144)^{-3}$. So you'd make it $(12)^{-3} \times (12)^{-3}$. That's neat! Wow!*

I pointed out that indeed we had hit on another property of exponents that transferred to the new domain, and that our explorations to this point seemed to confirm that the proposed definition of negative exponents ($a^{-b} = 1/a^b$) was compatible with all the major properties of exponents they were familiar with: $a^{b+c} = a^b \times a^c; (a \times b)^c = a^c \times b^c; (a^b)^c = a^{bc}$.

Even within the brief span of this activity, Katya and Mary were rapidly learning to become more independent students. At the beginning, in fact, Katya voiced her good ideas about reasonable values for 2^0 and $2^{(-1)}$ quite tentatively. By following her suggestions with phrases such as "I remember" or "Isn't that right?," she still showed a tendency to rely on "authority" (past teachers and myself) to verify her results. My refusal to say whether her suggestions were correct and Mary's initiative in questioning the truth of some of her hunches showed both students that it was indeed possible for *them* to answer their own questions, and to establish whether they were right or not, without needing to rely on my authority.

Episode 4.3: Constructing rules and meaning for fractional exponents

Their success in extending exponentiation to negative integers made the students quite eager to extend this operation to fractional exponents. I had initially planned to go through this extension quickly, but I changed my mind when Katya showed us her failed attempt to use patterns to evaluate $2^{1/2}$. She said, "I tried to do a pattern, but it didn't really work" as she showed her work: $12^{1/2} = \sqrt{12}$; $8^{1/2}$; $= \sqrt{8}$; $4^{1/2} = \sqrt{4}$; $2^{1/2} = \sqrt{2}$.

Katya's attempt revealed a fundamental uncertainty in the students' understanding of the heuristic of using patterns. It seemed worthwhile to slow down and go through the application of patterns and rules in a few concrete examples once again, so that we would not only find a reasonable definition for fractional exponents, but also clarify the fact that *useful* patterns and/or computations need to be set up in order to achieve the goal of extending a given operation.

Building on Katya's idea, I observed that in order to evaluate $2^{1/2}$ we needed a sequence in which we could move *from something we knew to something we did not know* by recognizing and continuing a pattern. I thus suggested a different sequence: $2^8 = ?$, $2^4 = ?$, $2^2 = ?$, $2^1 = ?$, $2^{1/2} = ?$.

The students were quick to recognize that for the first four terms of the sequence each term could be obtained by taking the square root of the previous one; once they understood this it was easy for them to continue the sequence: $2^8 = 16 \times 16$; $2^4 = 16$; $2^2 = 4$; $2^1 = 2$; $2^{1/2} = \sqrt{2}$; $2^{1/4} = \sqrt{\sqrt{2}} = \sqrt[4]{2}$.

We adopted a similar procedure to create a pattern with 4 as a base, which further confirmed the reasonableness of their definition for exponents such as $1/2$ and $1/4$: $4^4 = 16 \times 16$; $4^2 = 16$; $4^1 = 4$; $4^{1/2} = \sqrt{4} = 2$; $4^{1/4} = \sqrt[4]{4} = \sqrt{\sqrt{4}} = \sqrt{2}$. The students were now ready to accept the definition $a^{1/n} = \sqrt[n]{a}$, and furthermore $a^{m/n} = \sqrt[n]{a^m}$, though they still felt uneasy with their answer whenever it involved computations with radicals.

Episode 4.4: Discovering unavoidable problems in the extension of exponentiation[1]

After briefly reviewing our successive extensions of exponentiation I suggested the following comprehensive definition for this operation:

- If the exponent is a positive whole number, the exponent tells you how many times you have to multiply the base by itself. Example: $a^5 = aaaaa$.
- If the exponent is a negative whole number (say we have a^{-n}), it is the same as considering $1/a^n$.
- If the exponent is a fraction (say, $a^{m/n}$), it is the same as considering $\sqrt[n]{a^m}$.

When the students were asked whether they were totally satisfied with this definition, Katya showed considerable caution, along with some playfulness:

> **R:** *Do you feel that now we have the best possible definition of "exponent"? Do you think it is a precise definition?*
>
> **K:** For what we're working with now.
>
> **R:** *What do you think we might still want to do?*
>
> **K:** I don't know. Some tricky math thing. . . . Something nobody has come up with before, something we have never heard of before.

As these remarks show, the students, as a result of their previous activities exploring the definition of polygon and exponent, were able to appreciate the dynamic nature of mathematical definitions and the tentativeness of mathematical results. But they were not yet prepared to face the more radical challenges that the definition of 0^0 and of the exponentiation of negative bases were going to present.

Katya's expectation that we might eventually want to extend our notion of exponentiation further allowed me to introduce rather naturally the consideration of negative bases:

> **R:** *Before, we always got as a base a = 2, a = 3 or something convenient like that. What happens if we consider a = −2? Does our definition of exponent still work? For example, what would $(-2)^5$ mean?*
>
> **M:** $(-2) \times (-2) \times (-2) \times (-2) \times (-2)$! *Negative, actually.*

The students showed no hesitation in handling negative bases as long as the exponent was an integer. They also computed $(-2)^{-5} = \dfrac{1}{(-2)^5} = -\dfrac{1}{25}$ easily. They "got stuck," however, when I asked them to evaluate $(-2)^{1/2}$:

> **M:** *Maybe 1?*
>
> **R:** *Why?*
>
> **M:** *Because I was dividing it in half. Sounds really stupid.*
>
> **K:** No, it's not stupid.
>
> **R:** *Wait, wait. You should apply our definition of exponent, right? What is the problem here, though? What is the square root of −2?*
>
> **M:** *Isn't that something with an 'i'?* [Katya and Mary had been briefly introduced to imaginary and complex numbers in a course I taught the previous semester.]
>
> **K:** Neat.
>
> **R:** *That's the square root of a negative number.*
>
> **M:** *Brings an 'i'.*
>
> **R:** *Brings a complex number. I mean, you can't find any real number that squared gives you −2.*

Just as I was ready to observe that this is a case in which our extended notion of exponentiation breaks down and to suggest that we needed to limit its domain of application to positive bases only, Katya's next observation made me stop and reflect: "I think that, isn't that ['i'] an answer? It's just this. It's just that you can't go any further." Once again one of the students was presenting an alternative that I had not previously considered: why not further extend our system of numbers to include complex numbers? After all, that was exactly what we had done before. When exponents took on negative integer values we had to accept fractions as a possible result of the operation. Similarly, fractional exponents occasionally introduced irrational numbers.

Katya's ready acceptance of a further extension that would include complex numbers really challenged me to reconsider why mathematicians have decided to restrict the domain of exponentiation by considering only positive numbers as possible bases. The answer came to me only later, after some thinking and exploration involving real numbers as exponents that made me realize the fundamental problems negative bases would create in such a context.

At the time, the best course of action seemed to be to acknowledge the value of Katya's position while at the same time making both students aware of the alternative solution chosen by the mathematics community.

R: *You say you'll have to accept complex numbers as solutions then. Okay . . . That's one solution. What could another solution be? If you do not want to deal with unpleasant numbers . . .*

K: [After some silence] We change the definition!

R: *Change the definition, you say. In what way? Do you have any suggestion?*

M: [Quietly] *Suggestion?*

K: No.

R: *Well, generally, one way to deal with unpleasant things like these is to try to "cut them out." We say, "Wait a second, what kind of number is giving us this problem?" Two, three, four never gave us any problem, and they were all positive numbers. It's only when we consider negative numbers as a base that we seem to have some problems. So we may say, "This definition of exponents works only when the base a is a positive number." The advantage of this solution is that it assures that we get real numbers as a result of exponentiation. The advantage of Katya's solution, that is, to work with complex numbers, is that the base a can be any number.*

With this partial explanation, we concluded our discussion of exponentiation with negative bases and moved on to the evaluation of 0^0. When I first presented this task, Mary was at a loss, which made the activity more intriguing from the start.

R: *I'll show you another thing that gave me a problem. What do you think is 0^0?*

K: Zero?

R: *Why do you think that?*

M: It's not . . . it's undefined.

R: *How would you justify that it is undefined?*

M: Because . . . well, I can see how she's going to say zero times zero equal zero; but I would say undefined because you can't raise something to the power of zero; that makes it totally imaginary.

K: [Emphatically] You can!

Katya reminded Mary that in a previous lesson we had been able to evaluate 2^0 using patterns. Once we had recalled and applied the procedure for evaluating 2^0 and 3^0, a possible pattern for evaluating 0^0 suggested itself.

R: *Every number to the power of zero is one. Could it be that $0^0 = 1$?*

M: I'm being quiet . . . I'm not going to try.

K: . . . a pattern . . . equal zero [inaudible].

R: [Writing $5^0 = 1, 4^0 = 1, 3^0 = 1, 2^0 = 1, 1^0 = 1$] *All these numbers to the power 0 give you 1. So it seems reasonable that 0 to the power 0 gives you 1 too.* [R writes at the end of the sequence: $0^0 = 1$?]

The students were quite intrigued by this approach, though not yet ready to accept the rather unintuitive result $0^0 = 1$. My presentation at this point of the alternative pattern, $0^5 = 0, 0^4 = 0, 0^3 = 0, 0^2 = 0, 0^1 = 0, 0^0 = ?$, further confirmed their doubts, and caused considerable uneasiness and confusion.

R: *What about this new pattern?*

K: Equal zero.

R: *So we might also argue that 0^0 should be 0.*

K: Makes more sense to me that that would be zero.

R: *But this is really the kind of situation that I think makes mathematicians mad. . . . Patterns seemed to work so nicely before: we got all these nice extensions of the definition of exponentiation. But this time one pattern gives you one result, and the other pattern gives you another result. So, how do you think we can deal with a situation like this?* [Long pause]

K: I don't know . . . I don't know with this one . . .

M: I . . . I don't like it.

R: [Agreeing] *That's probably what the mathematicians must have said too: I don't like it!*

M: Pretend we never saw it. . . .

R: *Do you think that this means that we have to throw out our whole definition of exponentiation? Or, instead, maybe we just have to make an exception and say: 0^0 is undefined.* [Long pause.]

M: *The thing about this is, I sort of doubt . . . if we can't figure that out, who's to say the rest of our results are right? . . . And that's relatively simple, it's just an exponent. I'm wondering about all this stuff that we are learning, ten years from now we'll find out it's wrong! . . . It isn't really what you want to know! . . .*

R: **Well, I see your point . . . but then, what do you think mathematicians should do? It doesn't always work the way they want!**

M: *I think that they should be working toward a definition that is more universal, that included all of the exceptions. I don't know. What seems to be wrong with that is: how can this be right, if the entire negative part of the whole numbers is not included?*

R: *Yes.*

M: *It's . . . it's not right!* [Emphatically] *It's "prejudiced."*

Mary's concerns here are well articulated and, indeed, quite justified. Not surprisingly, neither my observation that in mathematics things do not always work out "right" nor my later consideration of the more familiar "undefined" expression 0/0 really succeeded in helping the students recover from the shock of encountering an unavoidable contradiction in what had worked so nicely up to that point. And these reactions are not surprising when we consider how careful the mathematics community is to present students with only the final "cleaned-up" result, which always works only because unpleasant exceptions and quirks have already been taken care of. This was confirmed by Mary herself in the following exchange:

R: **Was there any other time when, in mathematics, you had to deal with a situation more difficult than you really expected. Like a definition that didn't fit . . .**

M: *Just about every test I took for the last three years, actually!* [More seriously] *When a definition didn't fit?* [Thinking.]

R: **No? It never happened?**

M: *Not offhand, no, I do know it did happen . . . but I just don't remember it . . . I figure it was . . . but it might have been my fault . . .* [inaudible].

R: **But sometimes it may not be your fault. It may be because of the situation.**

Although at first the students did not seem very responsive to my analysis of this situation as an instance of the inherent limitations of mathematics and tried to hold on to their expectation that mathematicians should have "fixed" the situation somehow, it had a considerable impact on their views. This came out in their comments about this episode in the final interviews. In particular, further reflection caused Mary to look at the situation from a new perspective and to propose alternative solutions to the ones we had discussed so far.

R: **When we discussed 0^0, I was trying to show that there are some things in mathematics that do not work out in the way you want. I am really interested in knowing what you thought about that.**

M: *I think I understand. . . . I like concentrating on things that can't be solved in math. I know we came to that point with 0^0. I felt like if you hadn't said it was desperate, then I wouldn't have gone on thinking about it, I don't know. The way you made it seem . . . we had to fix it up.*

R: *Well, because if we have two equally good alternatives, either we arbitrarily choose one of the two (and that seems to give some problems here) or we have to give up.*

M: *Or we have to change to a new system . . . we invented zero to ten, and the whole number system and all the other number systems . . . it could have been invented in a slightly different way. And then I was thinking about, what if we had decided that it was one through ten, and there is no zero [laughter], then our problems would be solved!*

R: *Maybe some problems would be solved, but others would remain. In fact, some of those other problems would be so big that that's why zero was invented.*

M: *It would be neat, though, if some people just decided that that's the way their number system is going to be, so the whole world uses it. I don't know.*

Whether the decision to eliminate zero would indeed be a good solution to the problems we encountered is not really the issue here. Rather, what I think is remarkable in Mary's suggestion is her willingness to challenge the standard established system and her appreciation of the fact that mathematics is created in order to best fit our needs.

Concluding observations

More than any other component of the mini-course so far the activities developed around the extension of exponentiation allowed the students to share in what professional mathematicians do to expand the existing body of mathematical knowledge. As a result, Katya and Mary were able to experience the excitement and satisfaction, as well as the inevitable frustration and disappointment, that accompany genuine mathematical exploration. More than once they showed remarkable creativity and mathematical intuition, and even more important, a willingness to follow up their hunches with some sort of mathematical verification. Except for their uneasiness about working with radicals, one would never have guessed that either of them had experienced difficulty with school mathematics.

While experiencing the possibility and power of extending a known concept to wider domains (a moving force in much of mathematical research), the students also encountered, perhaps for the first time, some unresolvable limitations within mathematics itself. These limitations, and the contradiction they confronted in trying to evaluate 0^0 in particular, greatly disturbed them and forced them to come to grips with some of their prior conceptions and expectations about mathematical results. What is especially remarkable is how this episode seems to have influenced Mary to assume a more relativistic view of the discipline once she was able to overcome her initial disappointment that mathematics was less perfect than she had expected.

Unfortunately, the experiences in Episode 4 did not seem to have done much specifically to help the students refine their understanding of mathematical definitions. Perhaps they were so taken by the task of extending and reconceiving the *operation* of exponentiation that they did not look closely at its implications for the *definition* of exponentiation. In addition, I did not provide much opportunity to connect what we were doing with the overall theme of the unit. At the same time, I was a bit surprised by the students' easy acceptance of the fact that the original meaning of exponentiation as "repeated multiplication," employed in its initial definition, had to be relinquished in order to extend this operation. Yet I wonder whether this fact could just be the consequence of a conception of mathematics (and of arithmetic and algebra in particular) as a meaningless collection of symbols and rules—a view shared by most mathematics students.

Despite its limitations, I think that this episode was quite successful. At the very least, it confirmed the students' previous realization, acquired while working with the definition of polygon, of the tentative and dynamic nature of mathematical definitions. Even more important, it had a considerable impact on their conception of mathematics (as confirmed by their comments in the interviews reported in Chapter 9) and influenced the way they approached the remaining mathematical activities.

More on the Role of Context in Mathematical Definitions 6

Episode 5: The definition of circle revisited in taxicab geometry

As a result of their work with the extension of exponentiation beyond the whole numbers, Katya and Mary had encountered the unexpected fact that mathematical concepts and their definitions, far from being absolute, actually depend upon the context in which they are interpreted. In Episode 4 we had seen how the definition of an operation had to be modified if we wanted to extend it to a more inclusive domain. Now I hoped to make the students even more aware of the importance of the context for mathematical definitions by showing them that the very same definition (or to be more precise, the same wording) could take on new meanings and identify different sets of objects when interpreted in different contexts.

Taxicab geometry seemed an ideal environment for carrying out this plan. Taxicab geometry—or taxigeometry—is the name various mathematics educators (Borasi, 1981; Krause, 1986; Papy and Papy, 1973) have used to characterize the idealization of an urban area with a very regular pattern of streets, such as Manhattan. The usual plane Euclidean geometry does not serve well in describing the "geometry" of such an area from the point of view of a taxicab driver (or any driver), who cannot realistically measure distances "as the crow flies" (since cars cannot go through buildings!). Rather, to evaluate the distance between two points in a city we need to go back to the general definition of *distance* as "the length of the shortest path connecting two points." Given a pair of points, we must identify a minimal path connecting them along the streets of the city, measure its length, and use this measure as the *taxidistance* between the two points.

If we use a square grid (where the lines represent the streets and the squares the buildings of the city) as a simplified model of the city, we can easily evaluate taxidistances as shown in Figure 6–1.

The square grid, along with this redefinition of distance, constitutes a very simple "non-Euclidean" geometry accessible to secondary school students. By exploring taxicab geometry, students can discover interesting similarities and differences between it and the "standard" plane Euclidean geometry usually studied in high school and thus acquire a better understanding of the nature of geometry.

Taxicab geometry is of particular interest in a unit on mathematical definitions because here many of the most elementary concepts encountered in Euclidean geometry take on a new meaning and "shape" due to the different way in which distances are measured. The metric definition of *circle* found in most textbooks—for example, "a circle is the set of all points in a plane that are at a given distance from a given point in the plane"—interpreted in taxicab geometry identifies the shape depicted in Figure 6–2.

FIGURE 6–1

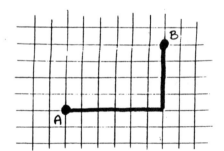

The taxidistance between A and B can be computed as:

$$t(A,B) = |x_B - x_A| + |y_B - y_A| = 6 + 4 = 10.$$

FIGURE 6–2

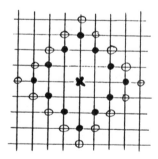

Taxicircles of radius 3 (full dots) and 4 (empty dots).

FIGURE 6–3

Taxiperpendicular bisectors. (Note that the first three figures comprise infinitely many points.)

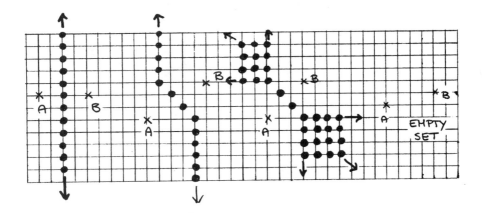

Similarly, the definition of *perpendicular bisector* as "all the points equidistant from two given points in the plane" could be applied to specific pairs of points in the taxiplane. Depending on the mutual position of the chosen points, the *taxiperpendicular bisector* can take on four very different shapes, as shown in Figure 6–3. Conic sections can also be reinterpreted in the context of taxicab geometry, since they too can be defined in terms of "distances":

- *Ellipse:* "All points in the plane such that the sum of their distances from two fixed points is a constant k."
- *Hyperbola:* "All points in the plane such that the difference between their distances from two fixed points is a constant k."
- *Parabola:* "All points in the plane equidistant from a given point and a given line."

Once again, however, when these definitions are interpreted in the context of taxicab geometry, each conic section loses the characteristic "shape" we associate with it in Euclidean geometry. In addition, each *taxiconic* will present different shapes depending upon the mutual position of the chosen fixed points and/or line. The most significant variations of *taxiellipses, taxihyperbolas* and *taxiparabolas,* are illustrated in Figures 6–4, 6–5, and 6–6, respectively.

FIGURE 6–4

Taxi-ellipses (where k is the sum of the taxidistances from each point of the taxi-ellipse to the two foci).

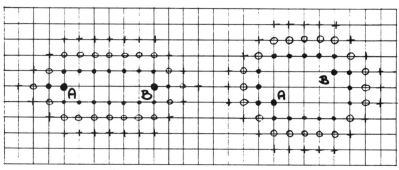

• K = 8
o K = 10
+ K = 12

FIGURE 6–5

Taxihyperbolas (where k is the difference of the taxidistances from each point of the taxihyperbola to the two fixed points).

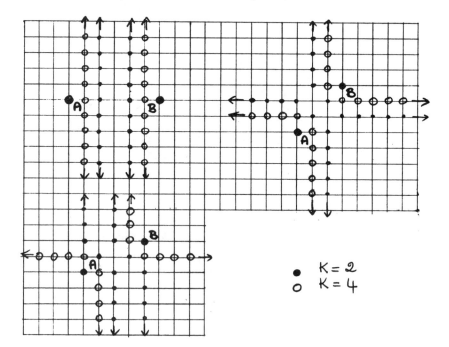

• K = 2
o K = 4

FIGURE 6–6

Taxiparabolas and their construction as intersections of taxicircles and taxilines (for convenience, the taxilines and taxicircles have been drawn as continuous figures instead of as points along the grid.)

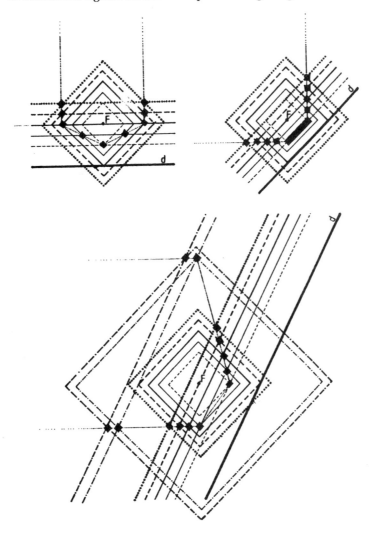

Figure 6–6 also shows how taxiparabolas can be constructed using a procedure analogous to that employed in Euclidean geometry to construct parabolas with ruler and compass. One can in fact reason that the "locus of points equidistant from a given point and a given line" can be determined

by finding the intersections of the loci consisting of "all the points at distance k from the given point" and "all the points at distance k from the given line," respectively, for all possible values of k. The first of these loci is easy to determine, since it will be a taxicircle of radius k centered in the given point. Determining the "locus of points at a given distance from a given line," on the other hand, is more complex and actually presupposes a number of things.

First, we need to agree about what a *line* is in taxicab geometry. Mathematicians studying this mathematical situation (Papy and Papy, 1973; Borasi, 1981; Krause, 1986) have assumed as taxilines the "traces" of the usual Euclidean lines on the taxiplane—that is, the points of those lines belonging to the grid. Other solutions, however, are also possible and justifiable. Given the definition of taxiline as a "trace" of a Euclidean line, the distance between a point and a line can then be determined by measuring "the length of the shortest path connecting the given point with a point on the line." Given these assumptions, it is easy to show that the locus of points at a given distance from a given line is another line, parallel to the given one.

The taxiconics illustrated in Figures 6–4, 6–5, and 6–6 may present a few surprises, given our image of what circles, parabolas, and ellipses should look like. In turn, these shapes raise interesting questions about mathematical definitions, since they require us to reconsider either the appropriateness of the traditional definitions of circle, perpendicular bisector, ellipse, hyperbola, and parabola, as well as many other figures, or the validity and domain of application of the standard criteria for mathematical definitions identified in Chapter 3.

Let us consider, for example, the case of the circle. Is the standard definition, "a circle is the set of all points in a plane that are at a given distance from a given point in the plane," really acceptable if it allows us to identify figures such as the usual "round" circles *and* the "diamond"[1] shapes of Figure 6–2? Would such a definition of circle meet the requirement of isolation of the concept? And what about precision in terminology, considering that the "problem" here is created by the possibility of interpreting the term *distance* in different ways?

The answers to these questions are far from being simple or straightforward. Even if we decide that we need to specify beforehand what *distance* has to be considered in the definition of circle, we may start wondering if other terms in this definition may later on require further clarification. Furthermore, even if we could modify the original definition in order to avoid all possible "misinterpretations," it is possible that such extreme precision could end up being counterproductive, since it could unnecessarily complicate even the definition of a simple concept such as circle and thus make it more difficult to understand its definition intuitively, and to remember and use it.

An alternative solution would be to recognize that a certain level of *ambiguity* is not only unavoidable but also valuable in mathematical definitions. Mathematicians have found it useful to generalize the notion of "the locus of points at a given distance from a given point" to contexts where *point* and *distance* may assume quite different meanings than they do in Euclidean geometry (think of the variety of metric spaces considered in advanced analysis[2]). Clearly, though, in this case one cannot expect that *all* the properties of the usual circle will transfer in these new situations. Indeed, investigating which properties do and do not transfer may clarify which characteristic elements of a circle are strictly due to its metric property of equidistance from a center point and which are not. This solution, however, raises a new problem, since it makes us question what we really want to consider as circles and on what grounds we should decide, thus challenging in an even more radical way the criterion of isolation of the concept previously accepted for mathematical definitions. In sum, I am suggesting that the interpretation of a mathematical definition cannot be totally objective and absolute, since it will to some extent depend on the specific mathematical context (or domain) in which one is operating. And even unsophisticated mathematics students can discover this important fact by studying what happens to some simple metric concepts in the nonstandard context of taxicab geometry.

Ideally, I would have liked to engage the students in an open-ended exploration of taxicab geometry before introducing the task of interpreting some familiar geometric definitions in this context. Unfortunately, the time allotted for our mini-course was quickly coming to an end, so I knew that I could devote at most one meeting to the topic (part of Lesson 8). Given this time constraint, I decided to introduce the students briefly to the nature of taxicab geometry (Episode 5.1) and then to focus on what happens when the usual metric definition of circle is interpreted in this new situation. I chose the concept of circle not only because it is one of the most fundamental and simple concepts that can be defined purely on the basis of a metric property, but also because of the considerable attention we had already devoted to this concept and its definition within Euclidean geometry in Episode 2.

My plan was to ask the students to interpret the definition of circle we had agreed on in previous lessons—"All the points on the plane equidistant from a single point"[3]—in the context of taxicab geometry (see Episode 5.2). In light of the discovery that the figures identified by this definition do not look at all like the "circles" we are used to, I then wanted to go back and reexamine the appropriateness of the definition of circle we had previously settled on (see Episode 5.3). I expected that at this point the students would be able to appreciate how the use of a "vague" term in our original definition of circle—the word *distance*—opened up a more general notion of circle, which could then be interpreted in *any* metric space, though each time characterizing a different "figure." In other words, I hoped that this experience could lead the students to appreciate the positive role occasionally played by *ambiguity* in mathematical definitions and mathematics more generally.

Episode 5.1: Becoming familiar with the context of taxicab geometry

For homework, the students had been assigned a short story, John Sheedy's "Moving Around the City" (see Borasi, Sheedy, and Siegel, 1990), introducing the environment of taxicab geometry. Since Katya and Mary did not have any strong reaction to it, I briefly reviewed the main gist of the story and suggested that we engage in our own exploration of the consequences of being constrained to move along the streets of a city. I then gave them some graph paper to use as a model for the city we were working in.

Drawing two points on the grid of the graph paper, I asked the students what the distance was between them. Mary immediately pointed out that you have to follow the lines and count the little squares as units. I supported her idea but also observed that in order to evaluate distances we must be sure that the path we are considering is a minimal one—one of the shortest possible paths that can connect the two given points. A lively exchange followed.

> R: *It seems reasonable to consider this* [the shorter path along the lines of the grid] *as the distance* . . .
> M: *But if you were an airplane, then the distance would just be* [indicates a straight line connecting the two points] : . . .
> R: *Right. But an airplane could not go through the buildings* . . .
> M: *No . . . but a helicopter could!*
> R: [Laughing] *Okay! But we are human beings, we have to* . . .
> K: [Jokingly] But what if we are . . . "superhero"!
> M: *Yeah!*
> R: [Laughing] *That would give you a different distance* . . .

I find this exchange remarkable for a number of reasons. The students displayed unusual initiative in challenging the given and looking at the consequences of changing some elements in the original situation, a problem-posing skill that is rare in mathematics students and that I was hoping would develop as a result of our unit. Furthermore, despite the playfulness of their comments, both students understood that the notion of distance depends essentially upon the constraints of the specific situation considered.

Later, I realized that I had missed a golden opportunity to take advantage of yet another instance of the influence of the context in interpreting a definition. It would have been worthwhile at this point to spend some time following up on the students' alternative suggestions to see how the definition of distance as "the length of a minimal path connecting two points" would hold in all cases yet assume a different interpretation (and, consequently, measure) due to the different constraints experienced by cars, helicopters, or superheroes. At the time, however, I simply acknowledged the reasonableness of the students' objections and tried to conclude the discussion by reaching an agreement about the new rules to be imposed in the nonstandard situation of taxicab geometry so that we could proceed to the crucial point of my original plan, reexamining the definition of circle when it is interpreted in a new context.

Episode 5.2: Identifying taxicircles

To begin our consideration of what happens to circles in taxicab geometry, I asked the students to "draw all the points at distance 5 from a given point in the city." Katya immediately recognized the usual definition of circle:

K: Maybe a circle?
R: *Sounds like a circle, right? Let's try to construct it. Would it look something like this?* [Using a compass, R draws a "usual" circle with radius 5 on the grid.]

Meanwhile, Mary had started figuring out her own version of the question and had drawn all the points at taxidistance 5 from the given point, thus obtaining the figure reproduced in Figure 6–7. She then commented: "I think it should be a diamond." Mary used the word *diamond* to refer to the shape of her taxicircle. I chose to let the students continue to use the word *diamond* rather than introducing the technical term *taxicircle*, since I value the use of a student-generated term for a mathematical concept. Indeed, the ambiguity built into the nontechnical term *diamond* turned out to be very productive (see Episode 5.4).

The difference between Katya's and Mary's interpretations of the problem I had posed and their solutions stimulated further discussion between them.

R: *Now we have two theories.*
K: But . . . you want all the points that are 5 away?
R: *Yes. Why is it not a circle?*
M: *Because you have to cut corners.*
K: [Objecting] You didn't say anything about this. You didn't say it couldn't cut a building in half.
R: *Even if it is reasonable to say you could only go on the roads?*

FIGURE 6–7

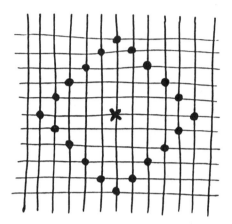

This brought us once again to try to clarify what was meant by *distance* within the context of taxicab geometry and which points could be considered "accessible" in this context. Still, this was not enough to settle the argument, as Katya was not yet convinced that the definition "all the points at a given distance from a given point" could give figures other than the usual circle, regardless of the specific constraints of the situation.

> **M:** *No, let's not do it that way!* [meaning: drawing the circle with a compass] *It is still the same town. There are no ways to go up and down the buildings.*
>
> **K:** So what? She said "5 points away."
>
> **M:** [Reaffirms] *It is a diamond.*

This discussion was going even beyond my most optimistic hopes! I took advantage of the strong disagreement between them to make an important (but often unrecognized) point about mathematical results: the truth of a mathematical statement may depend on the purposes and perspectives of the person evaluating it.

> **R:** *Can it be that both of you are right?*
>
> **M:** [Without hesitation] *Sure! It depends on what you want "distance" to be. It depends on whether you are on a graph or in a town. It's fun, I like this!* [She continues to embellish her graph paper.]
>
> **R:** *You are right, I have to tell you what distance I'm considering. You can argue . . .*
>
> **K:** [Teasingly interrupting] We don't want to argue. Why? We want to be friends.
>
> **R:** [Picking up the joke] *Why? Can't you still be friends and say . . .*

> **M:** [Mockingly] *I disagree with you, Katya!*
> **R:** **Maybe you don't even need to say "I disagree." You can say I agree with you. You are just considering a different "distance."**

It is amazing that Mary made her revolutionary observation—that definitions in mathematics may depend on the context in which one is operating—almost distractedly, as if it were obvious and trivial. Perhaps at this point she was not really aware of the implications of her statement (as is suggested by some of her reactions later in Episode 5.3).

I would also like to comment on Katya's joking "We don't want to argue. We want to be friends." While this remark could be seen as just one more example of the students' sense of humor and pleasure in being playful, it might also be more significant in light of the results of recent studies on gender differences in students' approach to knowledge and learning. If it is true, in fact, that most males (as well as the established scientific and academic environment) favor competition, while females feel more comfortable in a supportive and "connected" environment, Katya's remark may point to gender-related characteristics that could help explain why this capable female student, with an interest in social issues and the humanities, showed a dislike for mathematics. (I will return to the important issue of gender and mathematics in Chapter 11.)

Episode 5.3: A reevaluation of the usual definition of circle

Although the previous discussion might have satisfactorily settled the correct interpretation of the definition "all points at a given distance from a given point in the plane" in taxicab geometry, it raised another crucial issue (which was probably behind much of Katya's resistance in accepting Mary's "diamond" as a circle). We were, in fact, now forced to face the more complex question: Was the definition we had previously agreed upon still an appropriate characterization of the concept of circle?

This new question is indeed much more open-ended than the previous one. In fact, once the constraints of taxicab geometry have been clearly specified and agreed on, there can be no doubt that the figure corresponding to "all the points at a given distance from a given point on the grid" can only be the diamond or taxicircle exemplified in Figures 6–2 and 6–7. In contrast, deciding whether the usual definition is an appropriate characterization of the *concept* of circle will essentially depend on one's judgment of what circles should "look like," and though, of course, such a judgment is not arbitrary, different and justifiable solutions could be suggested depending on one's mathematical knowledge, values, and purposes.

In planning the unit I had not fully appreciated the implications of all of this. Rather, I expected that asking "Is the usual definition of circle still acceptable?" would simply lead Katya and Mary to see the potential for generalization embedded in the usual definition of circle, since that had been *my* reaction when I had addressed that question in my own preliminary inquiries. But because these students did not share my knowledge of mathematical analysis or my philosophical position regarding the critical role of ambiguity in thinking and learning, they did not see this as the only possible conclusion.

I began by commenting that the previous activity (Episode 5.2) had led us to identify two quite different figures that in different contexts would both satisfy the definition of circle. I then asked, "Can we call them both circles? They both satisfy the definition."

This question made Mary look at the situation in a new light. Although she was still ready to support her previous result—that her diamond represented all the points at the same taxidistance from the center point—she also began to realize that this figure did not satisfy many of the other properties of circles.

> **M:** *You could call that* [pointing at the interior angles of her diamond] *a circle, but if you went over it with properties, it wouldn't be a circle, because it's not 360°, is it?*
>
> **R:** [Deciding to point out that Mary is not stating the relevant property of circle correctly yet wanting to give support to her approach and intuition] *This is 360°* [pointing at the angle at the center of the diamond].
>
> **M:** [Disappointed] *Oh, gee!*
>
> **R:** *But other properties may not work in this case. For example, the circumference may no longer be 2πr, or the area πr².*

Mary's observations seemed to be based on her current understanding of the relationship between the *definition* and the *properties* of a concept, which she had stated on her first review sheet: "Definitions → overall identifier. Properties → 2nd opinions, reaffirm." In other words, she understood the basic principle that a mathematical definition should allow one to derive all the other properties of the concept in question and that when it does not, it means that there is something wrong with the definition, something that has to be identified and "fixed."

The realization that not all the properties of the usual circle may be shared by the taxicircles was starting to shake Mary's initial acceptance of this figure as a legitimate circle and led us all to consider the nature of definitions and their relationship to the properties of an object once again.

> **M:** [Pointing to the taxicircle previously drawn] *This does not look like a circle to me.*

> **R:** *But the basic idea of the points being equidistant from the center is there. So, would you say that the definition does not work? Or, what alternatives do we have?*
>
> **M:** *I think the definition works, but you have to use properties to make sure of things.*
>
> **R:** *But the whole idea behind definitions was to be able to identify the essential elements of the concepts—from which all the properties would follow—so that you didn't have to list all the properties.*
>
> **M:** *So we have to rewrite the definition of a circle?*
>
> **R:** *Not necessarily.*

In spite of my response, Mary returned to the original definition of circle we had been working with ("all the points on the plane equidistant from a single point") to determine whether any terms were vague (and might need a more precise definition) or whether *we* had misinterpreted any. Her attention was not caught by the word "equidistant," as I had expected, but rather by the interpretation of the constraint of being "on a plane." This led her to the following argument, which is both creative and logical:

> **M:** *We have not made a circle here. This is not . . . in the definition we said it was on a one-dimensional plane.*
>
> **R:** *Isn't this a plane?*
>
> **M:** *Yeah, but not "one-dimension" because of the buildings. That's more than one dimension.*
>
> **R:** *The situation is not the same.*
>
> **M:** *Yeah, I'm sure . . . in our definition we said "A geometric figure on a plane" . . . and this is not a plane . . .* [becoming silly] *this has chimneys . . . going way up. These* [pointing to the squares on the grid] *are all like buildings that are coming up in 3-D. So the diamond is not a circle.* [Pointing to a drawing of the usual circle] *That's a circle!*

What a nice way to describe the Euclidean plane! A plane with no obstacles! And Mary is absolutely right in her analysis here: by moving to the context of taxicab geometry, the first thing that changed, really, was that we were no longer considering the Euclidean plane but rather a "grid" of streets. Once again, the product of the students' own inquiry had provided new insights for me as well.

Here Mary resolved the potential conflict presented if both the usual circle and the taxicircle satisfy the same definition by finding a "mistake" in our interpretation of the usual definition of circle. Proud of her achievement yet as usual cautious and inquisitive, Mary did not stop here but looked for reinforcement of her argument by searching for other possible "flaws" in either the original definition or our interpretation of it.

> **M:** *It's a neat theory that everything is equidistant, but . . .* [still resisting the suggestion that her diamond might fit the definition of a circle].
>
> **R:** *Are you saying that our definition of circle works . . .*

M: [Interrupting] *Also, it would not work, because in the definition we said that it was a series of points . . . Did we say they were connected?*

R: **No. We said all the points, but we didn't say they were connected . . . It is a property of the circle, but we didn't need it in the definition.**

[Mary agrees with this argument, but seems a bit disappointed that her new criticism did not prove true.]

Mary's conclusions are obviously quite logical and well justified, once we accept her premise that a circle must satisfy certain properties in addition to being "equidistant from the center" as stated in the usual definition. As long as she was convinced of her own argument, she showed no hesitation in correcting a mathematical result established by the Authority—remember that the statement "all the points in the plane at a given distance from a given point" is reported as *the* definition of circle in most geometry textbooks. This once again confirms Mary's increased independence and confidence in her own mathematical and reasoning ability.

When I tried to suggest a different viewpoint, which would justify the use of a "vaguer" and more comprehensive definition of circle, my efforts did not meet with much success. The students had become interested in a different task: the creation of a "good" definition for the concept of *diamond*.

Episode 5.4: Defining diamond

Perhaps in an effort to prove beyond doubt that the taxicircle and the usual circle cannot share the same definition, Mary set herself the task of defining *diamond* precisely. In the process, she was actively helped by Katya, while I mostly observed and occasionally commented upon their activity. It became obvious from their approach that they had a clear idea in mind of what diamond should mean. That is, it seemed as if both students were confident that they could distinguish between instances and noninstances of this concept. It also became clear that they were not attempting to define the concept of taxicircle but rather trying to characterize precisely a shape they were familiar with, of which taxicircles just happened to be examples, although not necessarily the only possible ones.

There was still some concern at the beginning, however, about whether defining diamond would be considered a legitimate mathematical activity, a concern voiced by Mary when she proposed the task itself:

M: *I wonder how we define "diamond"? Or is that not a geometric figure?*
R: *It is a geometric figure.*

Indeed, I believe that any shape we may choose to isolate and abstract can legitimately be considered a "geometric figure," regardless of whether mathematicians in the past chose to focus on it or not. I do not know how Mary interpreted my answer here, but undoubtedly it gave her enough confidence in the value of her question to engage in its pursuit. Somewhat to my surprise, she immediately started to draw several figures and discuss whether they were instances of diamond (without ever dreaming of asking for the instructor's permission!).

During the ten minutes that followed, the two students were totally engrossed in their attempt to refine their tentative definitions of diamond in light of specific examples and counterexamples. It is difficult to convey the enthusiasm that went into this activity or to document the creativity and initiative the students showed in the process, since the dialogue that occurred as they worked was often broken and practically unintelligible unless one could follow the sequence of drawings to which they continually referred. The following excerpts provide at least a glimpse of the students' reasoning.

> **M:** *[A diamond]* *can be of all different shapes. It can be fat. It can be a parallelogram. It can have two really extreme, acute angles.* [She spends some time drawing different "diamonds" similar to the ones reproduced in Figure 6–8.]
>
> **R:** **What is characteristic then?**
>
> **M:** *Two angles are acute?*
>
> **R:** [Pointing at one of Mary's diamonds, which seems to have three obtuse angles] **What about this one?**
>
> [After some thought Mary continues.]
>
> **M:** *Two sets of equal sides. But then you could make it like that.* [She immediately draws a diamond that has four equal sides and gets a rhombus. Surprised, she continues] *Two sets of equal sides. Then you can make it a square* [draws a square]. *You can make it a rectangle* [draws a rectangle].
>
> **R:** **No, that does not [work].**
>
> **M:** *Two sets of equal sides?* [She seems to imply that the equal sides must be situated opposite each other in the quadrilateral.] . . .
>
> **K:** Oh, they have to be meeting? [She points at one of the angles.]
>
> **M:** [Ready to continue] *The two sides that share an angle are equal.*

Both girls continued to work in this fashion for a while, suggesting various examples and trying to refine their definition until they produced the following result, which Mary read aloud with considerable satisfaction: "Diamond is a geometric figure on a plane having two sets of equal sides which have a common angle." While the wording of this definition still leaves something to be desired, conceptually Katya and Mary had succeeded in capturing what is common to all the shapes reported in Figure 6–8 as well as to rhombuses and squares, yet excluding figures such as rectangles.

FIGURE 6–8

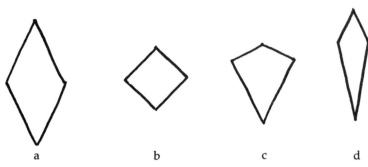

   a   b   c   d

Concluding observations

This episode provides remarkable evidence of the students' (especially Mary's) increasingly sophisticated understanding of the complexity of mathematical definitions and their growing creativity and critical stance within a mathematical learning context. First of all, the last, unplanned activity (Episode 5.4) provided the most valuable test of the students' working knowledge of the process of creating a good mathematical definition for a familiar concept: they themselves felt the need to come up with such a definition, they set the task, they independently proceeded in its solution, and finally, they evaluated the results. In this way they demonstrated their full understanding of the process of successively refining a tentative definition (illustrated in Episode 2.1 with definitions of circle). In addition, through their thinking and their actions they revealed their appreciation of the criteria established by the mathematics community for mathematical definitions, such as isolation of the concept.

Their work on taxicab geometry, even more than their experience on extending exponentiation to more inclusive sets of numbers, succeeded in making the students aware of the role played by context in the meaning of a specific mathematical definition. It also alerted them to the many surprises and problems that can occur when the definition of a familiar concept is reinterpreted in a new context. This is especially evident in the initial discussion about which distance would really be most appropriate in taxicab geometry (Episode 5.1), the debate between the two students about what a taxicircle should look like (Episode 5.2), and Mary's distress when she realized that taxicircles and "usual" circles apparently shared the same definition but not all the same properties (Episode 5.3).

Yet Mary's final resolution of the conflict in Episode 5.3 did not allow the students to fully understand some of the more radical implications of changes in context on one's *image* of the concept itself. Once Mary was able to establish the fact that taxicircles did not share some of what she considered the fundamental properties of the "usual" circle, she concluded that something was wrong with our interpretation of the metric definition of circle and proceeded to find and correct the perceived mistake, feeling totally satisfied that she had thus solved the problem. Her formulation of the problem itself, however, *avoided* rather than *solved* the more fundamental issue of what happens to the set of properties associated with a given concept when we reinterpret it in a new context. Indeed, such a move may have radical consequences. A set of properties that coexisted in a familiar context may become contradictory, logical implications that could be deduced in one system may no longer be possible, and properties that had been used alternatively to derive all the properties of a given concept may now identify a different set of objects and consequently, different concepts. In other words, changing the context may require us to reconsider what the characterizing properties of a concept really are and which of its properties we may be more ready to relinquish if necessary, a choice that may not always turn out to be easy or straightforward.

I must admit that I, too, had overlooked some of these implications. The contrast between Mary's resolution and mine made me seriously reflect on the situation and its implications for my own understanding of the notions of mathematical definition and mathematical concept. My initial simplistic conviction that a certain level of ambiguity in a definition is valuable because it allows us to extend the concept it defines into new domains was challenged to some extent by the realization that, in the process, our image of the concept in question may also need to be modified. These considerations made me think further about some of the criteria established by the mathematics community for the evaluation of mathematical definitions. In view of what may happen when we change context, for example, the requirement of essentiality took on a new meaning for me: by reducing the number of characteristic properties listed in the definition of a given concept, we also reduce the chances that in later extensions of this concept some of these properties might no longer coexist, which would make the concept itself impossible or meaningless in other contexts.

My surprise at Mary's solution—since it did not coincide with the one I had previously reached—also gave me considerable food for thought on a more strictly pedagogical level. When I asked the students to evaluate how well the usual definition of circle captured their notion of what a circle should be, I had presented them, perhaps for the first time in the unit, if not in my whole career as a mathematics teacher, with a genuinely open-ended question. This kind of question has no truly correct answer toward which I could hope to "lead" the students, since, as I have mentioned, the decision about whether the statement "All the points in the plane at a given distance from a given point" is an appropriate definition for the notion of circle is indeed a matter of judgment and depends on many factors. The fact that I had not fully realized this possibility and that I was taken by surprise when a solution different from my own was suggested, made me see how difficult it is in practice to be true to a style of teaching that lets students pursue genuine inquiry, in which they have a say in decisions about the directions worth following and the criteria to be used in evaluating the results. The lack of control over "what's going to happen next" that the teacher might experience in these circumstances is not easy to live with and radically undermines traditional expectations about teacher and student roles in a mathematics class.

Let me conclude this chapter with a brief comment on the remarkable degree of initiative and independence shown by the students—Mary in particular—throughout this episode. On the one hand, I think this can be seen as a result of the effect the new stance of learning assumed in this unusual mathematics course was having on the students toward the end of the experience. At the same time, it is interesting to see how a "non-standard" situation such as taxicab geometry, which had little resemblance to the students' past mathematical experiences in the regular classroom, might by its very novelty have contributed to letting Katya's and Mary's hidden mathematical ability finally flourish.

Looking at Definitions Outside of Formal Mathematics | 7

In the final episodes of the unit, my main goal was to lead Katya and Mary to recognize important similarities between mathematical definitions and definitions as they are used in other fields. As a step in this direction, I wanted to make them aware of the existence of concepts, even within mathematics, that do not really need a rigorous definition in order to be understood and used (Episode 6). For our final meeting (Episode 7) I planned a comparison among definitions across fields; unfortunately, only Mary was able to participate.

For a variety of reasons, I consider these last two episodes the least successful in the mini-course, and I would certainly modify them considerably in any future implementation of such a unit. Nevertheless, the activities in these episodes provided valuable learning experience and new insights for both the students and me, and an analysis of their limitations can serve to highlight several valuable pedagogical points.

Episode 6: "Unnecessary" mathematical definitions: The case of variable

All the mathematical concepts the students and I had considered so far—circle, isosceles and right triangle, polygon, multiplication, exponentiation—required a precise definition in order to identify instances of the concept and/or correctly perform relevant operations, logically derive the properties of the concept, and make use of these properties in problems, proofs, or algebraic manipulations. Not all the concepts employed in mathematics, however, are used in this fashion. In arithmetic and elementary algebra especially, there are a number of concepts—such as equation, operation, number, or variable—that students get to know intuitively and are able to use long before they have all the tools necessary to produce (or even appreciate) their rigorous definition. I thought that it would be important for the students to discuss at least one example of this type of concept in our unit.

Originally, I had planned to use the concept of equation to this end. An equation can be defined mathematically as a relationship between two expressions (each symbolized below by an uppercase letter) that satisfies the following properties:

- $A = A$ (reflexive property).
- If $A = B$ then $B = A$ (symmetric property).
- If $A = B$ and $B = C$, then $A = C$ (transitive property).

This definition of equation may appear too abstract and not very informative, yet such a generality is necessary in order to allow for the great variety of equations used in mathematics: identities, such as $(a + b)^2 = a^2 + 2ab + b^2$; algebraic equations, such as $x + 3 = 5$ or $\sqrt{x^2 - 4} = 1/x$; functions and formulas, such as $y = 3x + 1$ or $A = lw$; and even equations that do not involve numerical quantities, such as differential equations (example: $y' = y$), functional equations (example: $f(x + y) = f(x) + f(y)$), and equations dealing with sets (example: $A \quad B = B \quad A$).

While this definition of equation may satisfy all the requirements of a "rigorous" mathematical definition, it is not of much use if we want to understand the role and meaning of equations in mathematics, nor does it provide much help in actually working with specific equations to solve mathematical problems. In other words, mathematics students (and, in fact, most mathematicians) would not really gain much by "learning," or even creating, a rigorous definition of equation. A number of other elements seem much more crucial for success in most mathematical activities dealing with equations: understanding the meaning of the symbols employed, appreciating the difference between *variable* and *constant*, recognizing which equations should be solved and which ones cannot be solved, and mastering some techniques for manipulating specific types of equations.

My original plan to discuss the concept of equation and its definition along these lines, however, changed as our mini-course progressed because of an unexpected event that occurred during Episode 2.1. While we were attempting to derive the equation characterizing circles in analytic geometry by looking at Figure 7–1, Katya observed the striking similarity between the analytic equation of circles with center in the origin ($x^2 + y^2 = r^2$) and the equation describing a fundamental property of right triangles in the Pythagorean theorem ($a^2 + b^2 = c^2$): *"That's so neat . . . that's why! . . .*

FIGURE 7–1

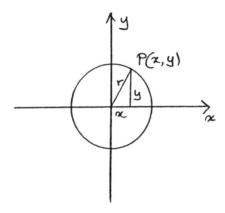

I always noticed that the circle formula is almost exactly like the formula in the Pythagorean theorem!"

Katya then raised an interesting question, which brought to our attention the various meanings that can be assumed by the same *symbol* in algebra: "But . . . how could you say that this is the equation for the circle when it is also the formula in the Pythagorean theorem for triangles?" Katya's doubts were quite justified, since the meaning assumed by the two syntactically identical formulas ($x^2 + y^2 = r^2$ and $a^2 + b^2 = c^2$) essentially depends on whether the letters used in these equations are interpreted as *variables* or as *constants* (an interesting example of *ambiguity* within mathematical symbolism).

When Katya first expressed her concern, it took me by surprise and caused me to look at the two equations in a new light. At the time, I was able to clarify her immediate concern by pointing out that in the equation for *circle* one of the letters (r) is a constant, a fixed number, while there is no such fixed number in the equation for the Pythagorean theorem. But I thought it would be worthwhile to come back to this example later to pursue a more in-depth analysis of the concept of variable and its definition.

Since the concept of variable can be intuitively understood and used well before a formal definition of the concept can be achieved, I thought I would use it instead of equation in Episode 6 to discuss "unnecessary" mathematical definitions. Because of Katya's earlier concerns, I hoped that using the concept of variable would present the added advantage of showing the students that I valued their observations and that they could generate worthwhile ideas to explore. Thus, part of our sixth meeting was devoted to a follow-up on Katya's "confusion" about the relationship between the analytic equation of circle and the formula for the Pythagorean theorem, which in turn led us to take a closer look at the concept of variable.

After reminding the students of Katya's question about the equations $x^2 + y^2 = r^2$ and $a^2 + b^2 = c^2$, I asked:

> **R:** *Do you think all of these—x, y, r, a, b, c—are variables?*
>
> **M:** *No, r—the radius—is not a variable. It's like an abbreviation. I don't really mean to say that a variable is a symbol . . . [continues] r is a constant. It's not a variable. It's like a universal abbreviation for radius.*
>
> **K:** Radius is an actual thing. It's like a number.
>
> **R:** [Perhaps misunderstanding what Katya meant by "actual thing"] ***Then a, b, and c are also "actual things," because they are the lengths of the sides of a triangle. Then x and y are also "actual things" that you can measure*** [R refers to Figure 7–1 illustrating the geometric meaning of x and y].
>
> **M:** *r is a part of the circle, just like the center . . .*
>
> **R:** *I agree with you that r, the radius, is different from x and y in this equation; but I would say it is because r stands for something that is constant, while x and y are variables because their value can really "vary." In order to create a circle you have to be able to think of many pairs of x and y, while r always remains the same.* [Moving to consider the equation $a^2 + b^2 = c^2$.] *What about a, b, c, here?*
>
> **M:** *Wouldn't these all be constants? If we're working on the same triangle?*
>
> **R:** *Yes, if I give you a specific triangle. But $a^2 + b^2 = c^2$ also works for any right triangle. In that case all three of them are variables.*
>
> **R:** *If you have a right triangle, then you know that the lengths of its sides a, b, and c will be a solution to $a^2 + b^2 = c^2$. If you take points on the circle, their coordinates (x, y) will be a solution to $x^2 + y^2 = r^2$. Does this clarify the difference between variable and constant?*

In this conversation it is obvious that I took on a much more directive role than usual. Yet I noticed it only long afterwards, when I was reading over the transcripts of this lesson. Indeed, this is one of the few examples in the entire mini-course when I led the students in a sort of Socratic dialogue and furnished explanations when they did not "get it" immediately on their own. The result, as Mary shrewdly pointed out to me later, after she had read this exchange in the manuscript, was that I did not let the students construct their own understanding of the difference between variables and constants, and when they left the lesson I did not really know what they had "learned" from it.

At the time, I assumed that the discussion had satisfactorily clarified the difference between variables and constants and decided that we could turn to the definition of variable. To do so, I suggested that we first go back and reexamine the definitions the students had proposed during our first meeting (see Episode 1):

> *M:* *A symbol or letter that represents an unknown element of an equation.*
>
> *K:* Used in algebra. What you are looking to solve for. The solution usually referred to as x. W + 1 = 3 in this equation, W is the variable.

Katya and Mary encountered numerous obstacles as they attempted to improve on these definitions by taking the result of our previous discussion into account—much as I had expected would happen. But this process proved valuable, since it led them to identify and further clarify some important aspects of the notion of *variable*.

> *M:* [Giving her original definition another try] *Being vague I could write again what I had here, but you gave us the impression that it was wrong.*
>
> *R:* **Not really.** [Referring to Mary's definition] **By "unknown" do you mean something that can vary?**
>
> *M:* [With humor] *No, even worse! It's used for representing a varying body or something!?*
>
> *R:* **Yet you know what a variable is.**
>
> *K:* [Reading aloud her new definition of variable] A letter or a sign for something representing a varying value.
>
> *R:* [Writing] **Suppose we take something like this:** • + 3 = 5. **Could the bullet be a variable? Or consider x + 3 = 5. Would x be the variable?**
>
> *K:* [Resorting to authority again] That's what we learned! [Pointing to x] Looks like a variable . . .
>
> *R:* **Then the bullet too should be considered a variable. I just used a different symbol, but I'm saying the same thing.**
>
> *M:* *We could have used a flower! It seems we should say a symbol in the definition.*
>
> *K:* A sign?

Another element in Katya's definition—a sign representing a varying *value*—led me to make the following observation, aimed at clarifying that a variable does not necessarily have to stand for a *numerical* value or quantity: "Do you think it should be a number, or could it be a varying value of something else?" When they did not reply, I continued, "Did you ever do something with sets? If I say $A \cup B = C$, or $A \cup B = B \cup A$, do you think A and B are variables? It could be a different set every time. So, 'value' may not necessarily mean a number. It could be other kinds of things as well."

By forcing the students to look more closely at their own mental image of variable and at several known instances of it, this discussion led them to see new aspects of this concept, such as the fact that a variety of symbols and values, as well as letters and numbers, can be associated with it. Thus, regardless of the "truth" or "rigor" of the definition they finally achieved, this exercise in refining a tentative definition once again proved useful in fostering a better understanding of the concept in question. This was not a result I had really expected when I was planning this part of the mini-course, and I realized that creating a definition for a given mathematical concept, even when a rigorous one might not be strictly necessary, was valuable in itself. At the same time, this exercise was not as successful as I had hoped in illustrating that rigorous mathematical definitions might not always be necessary.

When I asked the students whether having a precise definition of variable would indeed be useful, Katya expressed some doubt.

> *K:* I know that the radius is not a variable, and x and y are variables. But that's not going to help me do the equation!
>
> *R: We need to know what a variable is, because otherwise you don't know what to solve the equation for. On the other hand, we may not need a definition of variable that is as precise as that of a circle.*

Here I managed to make a double blunder. I missed the opportunity offered by Katya's remark to pursue the argument that formal, rigorous definitions of constant, variable, and equation are not always necessary in order to understand and work with these concepts, the very point of my lesson. And, partly because I had not listened carefully enough to Katya's expressed concern, my response missed its target. In order to be grasped by the students, the subtle point I was trying to make here needed more elaboration and illustration at the very least. Furthermore, contrary to what had happened when we dealt with the definitions of circle, polygon and exponentiation, creating a definition for variable lacked a specific purpose. Since Katya and Mary did not need to *use* the definition they were working at, how could they truly decide whether their result was acceptable or not? In the circumstances, they could only reach such a conclusion on the basis of my authority.

Perhaps a better way to achieve my original goal would have been to search through a few high school mathematics textbooks to locate definitions for some key concepts the students were familiar with—such as number, variable, constant, equation, geometric figure, and operation. Analyzing how these concepts were defined—if they were defined at all!—might have provided a more compelling starting point for a discussion of when and why a specific mathematical concept would require a rigorous definition.

Episode 7: Looking at definitions across fields

I had originally planned to conclude our instructional sessions by comparing definitions in various fields in order to show Katya and Mary that mathematical definitions are not so different from those used in most other domains. Our inquiry so far had already provided many good reasons to doubt the popular belief that mathematical definitions should always be "perfectly rigorous and precise." We had dealt with mathematical definitions that could be considered vague or ambiguous—inasmuch as the interpretation of some of their terms might depend on the mathematical context in which we were operating or on the mathematical background of the person reading it—as had been the case for circle. We had realized that mathematical definitions are not "written in stone" and might need to be modified in light of new discoveries or circumstances, as happened with polygon and exponentiation. Our encounter with the definition of variable, despite the limited success of the activity, had prepared the students to see that formal mathematical definitions may not always be needed. I hoped that considering some of these "limitations" would make the students feel less intimidated by mathematical definitions. At the same time, I was also interested in seeing whether they would feel inclined to apply some of the procedures they had learned in this unit to areas outside of mathematics.

With this goal in mind, and also in part to conclude by coming full circle, I thought it would be worthwhile during our last meeting to ask Katya and Mary once again to write a definition for the nine concepts (circle, square, polygon, variable, exponent, equation, cat, crazy, and purple) we had discussed at our first meeting. I expected that the product, as well as the process followed by the students, would motivate a discussion about similarities and differences between definitions in mathematics and in other fields. It was a real disappointment when I learned that only Mary would be able to attend this last session and that for various reasons it would be impossible to reschedule so that both students could participate. In the end, however, Mary's performance was remarkable and initiated quite an interesting discussion.

Mary approached the assigned task without comment, working on each item in the list in the order in which it had been presented to her. But soon she started feeling uneasy.

> M: *What do you call the plane?*
> R: ***Just call it the plane. If you'd prefer call it the usual plane if you have doubts . . .***
> M: [To herself, while writing] *For polygon I have: "A closed geometric figure comprised of straight lines." I can't remember what else . . .* [inaudible]

In writing definitions for the first six mathematical terms on our list, Mary was mostly trying to recall the "final" definitions produced in our previous lessons. She did not even consider the possibility of going over some of the processes we had established for creating and evaluating definitions during the mini-course, such as checking whether the tentative definition she had initially produced succeeded in including instances of the concept and excluding noninstances. This contrasts markedly with the ability she had demonstrated in Episode 5.4, when she independently initiated and led the activity to create an appropriate definition for diamond.

The most likely explanation for this rather disappointing performance lies in the nature of the task itself. As I remarked in my comments on Episode 1, asking students to produce definitions for given concepts *without providing a specific purpose and context for doing so* is unlikely to inspire them to approach the task in a constructive way. In addition, the request to write definitions for circle, polygon, variable, and exponent *at the end of the unit*, after we had spent a considerable amount of time discussing the definitions of these very concepts, may have contributed to Mary's perception of the task as a sort of "test"; hence her "recalling" approach.

The results of Mary's efforts to define the six mathematical concepts are as follows:

Circle: the locus of points in the plane equidistant from a fixed point.

Square: a closed four-sided geometric figure on a unorganized plane having four 90° interior angles. All sides are of equal length, opposite sides are parallel.

Polygon: a closed geometric figure comprised of straight lines.

Variable: a symbol representing a given value.

Exponent: $a^h = a \times a \times a \times a \times a \ldots \times a$; a number or variable that signifies the base value in a more complex form (example: $5^2 = 5 \times 5 = 25$)

Equation: a mathematical sentence stating equality, inequality, or some balance of numerical value.

While, as I argued before, I do not think that these definitions are an appropriate measure of Mary's improved understanding of mathematical definitions, most of them come closer to the "textbook" definition than her first attempts in Episode 1. It is also interesting to note some elements that clearly reflect the effect of the earlier activities in the unit. In particular, her use of the phrase "an *unorganized* plane" in her definition of square reveals her awareness of the surprises that can occur when we move away from Euclidean geometry.

The assignment became more lively and interesting as soon as Mary hit upon the definition of cat. In this case, when she tried to apply the criterion of isolation of the concept, which we had emphasized in mathematical definitions, she encountered unexpected obstacles.

> **M:** *The thing about cat . . . I'd like to say all these things about it, but there are so many exceptions . . . and we shouldn't include exceptions, right?*
>
> **R:** *Well, remember what happened when we worked with exponents . . . there were exceptions, right?*
>
> **M:** *[Continues to write, groaning] How heavy would you say a cat is?*
>
> **R:** *Well, I think it depends.*
>
> **M:** *I can define a breed of cats.*
>
> **R:** *Well, maybe you can skip this definition and go to the others . . . and then come back.*

Taking my suggestion, Mary abandoned the definition of cat for the moment and proceeded to the remaining two items on the list, *crazy* and *purple*. As in Episode 1, she found no problem producing good "dictionary" definitions for these more complex concepts.

> *Crazy:* a state of mental health not considered "normal" in a given society; a state of emotional/mental unbalance legally proclaimed by a psychiatrist.
>
> *Purple:* a color comprised by the balance of red and blue equally mixed, the color of grape juice.

Mary was also able to respond well to some of my critical remarks on these definitions.

> **M:** *This is much easier . . .*
> **R:** **What did you write for "crazy"? "A state of mental health . . . "**
> **M:** *" . . . not considered 'normal' in a given society; a state of emotional/mental unbalance legally proclaimed by a psychiatrist."*
> **R:** **It's interesting that what I consider abnormal mental health may not be not the same thing as you do.**
> **M:** *That's why I wrote "normal" in quotes. But, you know, in a given society there are basic outlines of what is considered normal.*
> **R:** **Okay, so that's why you wrote "in a given society" . . .**

Here is good evidence that Mary had internalized the importance of the context in interpreting a definition, even outside of mathematics.

She was still considerably bothered by her previous inability to write a "good" definition of cat, and thus came back to this item as soon as she had finished with the others. When I tried to explore the reasons for her difficulty, a very thought-provoking conversation followed.

> **R:** **Can you tell me why you have so much trouble with "cat," while you seemed to go very quickly through the other definitions.**
> **M:** *Kitty-cats . . . I can't say they have a tail . . .*
> **R:** *[Agrees.]*
> **M:** *I can't say how long their fur is because . . . I can't say they have a tail because it can be cut off by cars . . . Sometimes they have only three paws! And I rarely see a cat with the normal amount of toes on its feet! . . . and I said, usually they have all five senses. Five senses, it could be a dog, so . . . I can't say they have whiskers. My St. Bernard has whiskers . . .*
>
> **M:** *[chuckles] I can draw a little picture.*
> **R:** **But again, not all cats would look like your picture . . . but I guess people would be able to recognize it's a cat then.**
> **M:** *Charming . . . Hmm . . . I could give the Latin term for what a cat is . . .*
> **R:** **Do you think that you would be able, given any animal, to decide whether it's a cat or not?**
> **M:** *How I decide it's a cat?*
> **R:** *[agrees] Maybe what you're saying is that there are a lot of characteristics that kind of go together. It's more difficult . . .*

M: [Interrupting] *How would I know it's a cat . . . all right . . .* [starts writing seriously again] *I want to describe all the mess of kitty-cats, that they are inquisitive, flappy . . . I'm thinking of myself walking down the street: I see a cat. How do I know it's a cat? . . .* [laughter] *Because it's a cat . . . because it's not a dog . . . oh . . .*

Despite the playfulness of some of her comments, Mary demonstrates a considerable appreciation of the complexity of finding an appropriate definition for what initially seemed a simple concept. She was obviously trying to create a definition of cat by identifying a set of characterizing properties that would belong to *all* cats and to cats *only,* much as we had done in the case of circle in Episode 2.1, polygon in Episode 3.1, and diamond in Episode 5.4. While she did not have any problem deciding whether a specific "object" was a cat or not, she found it difficult to identify properties common to all cats. She realized that there are considerable variations among members of the species (later in the conversation, she explicitly mentioned the many breeds of cats she knew of). She also realized with dismay that not all cats comply with even the most fundamental characteristics of the species, since, due to all sorts of accidents, some cats may lose some of their toes, paws, or tail. Yet any of these "shortcomings" would not make them any less a "cat."

Mary's observations about the definition of cat point out some fundamental problems embedded in the notion of *definition* itself. When we think carefully about it, the intuitive and appealing idea that the definition of a concept should "capture" the set of properties that *all* of its instances share (what I would call a *definition by abstraction*) may not always work for complex concepts. Using the concept of game as an example, Wittgenstein (1968) in fact argued that the instances of a concept may present such variations among themselves that the intersection of all their properties may actually be the empty set!

Consider for example the proceedings that we call "games." I mean board-games, Olympic games, and so on. What is common to all of them?—Don't say: "There must be something in common, or they would not be called 'games' "—but look and see whether there is something in common to all.—For if you look at them you will not see something in common to all, but similarities, relationships, and a whole series of them at that. [. . .] I think of no better expression to characterize these similarities than "family resemblances" for the various resemblances between members of a family: build, features, colour of eyes, temperament, etc. etc. overlap and crisscross in the same way.—And I shall say: "games" form a family. (pp. 31–32)

Defining a concept on the basis of *family resemblances* among its instances rather than *by abstraction* is certainly a revolutionary notion, especially in mathematics. Yet when we look at mathematical concepts such as number, infinity, or even exponent, the alternative of looking at *family resemblances* is worthy of consideration (see Borasi, 1984).

At the time this conversation took place, I did not fully realize the potential of Mary's observations about the extent of variations among cats and thus was not able to take advantage of them to initiate reflection on "what a concept is" and "how we can characterize it." Adhering to my original goal for this lesson, I instead suggested that Mary compare her difficulties with the definition of cat and some of our earlier experiences in dealing with mathematical definitions. Indeed, Mary was able to draw some interesting connections between this situation and what she had learned about mathematical definitions, although throughout the conversation she never abandoned her foremost concern—to improve her definition of cat. Specifically, she recognized the key role played by *context* and *purpose* in the creation and evaluation of definitions in all fields.

R: *What do you think . . . about equations? Couldn't you say that there are lots of kinds of equations? Some equations have a square; some equations don't; some equations have only numbers; some equations have symbols. How were you able to come up with something that describes equations, considering all the variety within this concept?*

M: *I just put down the basic . . . [inaudible]*

R: *But it's more difficult to do it for "cat"?*

M: *Yeah . . . when you're trying to define a cat in logical terms . . . A basic cat structure!*

R: *Let me ask you a different question. Do you think there are things in mathematics that you can recognize . . . but that you have difficulty coming up with a definition for?*

M: *Oh sure.*

R: *Can you give me an example?*

M: *An exponent?*

R: *Okay, how would you write a definition for it?*

M: *I gave a first definition of exponent as something that sits on top of a number.*

R: *So, if you see something like this, you know it's . . .*

M: *Wait . . . to define it . . . you need to agree on what the purpose is.*

R: *I think you're right in saying that you can describe an exponent by saying "whenever you see a little number on top of another one, that is an exponent." But you weren't satisfied with it, because you were saying . . .*

M: *So what do you do with it?*

R: *Right!*

M: *[Groans] Especially as you did in class before . . . a circle is like the outside of a doughnut . . . Sure! It looks like the outside of a doughnut, but you can't really use that in the definition, because a definition shows the purpose . . . it should have. Its own purpose . . . [Chuckles] I just painted one kitty-cat . . . I'll bring it in . . . [Mumbling] It gets hard.*

R: *It gets hard, yes. Perhaps it seems more difficult in the case of "cat" because there are so many properties . . . Do you think that definitions are different in mathematics?*

M: Yes, because, as far as I know, there aren't as many different kinds of exponents as there are cats . . . And they don't get hit by cars. Because when you find a lump of flesh on the road . . . you know it should be a cat, but it shouldn't have those characteristics. You can't do that to exponents.

R: But there are different kinds of exponents, right? We know that if you have a positive integer as an exponent, it has a different meaning than if you have a negative integer and all that . . .

M: And also what we were doing about a circle, in a different context, that if you drew it a little different that it's still a circle?

R: [Agrees]

M: So I should find a definition that fits kitty-cats in all different contexts . . . domestic cats . . . I would have to go to everybody's house and look at their cat . . . and I know enough cats to know that no two cats are alike! [Chuckles]

R: But then, in a sense, no two exponents are alike! Every exponent means a different thing. But still you were able to come up with something general about them. Even if you have exceptions, and even if you have differences among exponents. So, maybe it's just a question of a difference in degree [between mathematical definitions and definitions in other fields].

The level of this conversation is amazing for a secondary school student. Here, Mary was able to relate her present difficulties in creating a definition for cat to her earlier experiences with mathematical definitions in our unit. Not only was she able to respond thoughtfully and to the point to my suggestion to draw connections from our previous work with exponents, she also brought in the surprising results she encountered with circles in taxicab geometry. In this conversation Mary clearly showed her understanding of many of the crucial elements addressed in the mini-course, such as the fact that a definition should have purpose and meaning, and that it depends on the context. She also seemed quite able to transfer the process for improving an initial tentative mathematical definition (by verifying whether it succeeded in distinguishing instances of the concept from noninstances) to definitions in other fields.

Mary commented about this very activity.

M: I like starting with this and ending with this. I think I've learned a lot about these definitions.

R: Well, we didn't do too much with the nonmathematical definitions.

M: But, you know, if I sat down with "cat," "crazy," and "purple," I could get a better definition of them just because of the processes we went through to get the other definitions.

The lesson ended by coming back once again to the problem of defining cat, which Mary clearly felt still compelled to resolve:

R: Maybe that's really what the scientists do when they characterize "cat." They might have found out that there are some common characteristics.

M: Watch for patterns.

R: **Right. It would be easier . . .**

M: [Interrupting] *That's why I was getting the "silky, sultry" stuff, because a cat is really smooth, and I can see doing a survey of kitty-cats finding general traits that they all have. But I don't know if I could make a definition from which someone could draw a cat, or recognize a cat . . .*

R: **It might be quite difficult.**

M: *And the list of exceptions would scare people from reading a definition* [laughter].

R: **That's a good point too.**

M: *That's why they go into defining kinds of cat—a Burmese, or a Siamese . . .*

R: **It seems also that in some cases it's more interesting to see what all the different kinds or breeds are, rather than to get a definition that says all the general things.**

M: *Like what we did with exponents.*

R: **Right. And in a sense also "equation." You have to know quadratic equation, and linear equation, and the ones you can graph. Getting to know all the different types of equations may be almost more interesting than getting the definition of equation.**

M: *Yeah. I'm sure they are more interesting than the definition.*

Once again, Mary's comparison between types of exponents and breeds of cats speaks for her ability to transfer what she has learned about mathematical definitions across fields and suggests that her perception of the difference between mathematical definitions and real-life definitions is more a "difference in degree" than a "difference in kind."

8 | *Working Independently: The Final Project*

Episode 8: The final project

The problem of how to evaluate what Katya and Mary had learned in our mini-course troubled me for a long time. Throughout the unit, I had tried to encourage them to question, doubt, inquire, and pose problems in mathematics, rather than simply acquire knowledge and skills to solve specific problems. Thus, I was aware that a typical in-class test, with its time constraints and closed questions, and the expectations it was likely to inspire because of the students' prior scholastic experience, was not an appropriate measure of their growth in terms of my instructional goals.

A take-home project seemed a better choice as a "final evaluation" tool. I believed that this format would allow me to assign a real open-ended task, and thus provide the students with the opportunity to be inquisitive and creative while they applied their newly acquired knowledge about mathematical definitions. By doing the project on their own at home, the students could also show me what they were able to do *without my guidance*. Finding an appropriate project, though, was no easy task, and the one I finally decided upon did not leave me completely satisfied even if it did enable me to gather some interesting information about the students' learning.

Before I describe the nature of the project, I would like to report on the genesis of the task itself. The students played an unexpected role in its formulation, and their participation was one of the most valuable elements in the course, since it revealed a high degree of independence and creativity on their part.

My first idea had been to find a mathematical situation different from those we had covered in our instructional sessions and yet of a similar nature to see what the students were able to transfer from their work in the unit. Finding such a situation, however, turned out to be quite difficult, and I soon moved on to an alternative task: asking the students to write a comprehensive essay about "mathematical definitions" in which, assuming other high school students and prospective mathematics teachers as their audience, they would attempt to synthesize what they had learned.

To my surprise, the students responded to this idea with little enthusiasm and even some disappointment! They had no qualms about explaining these negative reactions and stating what their expectations had been.

> *K:* Is this something . . .
>
> *M:* *Is this the project you meant?* [Both seem surprised.]
>
> *R:* **Yeah.**
>
> *M:* *Because I had a totally different idea . . .*
>
> *R:* **Okay, what did you think?**
>
> *M:* [Almost talking over R] *. . . last night, in fact* [laughter] *. . . I was talking with* [my boyfriend] *about how much work I will have coming up next week, as we were talking about doing some things. I said, "I've got a big project coming up," and he said, "Well, what do you have to do?" and I said, "Well, I think that she is going to give us a figure, or something that needs to be defined, and then we have to define it and give all of its properties, by figuring out . . . And I thought, that would be fun, but hard work . . . it would probably be something really complex, and I would have to work on it for hours and hours and hours* [laughs] *. . .*
>
> [During this time, R makes encouraging sounds.]
>
> *K:* I thought something like that, too, or else . . . that you would give us graph paper or something, and we would have to construct a little town or something, and tell a story about how long it would take to get . . . [everybody is laughing supportingly] . . . I don't know!
>
> *R:* **Would you prefer something like that?**
>
> *K:* I don't know.
>
> *M:* *Yeah! This* [meaning R's idea for the project] *is interesting . . . but it's just . . . kind of review . . .*
>
> *K:* This will be just like rounding everything which we have learned, and just like putting it on paper . . .
>
> *R:* **Right.**
>
> *K:* But instead, doing something . . . taking everything that we have learned and actually applying it to something else . . .
>
> *M:* *That's why I thought you would take all this, and then we would have to apply it to something new. . . .*
>
> *R:* **I like your ideas for the project very much, so . . .**
>
> *M:* *Maybe we could incorporate them? So that Katya could make a little town, and I can make a little* [inaudible]?

R: *Well, why don't you elaborate, each of you, on what you were thinking, and maybe we can compromise. . . .*

K: I was thinking . . . maybe even just constructing something, like making a little place or something, but, . . . like the thing about the circle, planes and stuff, and . . . something like "Sesame Street," like circles and other pictures, and there are all those other buildings, and you can define them . . . Like the taxi-driver story . . . Like how distance can be counted . . . [laughs and stops].

M: *My idea, was . . . that we would be given something that we would not be familiar with, either a geometric figure, or something in arithmetic, or algebra, which we had to find a definition for, going through trial and error, and . . . after we had build up all of the possible properties, and . . . a good definition that we were . . . safe with, or two definitions, apply it to problems that we find in mathematics and show its properties and . . . what we use it for.*

R: *This is something that needs some thinking on my part. I will try to think up something and then maybe suggest some new project.*

And indeed, I took the students' comments seriously. I went back to my very first idea, elaborated it while also trying to incorporate some of the concrete suggestions they had made, and finally came up with the text of the project reproduced below.

I remained impressed by the students' participation in the formulation of this project. It is unusual for students to challenge a teacher's decision about what should be on a test, especially in mathematics. Katya and Mary's initiative in this regard seems to me to be a clear result of the different roles they as students and I as teacher had assumed in this mini-course. What I find even more remarkable is that the students seemed totally unaware of the significance of their gesture and brought forth their criticisms and alternative suggestions very simply and spontaneously. In addition, while expressing their disappointment in the initial project they were able to describe what their expectations had been. These expectations, Mary's in particular, demonstrated their realization that what they had learned could be "transferred" and that a mathematical task could provide an opportunity for creative activity.

The final text of the project

The project I finally assigned Katya and Mary consisted of three parts. The first part asked the students to prove the equivalence of three definitions of perpendicular bisector; the second part asked them to explore the differences between circles, ellipses, parabolas, and perpendicular bisectors in the context of Euclidean geometry and of taxicab geometry; the third part was even more open-ended and involved the creation of a story or a map reflecting what they had learned about taxicab geometry.

To make such a complex task more understandable, I provided the students with a handout, describing in detail the three components of the project and what they were expected to do within each of them. Following is the text as it was given to the students, although later I discovered some small mistakes and imprecise wording which I will comment on further. Page breaks in the original document are indicated by asterisks.

Final project

This projects comprises three parts, which are related to each other, but do not necessarily need to be done in the order they have been presented here.

You can collaborate on this project at any point and come to me for help or suggestions, but I expect each of you to work on the project individually and to give me an individual written report on your work on Part 1 and 2. For Part 3, instead, you can decide whether you prefer to work together or separately, and end up with a common report or two separate ones as you wish.

Part 1
Given a definition, try to know all you can about the object it characterizes
DEF.1: *The locus of points equidistant from two given points.*
DEF.2: *The line perpendicular to a segment and passing through its midpoint.*
DEF.3: *The locus of the centers of the circles passing through two given points.*
What "geometric figure" corresponds to each of these definitions?
How could you try to construct the figure described by each definition?

(Hints:
- for def.1, remember the definition of the circle as "locus of points equidistant from one fixed point"
- for def.3, look back at your notes/review sheets regarding the problem of finding the circle passing through three given points)

DO NOT TURN TO PAGE 2 UNTIL YOU FEEL YOU HAVE DONE ALL YOU CAN HERE. ON THE OTHER HAND, IF YOU WANT TO TAKE A BREAK FROM THIS EXERCISE, TURN TO "PART 2" ON PAGE 3

* * * * *

It looks as if the three definitions given in the previous page all describe the same geometric figure. Can you prove that they are (or are not) equivalent definitions?

(In order to do so, first state in writing what you think has to be done in order to prove that three definitions are equivalent. Then you can try to actually prove each of the "steps" you have identified for this specific case. This may be quite difficult and require some imagination. Give it a try, and I can give you some help too later on.)

Let us call the object identified by either of these definitions the PERPENDICULAR BISECTOR.

Here are some instructions telling how to draw a perpendicular bisector of two points A and B, using only a straight edge and a compass:

Place the fixed end of the compass on point A and the moving end on point B, and draw the circle; then place the fixed end of the compass on point B and the moving end on point A, and draw the circle; use the straight edge to draw the line passing through the two points which are common to both circles; this line is the perpendicular bisector of A and B.

What do you think of these instructions?

(Note: the ancient Greeks were particularly fond of this kind of exercise, which can require a great deal of creativity—it is much more challenging than using a computer!)

List as many properties of the perpendicular bisector as you can (including those stated in its various alternative definitions).

* * * * *

Part 2
Exploring how the context may change the meaning of a definition

Here are the definitions of some interesting geometric figures:

CIRCLE: *the locus of points equidistant from a fixed point.*
PERPENDICULAR BISECTOR: *the locus of points equidistant from two fixed points.*
ELLIPSE: *the locus of points such that the sum of their distances from two fixed points is constant.*
PARABOLA: *the locus of points equidistant from a fixed point and a fixed line (surprised?).*

Explore what geometric figures these definitions characterize:

• in the usual plane
• in taxigeometry

(Note: in taxigeometry especially, try out the definitions in more than one situation, choosing different points and locations—you might get different results!)

Can you also think of other contexts (besides the regular plane and taxigeometry) where these definitions could be applied? What figures would they characterize in that context?

* * * * *

Part 3
Be creative and humanistic

Through the exploration conducted in Part 2, you now know a lot more about the geometry of a city (where we have to accept the disturbing limitation of not being able to walk through buildings and walls).

Can you create a map and/or a story about a city that makes use of some of the knowledge you have gained? You may state problems or situations that may have surprising results because of the different properties of this situation; or make fun of the consequences of using usual geometric results in this situation; or just use some of the shapes you have discovered—if you find them appealing—in your "planning" of the city.

These are just some suggestions . . . let your imagination free, and do not be too bothered to create something "mathematically" interesting. Rather, it is important that your result be, as much as possible, artistic and appealing.

HAVE FUN!!

Comments on the text of the project

The educational potential of the assigned project seems more interesting to me than the results it actually produced when the students engaged in it, partly because of the nature of the task itself and partly because of the students' uneven performance on any out-of-class assignment. I would thus like to comment on my rationale for the various components of this project and on the learning opportunities inherent in each.

Part 1

In general, the task of proving the equivalence between three alternative definitions of the same geometric object was intended to measure to what extent the students had understood the "ideal" requirements for mathematical definitions when used within a formal mathematics system such as Euclidean geometry. I thought that its various components would give the students an opportunity to demonstrate whether they were able to:

- Use the information provided by a given definition to identify a mathematical concept.
- Distinguish between the *set of properties* and the *definition* of a given mathematical concept and derive some mathematical properties of the concept in question from its definition.
- Recognize the possibility of alternative definitions for the same mathematical concept.
- Prove the equivalence of two alternative definitions (by showing that the set of properties stated in one of them implies the set of properties stated in the other, and vice-versa).
- Discover the minimum number of proofs necessary to verify whether *three* definitions are equivalent.

The concept of perpendicular bisector seemed especially suited to this exercise. The students were familiar with the figure it described, since we had used it in Episode 2 when working on problems involving circles, but we had not discussed its definition. It is an elementary geometric concept, yet it can be defined in at least three different ways. And, it is an interesting notion to explore in the context of taxicab geometry (as the students were asked to do in Part 2).

Only later when it was pointed out to me by an outside reader did I realize that throughout Part 1 I assumed that we were operating within the context of the Euclidean plane, although I never explicitly said so. This omission did not matter to Katya, who (like me) also assumed the Euclidean plane as the context for her work. Mary, in contrast, was able to recognize and take advantage of the ambiguity I had built into the task (however involuntarily), thus making the task itself more worthwhile than I had originally intended it to be.

Part 2

Here the students were asked to explore the geometric figures corresponding to the metric definitions of circle, perpendicular bisector, ellipse, and parabola—that is, the characterization of these loci solely in terms of properties involving distances—in two contexts, Euclidean plane geometry and taxicab geometry. My objective was to probe how well the students could interpret the same definition in different contexts, and to provide a situation that would offer room for open-ended mathematical exploration.

I also wanted to see to what extent each student would:

- Be able to interpret definitions with which she was probably not very familiar, such as those of ellipse and parabola.
- Attempt to see if the choice of different positions for the fixed points would make a difference in the "shape" of the figure described by the definition (in Euclidean geometry and in taxicab geometry) and what conclusions this would trigger.
- Be able to transfer to taxicab geometry some of the results and constructions she had learned in Euclidean geometry (for instance, realizing that the perpendicular bisector in taxicab geometry could be found by using the same idea described in Part 1 for the construction of the perpendicular bisector in Euclidean geometry, provided that she reinterprets each term correctly by taking into consideration the new constraints presented by taxicab geometry).
- Create further questions and pose further problems about these geometrical objects on her own.

The contexts of Euclidean geometry and taxicab geometry seemed ideal for all these purposes, because both are quite elementary and yet their exploration can lead to some surprising results, especially when one compares the "shapes" assumed by the same metric locus in these two contexts. My choice of the four concepts was based on the facts that they are among the simplest metric loci, they can be easily constructed by applying the given definition, and they present some interesting differences in the two contexts (see Figures 6–2 to 6–6 in Chapter 6 for examples of taxicircles, taxiperpendicular bisectors and taxiconics).

Part 3

The last part was designed to appeal to the students' creativity and to see how they could relate what we were doing in mathematics to their abilities and interests in the arts and humanities. For this reason—but also because I could not come up with anything better at the time—I left the task very open-ended. I hoped that the students would use this opportunity to create a "real-life" context in which some of the new notions we had explored in taxicab geometry would make sense.

The students' work

In the following pages, the projects produced by Mary and Katya—redrawn and rewritten for readability—are presented in their entirety to demonstrate the quality and extent of their independent work.

MARY'S PROJECT

PART I

DEFINITION 1: THE LOCUS OF POINTS EQUIDISTANT
FROM TWO GIVEN POINTS

A) IMMEDIATE ASSUMPTION : A STRAIGHT,
INFINITE LINE

(ASSUMING THE DEFINITION IS APPLIED
TO A SINGULAR, MEASUREABLE PLANE.)

LETTING POINTS A & B REPRESENT THE
TWO POINTS,

I MEASURED A POINT WHICH IS OF
EQUAL DISTANCE FROM A AND B. (C)

FOLLOWING MY
ASSUMPTION,
I LOCATED LINES
ON THE PLANE
THAT SEEMED TO
BE EQUIDISTANT
FROM POINTS A & B
AND MEASURED THEM.

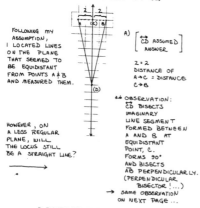

A) $\overleftrightarrow{CD}$ ASSUMED
ANSWER

2 = 2
DISTANCE OF
A→C = DISTANCE
C→B

** OBSERVATION:
$\overleftrightarrow{CD}$ BISECTS
IMAGINARY
LINE SEGMENT
FORMED BETWEEN
A AND B AT
EQUIDISTANT
POINT, C.
FORMS 90°
AND BISECTS
$\overline{AB}$ PERPENDICULARLY.
(PERPENDICULAR
BISECTOR! ...)
→ SAME OBSERVATION
ON NEXT PAGE ...

HOWEVER, ON
A LESS REGULAR
PLANE, WILL
THE LOCUS STILL
BE A STRAIGHT LINE?

→

MARY'S PROJECT
PAGE 1

B) TAXIGEOMETRY →

ASSUMING A NEW PLANE,
ON WHICH DISTANCE CAN ONLY
BE MEASURED ON THE LINES
OF THE GRAPH AND ALL CUBES
CANNOT BE TRANSVERSED, TWO POINTS
ARE PLOTTED. (A AND B)

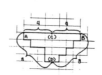

AN IMAGINARY
LINE SEGMENT
IS FORMED
AGAIN IN GUESSING
APPROX. EQUIDISTANCE.
(C)
IT IS PROVED
TO BE THE FIRST
EQUIDISTANT
POINT.
HOWEVER,
CHOOSING ANOTHER
POINT (D)
I FOUND THAT
A PARTICULAR
ROUTE DOES NOT
HAVE TO BE
TAKEN TO SHOW
D AS EQUIDISTANT.
D IS OF A
COMMON DISTANCE
FROM A & B
BUT NOT OF
AN EQUAL
ROUTE.

*** COMPLICATIONS
ARISE WITHOUT
CLARIFICATION
OF WHAT IS
THE FASTEST
MOST APPROPRIATE
ROUTE TO FIND
DISTANCE.

HOWEVER A FIGURE
IS FORMED

** PERPENDICULAR
BISECTOR!

$\overleftrightarrow{CD}$, AN INFINITE STRAIGHT LINE,
IS THE FULL LOCUS OF POINTS
EQUIDISTANT FROM
POINTS A AND B.

? HOW CAN I USE
THIS TO IDENTIFY
A STRAIGHT, INFINITE LINE?

PAGE 2

ASSUMPTION:
THIS GEOMETRIC FIGURE IS UNKNOWN TO ME.

GUESS: STRAIGHT LINE

FIND TWO POINTS
WHICH ARE
OF EQUAL DISTANCE
FROM ALL THE
POINTS ON THE FIGURE
IF TWO POINTS CAN
BE FOUND, IT IS A
STRAIGHT LINE

(TURNING THE FIGURE
TO PROVE UNIMPORTANCE
OF GRAPHING)

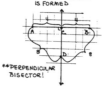

$\overline{ZW} = \overline{YW}$
BUT
$\overline{ZX} \neq \overline{YX}$,
∴ NOT
EQUIDISTANT

$\overline{MD} = \overline{DN}$
$\overline{ML} \neq \overline{LN}$
∴ NOT
EQUID

TWO POINTS THAT
ARE EQUIDISTANT
FROM ALL THE
POINTS ON THE
FIGURE ARE FOUND
(THERE IS AN INFINITE AMOUNT
OF THESE PAIRS)

** DRAWING AN IMAGINARY
LINE SEGMENT FROM A TO B
SHOWS THAT THE
STRAIGHT LINE IS ALSO
A PERPENDICULAR
BISECTOR ...

PAGE 3

DEFINITION 2: THE LINE PERPENDICULAR TO A
SEGMENT AND PASSING
THROUGH ITS MIDPOINT.

1) STARTING WITH A LINE SEGMENT, $\overline{AB}$;

2) FINDING ITS MIDPOINT (POINT EQUIDISTANT FROM
A & B ON SEGMENT)
(C)

3) DRAWING LINE PERPENDICULAR TO $\overline{AB}$
(FORMING 90° ANGLE) WHICH WILL
PASS THROUGH THE MIDPOINT OF $\overline{AB}$ (C).

4) OBSERVE THAT THIS LINE HAS BISECTED
$\overline{AB}$ WHILE BEING PERPENDICULAR TO $\overline{AB}$;
DEFINITION IS OF A PERPENDICULAR
BISECTOR

HOW DO I FIND OUT IF A FIGURE
IS A PERPENDICULAR BISECTOR??
→

PAGE 4

Continued

TO CHECK IF A FIGURE IS A PERPENDICULAR BISECTOR, ONE MUST REFER TO THE DEFINITION IN QUESTION FORM.

i)

A) IS THERE A LINE? A SEGMENT? ARE THEY PERPENDICULAR? ($\perp$)

a: YES
b: NO

B) DOES THE LINE PASS THROUGH THE MIDPOINT?

IF ALL ANSWERS ARE ANSWERED CORRECTLY, THE FIGURE IS CORRECT. ALWAYS DOUBLE-CHECK.

2)

ANSWERS:

a: NO
b: YES

PAGE 5

DEFINITION 3: THE LOCUS OF THE CENTERS OF THE CIRCLES PASSING THROUGH TWO GIVEN POINTS.

GIVEN TWO POINTS, A and B DRAW ALL POSSIBLE CIRCLES PASSING THROUGH THE TWO POINTS.

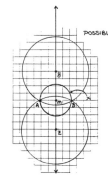

THREE CENTERS ARE MADE FROM THE PASSING OF ALL POSSIBLE CIRCLES THROUGH TWO POINTS. THE TWO POINTS FORM AN IMAGINARY LINE SEGMENT WHOSE MIDPOINT (m) IS THE CENTER OF THE FIRST CIRCLE, OX. THE CENTERS OF CIRCLE Y AND CIRCLE Z PASS THROUGH THE MIDPOINT OF SEGMENT AB IN AN IMAGINARY LINE, BECOME A PERPENDICULAR BISECTOR.

PAGE 6

THE THREE DEFINITIONS GIVEN ARE NOT EQUIVALENT DEFINITIONS FOR A PERPENDICULAR BISECTOR. THOUGH THEY ALL CAN BE DRAWN INTO THIS GEOMETRIC FIGURE, THE FIRST AND THIRD DEFINITION ARE NOT OF PERPENDICULAR BISECTORS (PB). RATHER, THEY ARE DEFINITIONS OF SITUATION IN WHICH THE ACTUAL DEFINITION OF A PB CAN BE APPLIED.

THIS POSES A PROBLEM, HOWEVER, BECAUSE IF I AND 3 ARE NOT DEFINITIONS BUT PROPERTIES OF PBS, THEN WHAT ARE THEY DEFINITIONS OF? OR IS THIS A TRICK OF THE ASSIGNER TO BAFFLE US BY CONFRONTING US WITH THE MASSIVE IMMOVABLE WORD DEFINITION THAT HAS NEVER TAKEN ANY LIP FROM US FOR YEARS? (NOT OUT OF CHOICE, I MIGHT ADD)

I PROPOSE THAT THE SECOND DEFINITION IS IN FACT THE ONLY ACTUAL DEFINITION, THE TWO REMAINING BEING INTERESTING PROPERTIES OF PBS WITH WHICH ITS SWORD IS WEILDED.

THE INSTRUCTIONS ARE ALRIGHT. THIS IS THE WAY I WAS TAUGHT TO DO IT RIGHT AND DO WELL ON FINALS, ETC. ETC. I WOULD SUGGEST DRAWING A LINE BETWEEN THE TWO CENTERS TO FORM A SEGMENT TO BE BISECTED... NOT MUCH OF A BISECTOR IF ITS NOT BISECTING ANYTHING MORE THAN SPACE.

PAGE 7

PROPERTIES OF THE PERPENDICULAR BISECTOR:

FOUND IN THE MAKING OF A STRAIGHT LINE

FOUND IN THE CROSSING OF PATHS OF CENTERS FORMING IMAGINARY LINES FORMED BY THE TOTAL CROSSING OF TWO GIVEN POINTS. (!?) *FIX

FORMS 4   90° ANGLES (MORE THAN 2)

EACH OF THE POINTS OF THE BISECTOR EQUIDISTANT FROM THE TWO POINTS OF THE SEGMENT

PAGE 8

Continued

PART II

"EXPLORING HOW THE CONTEXT MAY CHANGE THE MEANING OF A DEFINITION."

THE CIRCLE: Locus of points equidistant from a fixed point

In the usual plane

IN CIRCLE M, LET M BE THE FIXED POINT (CENTER)

DISTANCE: 3 cubes

NOT A CIRCLE
DOES NOT MATCH DEFINITION
NOT EQUIDISTANT

$r_{xy} \neq r_{yz}$

WHAT ABOUT IN TAXIGEOMETRY? →

TAXIGEOMETRY : CIRCLE

ASSUMING A NEW PLANE ON WHICH DISTANCE CAN ONLY BE MEASURED ON THE LINES OF THE GRAPH AND ALL CUBES CANNOT BE TRANSVERSED, A FIXED POINT IS PLOTTED (POINT T)

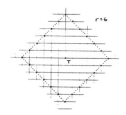
r=6

POINT T IS THE LOCATION OF A TAXI. THE DRIVER IS ASKED HOW FAR AWAY FROM POINT T HE WILL DRIVE FOR A SPECIFIC AMOUNT OF MONEY.

THE DRIVER SAYS IN REPLY:

"FOR THAT MUCH MONEY I WILL DRIVE YOU A SIX BLOCK RADIUS IN ANY DIRECTION."

HOW MANY POINTS MIGHT THE TAXI REACH?

THIS WILL BE A CIRCLE IN TAXI GEOMETRY.

In the usual plane again:

r=6

IT HAS A COMMON RADIUS AND A LOCUS OF POINTS EQUIDISTANT FROM A FIXED POINT, BUT IT IS NOT A FIGURE THAT WOULD BE A CIRCLE IN ANY OTHER CONTEXT.

WHAT ABOUT IF THE POINT WERE THE BOXES & NOT THE CORNERS?

CIRCLE F HAS A RADIUS OF 6 ALSO

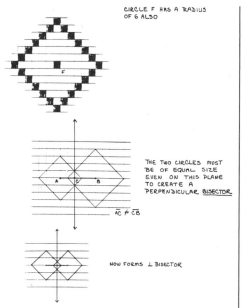

THE TWO CIRCLES MUST BE OF EQUAL SIZE EVEN ON THIS PLANE TO CREATE A PERPENDICULAR BISECTOR

$\overline{AC} \neq \overline{CB}$

NOW FORMS ⊥ BISECTOR

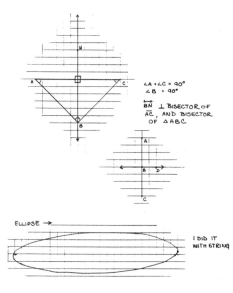

∠A + ∠C = 90°
∠B = 90°

$\overline{BN}$ ⊥ BISECTOR OF $\overline{AC}$, AND BISECTOR OF △ABC

ELLIPSE →

I DID IT WITH STRING

Continued

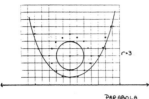

PARABOLA

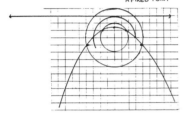

A PARABOLA FORMED
BY THE EQUIDISTANT
POINTS BETWEEN
A FIXED LINE &
A FIXED POINT

r=3

TAXIGEOMETRY ⟶

PAGE 13

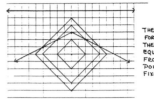

THE PARABOLA
FORMED BY
THE POINT
EQUIDISTANT
FROM A FIXED
POINT AND A
FIXED LINE

PAGE 14

PART III

A RIVER FLOWS. WANDERING, STRAGGLING THROUGH THE
FIELD OF SHRUBS, IT WINDS A PATH IN THE
WISHY-WASHY MANNER OF AN INDECISIVE TRAVELLER.

A MAN CAME. HE MAPPED A QUADRANT OF THE FLOWING
TRAVELLER, AND FOUND A PATTERN IN ITS PATH. IT RAN
IN A SERIES OF HALF-CIRCLES, ALMOST GEOMETRICALLY
PERFECT, AND HE FOUND SOME INTERESTING RESULTS.
HE HAD TO MEASURE IT IN SQUARES OF 10 METERS;
THE MAP BECAME INACCURATE, BUT STILL CORRECT.

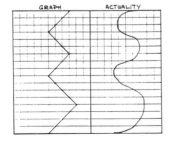

GRAPH   ACTUALITY

PAGE 15

Katya's Project
Part 1

Graph 1a: construction of a line

an arc was swung from point a and point b
and a line was drawn through the
two points of intersection of the arcs

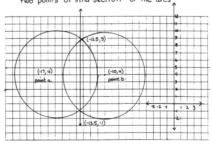

(-13.5, 9)

(-17, 4)
point a.

(-10, 4)
point b

(-13.5, -1)

*note: the radius of the compass was not
altered during the interval between drawing
the arc between pt. a and pt. b

KATYA'S PROJECT
PAGE 1

Continued

Graph 1b:

assuming line ab is a straight line, (which it is) to find the midpoint of this line you must do the same as was performed in graph 1a. That is to place the metal end of the compass on point a and swing a large arc with the pencil end. without adjusting the radius of the compass, place the metal end of the compass on point b and, again, swing

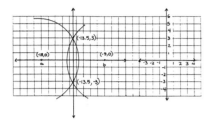

an arc. These two arcs will always intersect at the two points and now draw a line through these two points. This line always passes through the midpoint of points a and b.

Graph 1c:

This graph is also very similar to graphs 1a and 1b. In fact, it is constructed in almost the same manner. All the same steps are followed except - in swinging the arc let the arc continue and then you have a circle. So

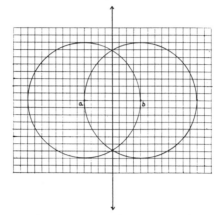

this is merely an extension of graphs 1a & 1b * look back to graph 1a and observe the dotted line. The pictures are the same.

Part 1 continued:

There are several ways to prove that all three of these lines are perpendicular bisectors. One is, supposing the two lines are nonvertical lines, you can prove that they are perpendicular if the product of their slopes is -1. Then to prove this perpendicular line is the bisector, we use the distance formula. The slope formula is $\frac{y_2 - y_1}{x_2 - x_1}$

for example:

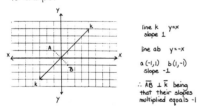

line k   y=x
    slope 1

line ab   y=-x

a (-1,1)   b (1,-1)
    slope -1

∴ $\overline{AB} \perp \overline{k}$ being that their slopes multiplied equals -1

another way to go about proving this is to prove that a right angle is formed. You can do so by creating a third line and forming a right triangle (3,4,5)

Part Two

Part 2a
circle: locus of points equidistant from a fixed point

on a usual plane:

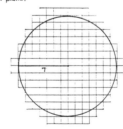

in taxigeometry:

Part 2b
perpendicular bisector : locus of points equidistant from
two fixed points.

on a usual plane:

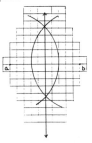

taxigeometry:
same. except when the points are on diagonals.

Part 2c
ellipse: the locus of points such that the sum of
their distances from two fixed points is
constant

on a usual plane:

when all points are connected, it will form a circle

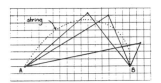

taxigeometry

sum = 10

Part 2d
parabola: the locus of points equidistant from a fixed
point and a fixed line.

in the usual plane

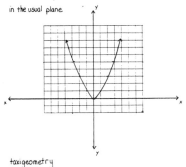

taxigeometry

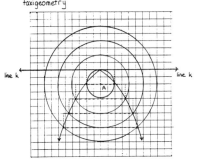

Part 3

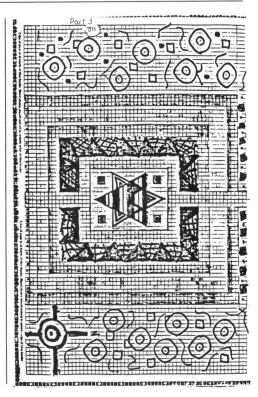

Comments on the students' results

Before I discuss the students' performance on the final project, I want to mention again a problem I noted in Chapter 2: their uneven commitment to their homework. This problem was obviously amplified in the case of the project, since the tasks assigned were complex and demanded considerable effort and careful management of time. Mary took the project very seriously and was sufficiently intrigued by some of its aspects to invest a good deal of time and energy in it. Katya, however, was not able to give the project her full attention, since she was trying to deal with other aspects of her life that obviously took priority. This situation needs to be taken into account in order to see the students' performance in a truer perspective. In addition, they both worked on the project essentially on their own. After I had given them the assignment, I was, for logistical reasons, unavailable during the two weeks in which they completed it.

Let me now briefly summarize and comment on their work. The results in Part 1 of the project are a bit difficult to evaluate, because neither student (although each in a different way) interpreted the task as I had intended it. Even though they both ended up drawing correctly the perpendicular bisector of the two given points as the locus described by all three definitions, the procedures they followed and their rationale were not always clear.

Mary's project reveals an overwhelming concern for *justifying* her conjectures—although the product of her work is not always rigorous. Her discussion of whether the three given definitions are equivalent is thoughtful and logical even if, because of her own idiosyncratic interpretation of the meaning of *equivalent definitions*, she reaches a conclusion that does not coincide with that accepted in the mathematics community. What I find most remarkable about Mary's performance in the first part of the project is her appreciation of the ambiguity inherent in my definitions of perpendicular bisector, since I had not explicitly stated that we were working in a Euclidean plane. She was able to exploit this ambiguity by questioning what would happen if we were not working in the "usual" plane and setting off to explore the problem within the context of taxicab geometry. Mary's initiative in generating new questions is also evident in her exploration of what would happen if the location of the fixed points were to change, although, unfortunately, she examined it only in the context of the Euclidean plane, where (unlike taxicab geometry) the shape of the perpendicular bisector does not change, whatever the mutual position of the fixed points.

Katya's work also presents evidence of careful mathematical reasoning and creativity. A good example is her analysis that, in order to prove that a line is the perpendicular bisector of a segment AB, one should first show that the line is *perpendicular* to the segment and then that it intersects the segment in its *midpoint*. She also displays some initiative in using some of the tools of analytic geometry—the relationship between the coefficients of perpendicular lines and the formula to evaluate distances—as a means of verifying these facts. Most students fail to relate what they have learned in different areas of mathematics and thus cannot make full use of their mathematical knowledge to solve novel problems, as Katya proved she is capable of doing here.

In Part 2 of the project, the two students' performances differed considerably, although once again, given the circumstances, I would argue that the extent of Katya's learning in the unit cannot be judged solely on the basis of her performance on this particular occasion.

Katya was able to construct all four loci correctly in the context of Euclidean geometry. She achieved only limited success, however, when she tried to interpret the same definitions in taxicab geometry. Her drawing of the taxicircle (the one locus we had already discussed) is correct, despite her earlier resistance (in Episode 5) to accepting this solution. I cannot fully understand the illustration she provides to support her conclusion that the taxiperpendicular bisector would look the same as the Euclidean one "except when the points are on diagonals," although this conclusion is correct if we interpret it to mean that the taxiperpendicular bisector is a line perpendicular to the line determined by the two points when these belong to a line on the grid, but it has a different shape when the two fixed points form the corners of a rectangle on the grid. In the case of the taxi-ellipse, Katya was able to mark only a few points belonging to this locus, but the points she identified do indeed satisfy the definition. In working on the taxiparabola, Katya displayed sound intuition and reasoning as she attempted to find this locus as the intersection of circles with center in the fixed point (representing all the points at a given distance from that point) and lines parallel to the fixed line (representing all the points at a given distance from the fixed line); this is the procedure used in Euclidean geometry to construct parabolas. But she failed to realize that in taxicab geometry "all the points at a given distance from a given point" and "all the points at a given distance from a given line" take on different shapes than the same locus in Euclidean geometry, a subtle, but important difference that Mary was able to appreciate.

Mary took full advantage of the open-ended nature of Part 2. Indeed, I think that the tasks proposed here allowed her to show the full extent of her understanding of the importance of the context in the interpretation of a definition and her appreciation of the value of "vague" definitions, as well as her inquisitiveness. Not only was she able to produce correct examples of all the loci required except for the taxi-ellipse but on her own tried to "justify" the figures she had obtained. In the familiar case of the taxicircle, Mary provided a beautiful justification of why the figure satisfying the metric definition in taxicab geometry does not resemble the usual circle.

She also generated a new problem with respect to this locus by asking, "What about if the points were the boxes and not the corners?" While the taxi-ellipse still eluded her efforts, Mary's results were remarkable in the cases of both the taxiperpendicular bisector and the taxiparabola. Mary drew those figures correctly in the particular cases she considered and provided a creative mathematical justification of her results by correctly transferring the procedure used in Euclidean geometry to construct those loci to the new context of taxicab geometry. It is worth noting that such a transfer is not obvious: it took me some time to reach it when I explored taxicab geometry as a graduate student in mathematics, and a good number of mathematics teachers to whom the situation was presented never thought of it! Katya's lack of success with the same task is further evidence of the difficulty of this transfer.

Unfortunately, neither student followed up on my suggestion to explore what happens when the mutual position of key points (such as the foci of the ellipse and the two fixed points in the case of the perpendicular bisector) changes in taxicab geometry. Thus, neither realized that in taxicab geometry one can have more than one shape corresponding to each of the loci considered.

The students' responses to Part 3 of the project were a bit disappointing, since I felt that neither of them went very far with it. Katya indeed produced something "artistic" and appealing, just as I had requested, but I must admit that the task itself was probably too vague and too unusual to hope for better results.

Concluding observations

When an instructor assigns a rich, open-ended task such as this final project, it is difficult ever to feel satisfied with what students turn in, since they will inevitably leave many of the valuable learning opportunities offered by the assignment either unexploited or exploited only in part. The students, too, may feel frustrated by the fact that their work is never really "finished" and they have to hand in a necessarily incomplete product.

As I looked back at the text of this project, I realized that it was unrealistic to expect Katya and Mary to comply fully with all the tasks assigned. Even a college student might have needed a few weeks to work out all the details necessary to address Part 1 satisfactorily and to explore the metric loci suggested in Part 2. I also realized that I sometimes expected too much of the students, given the limited experience our unit had provided them. This was certainly the case in Part 1, since I was expecting them to be able to derive properties from given definitions and to "prove" the equivalence of alternative definitions when we had not spent much time or given much attention to these difficult exercises in our instructional sessions. In evaluating the students' performance on this project, it is indeed crucial to keep in mind the highly demanding nature of the tasks assigned.

At the same time, it is also important to appreciate the pedagogical value of an "overly demanding and open-ended" project like this one, provided that appropriate expectations in terms of students' output, and in terms of the criteria and standards for evaluating them, are assumed by both teacher and students. By putting no prior boundaries on what the students are expected to accomplish, a project like this can provide ample opportunity for demonstrating initiative and creativity. Indeed, on a few occasions Mary's results went even beyond my expectations, although at the same time she skipped over or was not able to do other parts of the project.

In view of these considerations, I see my initial disappointment in a different light. At the time I did not fully appreciate the need for different standards in evaluating the students' work. I also focused my attention almost entirely on *the product* the students handed in and not on *the process* they went through in doing the project. Part of the problem, of course, lies in my decision to make the project a take-home assignment rather than to devote "class-time" to it. Although this decision was influenced by scheduling and time constraints as well as pedagogical reasons, it overlooked the value of monitoring the students' process as well as their final product. I had wanted to make sure that their completed assignment would be the result of their own work, uninfluenced by my input and guidance, and I still believe that it was important for them to have an opportunity to work independently and thus experience greater control over how they interpreted the task, where most of their efforts should go, and what strategies could be used. At the same time, I think I was overly concerned with the *evaluation* aspect of the project and thus did not take full advantage of the *learning opportunities* it could have offered if it had been better integrated with the instructional component of the unit. For example, we might have devoted some sessions to brainstorming ideas and approaches to comply with the assigned tasks, to sharing preliminary results and problems, to discussing the process and, finally, to having the students report on their results and evaluate them together. In other words, integrating the project with "regular instruction" instead of isolating it as an evaluative activity that occurred after our unit had concluded could have allowed the students to benefit more and produce better results, since they could have taken advantage of the support and encouragement of the teacher and each other, and received the stimulus to try new ideas and approaches. This is an interesting example of how sometimes the concern for evaluating students may interfere with our ability to provide them with the best possible learning experience—something worth thinking about in the context of regular mathematics instruction as well.

9 | *From the Students' Perspective: Reflections on the Experience*

To conclude the story of our inquiry into mathematical definitions I would like to report on the students' own impressions and evaluation of the experience. I had solicited Katya's and Mary's opinion about what was happening in the mini-course as well as about its impact on them as mathematics students on many occasions—after a specific activity had taken place, on the review sheets, and especially during a series of interviews after the experience had been completed. On all these occasions, they seemed very open and sincere and did not hesitate to criticize a specific element of the experience if they had disliked it, nor did they hold back their appreciation for aspects they had found particularly interesting or effective. And more than once, their comments contributed new perspectives and insights.

In this chapter, I have collected many of the thoughts that Katya and Mary expressed, in various circumstances and at different points, about the experience as a whole and its impact on their learning and thinking. To let them speak for themselves as much as possible, I have tried to limit my intervention here mainly to a few linking sentences intended to make these excerpts read more fluently.

Comments on the nature of the teaching experience

When I asked Katya and Mary to comment on the instructional sessions we had just concluded, their first observations were directed at the unusual approach toward "doing mathematics" we had assumed in our meetings.

> *R:* **What do you think was different in what we did? I think it's very nice to see pros and cons, so please be open . . .**
>
> *K:* Well, in starting out with not knowing anything. Instead of you saying, "This is the definition of a circle now, you know, you apply it to this" . . . [We were] starting from the very scratch. And you're not saying, "This is right or that's wrong" . . .
>
> *M:* *We're more into logic, and if possible, it's more like a hands-on experience. . . .*
>
> *M:* *It seems like . . . we were looking at it from the eyes of a mathematician. And instead of being taught something, we were learning it and discovering it as we went along. I felt that, instead of having a teacher that was standing up in front of the room and dictating and saying, "No, you're wrong. Yes, you're right," it was more like, "Well, maybe, let's try it." And it was a lot more liberal and I liked it. . . . I learned a lot more, because I tend to learn a lot faster when I do it wrong first . . . if I was just handed on a silver platter exactly how to do it, I probably wouldn't have learned a great lot. But instead I was given it—or, not even given it, just posed it—and then we worked it through.*
>
> *M:* *Before . . . in class I said something about how we were presented with errors. But we weren't really, we were presented with a question like "How?" And then we would try to figure it out and we would make errors first. Which is a regular way of learning things: you make an error and you try to correct it and you just work it through . . .*

Although the students voluntarily mentioned various aspects of our unusual *approach* to learning mathematics, it is interesting that they never questioned or commented upon our choice of *topic* for the unit—the notion of mathematical definition. Perhaps this by itself is noteworthy, since students rarely expect to be consulted by their teacher about content decisions in the curriculum. Yet both students freely expressed their preference for certain types of content and activities as opposed to others. Initially, for example, they both showed some uneasiness in dealing with algebra:

> *M:* *. . . the equations . . . I'm not really steady with that yet and I sort of get scared . . . Because I have never really concentrated on that and [it] is one of my problem areas . . . But I always liked equations even if I couldn't do them well. . . .*
>
> *R:* *Katya, do you like systems of equations, or algebra?*
>
> *K:* No!
>
> *R:* *You prefer pure geometry?*
>
> *K:* Yeah!

On another occasion, Mary expressed her appreciation for the way we had dealt with geometry in the unit: "I liked it. In particular geometry. When we used all the different mediums for learning geometry, that was great! I really learned it more, because I saw the different angles of it."

In general, they preferred more "concrete" activities, whether they involved solving problems or refining a definition by checking it against specific instances, to more abstract discussions on the nature of definitions:

> *M:* *I think we were kind of "abstract" with properties and definitions [she is probably referring to Episode 1 in particular], and then we got into the work itself, this stuff with the properties [Episode 2.1] . . . and we got down to details, the circles and the half circles [Episodes 2.2, 2.3, and 2.4] . . . I thought they were more interesting than "talking about" definitions.*
>
> *R:* *Is it because they're more concrete?*
>
> *M:* *No, more like we were explorers, and we were finding out what would happen. I was afraid that when writing definitions we were going to be right or wrong, according to a book. You didn't make us feel that way, but I felt that way myself. I felt it was going to be like right or wrong, according to what the classic idea was. . . . I liked instead when we were discovering things about circles and half-circles . . .*
>
> *R:* *I was very happy about this experience, and I hope you enjoyed it as much as I did. I think you were really working as mathematicians and it was more so the more we were moving toward the end . . . I don't know why.*
>
> *M:* *You mean, that we were doing it better toward the end?*
>
> *R:* *It seems to me that you were much more open and more willing to . . .*
>
> *K:* The further we got into it, the more we studied, the more interesting it got. But in the beginning it was so basic and general, we were kind of lost, I don't know. Then when we started in a specific direction it became more interesting.

About the more open-ended activities in the unit, Mary expressed considerable enthusiasm:

> *R:* *How did you feel about the fact that we really were not able to come up with a perfect definition of exponent? That the negative numbers couldn't be used as bases; and zero to the power of zero didn't work out? . . .*
>
> *M:* *I don't know. It made me doubt all of the definitions, as I told you. It made me doubt a lot of the extension of exponentiation we had achieved . . . I don't know. I kind of like it, because it's challenging. I just wonder if we're going to find exceptions to the rest of them eventually.*
>
> *R:* *Well, in a sense, even with the definition of "circle" we did find an exception—if you want to consider the diamond in taxigeometry a circle. Do you feel that we should find a perfect definition?*
>
> *M:* *It would be nice . . . as far as math goes, but I don't need a definition for "cat," or "crazy," or "purple," because each person has his own definition for it.*
>
> *R:* *Would you have preferred not to know about the limitations in mathematics, so that at least you could have more security left?*
>
> *M:* *No. I'm glad I know about it, but I don't think that definitions ever made me secure really. I think definitions make me insecure.*
>
> *R:* *Why?*

M: *Because they are like labels . . . Well, I guess . . . I'm glad I found out about the exceptions. But I think that there should be someone out there that is going to perfect the definitions, because it would be nice to know that, in math at least, you can always go by it. Because if a definition is what you'll go by in all your work and then you find an exception and you can't do anything with it, I imagine that'll be frustrating. We found some of those and it was very frustrating. But it's like, where do you go when the definition written "in blood" isn't right?*

R: *[Laughs]* **So, what do you think is the value of what we got? If we were not able to have all the exceptions taken care of . . . do you think that this is still valuable?**

M: *Yes, because it's like opening doors to find out what is there.*

R: **So . . . you cannot be totally sure of your results, and you have to be alert.**

M: *Yeah.*

R: **And that's the disturbing part of it?**

M: *Um . . . not really. The thing is, it's not really disturbing to me . . . I guess I was using words too harshly. . . . It's interesting. It's really interesting to find these things we don't know about and then learn about them, like teaching ourselves about them. But, it doesn't disturb me when it turns out that something is wrong, then I would just modify it.*

R: **What did you think about the topic, the fact that we worked with definitions, and the fact that especially toward the end we were kind of shaking some of our hopes about definitions in mathematics being so precise and nice and always working out fine.**

M: *[I liked it] a real lot! . . . when we find things that don't work, I'm not disturbed, but I was thinking about it, you know, Friday night . . .*

R: **Boy! If you think about math on Friday night then this was a real success!** *[Laughter]*

M: *Anyway, what I was thinking about was . . . when we come to an equation like that, when it just cannot be figured out by me, or by the next person, and then it just reminds me that this was all invented by people. It's not something like we are born and there is a tree and it has been there forever. It's like we invented this, out of our minds.*

Comments on the effects of the experience

When asked about it specifically, both students declared that this learning experience had considerably affected their view of mathematics and elaborated on the theme by describing how they now conceived of the nature of the discipline (*I* in the dialogues that follow refers to the nonparticipant observer who conducted some of these interviews.)

I: *Does this experience now encourage you to look at mathematics in a different way?*

M: *I would say yes. I have never been in a class like this. I never had any kind of experience with anything beyond the clear-cut, out-of-the-book stuff. I look at it differently just because we theorized a lot, a lot more than I'm used to.*

I: *Was that something that you found enjoyable?*

M: *Oh, yes, and I liked relating it to real life because that has always been a big problem with me. Mathematics is . . . like in a closet somewhere and it has nothing to do with anything else. I'm just going to open the door . . .*

I: *What do you think mathematics is? Can you say a little about that and perhaps in what way this course has changed that?*

M: *It's difficult. I can't really explain what mathematics is but . . . It's kind of like an art, but it serves a purpose . . .*

I: *It serves a purpose in what way?*

M: *Well, it solves problems. Geometry solves problems in real life. Equations solve problems in real life . . . Just like writing serves a purpose . . . It's enabling us to see, just like reading a good novel enables you to see something. Good art should be able to help you see something. And mathematics, when correct, should help you see something, and even when incorrect, because then you can see what's right and what's wrong about it. Some sentence! Nature of mathematics . . . before I thought mathematics was just something that was as multifaceted as a new foreign language I haven't learned yet. It's just like learning a language. I start to see the patterns in it and I start to see how everything fits together. And especially this class, we did link all the different areas together: geometry came right into algebra, and algebra came right back in, and it was just all together, rather than little separate parts of it. And the separate rules, all the rules seem to be pretty regular. . . . So I think the nature of it is that it is well-patterned and there are exceptions just like in everything, as in languages. But it still . . . it holds a definite shape and it does have a purpose and it can be figured out, even by me! I didn't think I could figure math out before . . .*

I: *Do you think the mini-course with Raffaella has affected your perception of what mathematics is? And, if so, in what ways?*

K: Oh, yeah, definitely. Even from the very beginning, when she was teaching the classes last semester . . . our whole outlook on math . . . has changed. I guess it started changing just last year, when I started to go to the School Without Walls . . . seeing how math applies to real things . . . challenging us to really think for ourselves instead of just accepting things from a textbook . . . or else seeing that it is something where you can discover things. I thought math . . . everything that was going to be discovered in math has already been discovered and being a mathematician would be a really stupid thing to do because everybody already knows everything there is to know. But even the smallest thing is questionable.

I: *Do you think that that's the case only with the mathematics that already exists or is there, or do you think new mathematics is being discovered in this way?*

K: I think it is definitely being discovered this way or else people wouldn't become mathematicians, right? . . . I mean, if you get frustrated with something, like accept the definition of a circle, you know, like with the taxigeometry, and stuff. The same definition could get you something completely different. There's all these questions . . .

To appreciate the dramatic change in conception of mathematics that occurred as a result of the mini-course, compare these views to what Katya and Mary wrote about mathematics before the course (see Chapter 2): the contrast is indeed remarkable!

Both students revealed that this change in their conception of mathematics had made them look differently at the way mathematics is traditionally taught in school:

K: I really got frustrated now that I'm studying for SAT's and I'm looking at the SAT book, which is really traditional, it's different from: "Please write an essay about what you think a circle is." That's real traditional and I get real frustrated and I want to do something that might be a little more creative or a little more interesting. There always seems to be just one right answer when you look at the back. And you see the answers, and you correct yourself . . .

M: *In general terms now, sadly, I dislike my other math class even more.*

I: *And why is that? What's the contrast?*

M: *The teacher's teaching style and . . .*

I: *Which is what?*

M: *Very clear-cut, and she presents it, and we learn it, and we use it, and then we move on.*

I: *Are you saying that there are no opportunities to question why?*

M: *Oh, we have opportunities to question why, but it seems like a totally different way of looking at math.*

I: *Why do you suppose so many teachers present these materials in such a strict, one-directional way?*

M: *Because that was the way it was presented to them.*

I: *Do you think that's it, or do you think it has something to do with the material itself?*

M: *I used to think that the material was to blame, but now I really think it is the way people were told to teach it. And I think that it is the way they were taught. And many math teachers go under the assumption that [mathematics] is something you have to work for. They say that in languages too. It's not something you can really philosophize about. It is just something that you learn and memorize and get tested on. I've heard teachers say something to the effect of: "Well, not everybody is going to get it. Math was not meant for everyone. But I'm just teaching for the few kids that will end up like me and really get into it. And it will just click in their heads and they'll have it, and the rest of the kids will struggle with math for the rest of their lives." Yes, I've been told that. My mother even sort of believes that.*

I: *What if you encounter again what you call a clear-cut, "this is what it is" presentation then?*

M: *They're boring, but I feel like I can look at them in a different way and I can . . . instead of having Raffaella pointing all those things out, I can point them out to myself. And it is like a new way of learning it, and it is not a new way of . . . yes, it's a new way of teaching it but in a situation when it is not being taught that way I can still learn it that way. And not totally ignore my teacher but be able to look past what my teacher is saying.*

I find Mary's last remark quite encouraging, since I sometimes worried that my attempts to make the students see mathematics differently would end up creating problems for them once they went back to the traditional mode of mathematics instruction.

Katya, too, mentioned that the experience had provided her with some new strategies for learning mathematics:

I: *Do you think there is some carryover from what you did with Raffaella to other work?*

K: Maybe my other math class. I'm asking more questions, and . . . when the teacher says, "This is the rule"—well, she usually doesn't say that if somebody says, "Well, why does it turn out that way?" she almost never says "Well, it's because that's the rule"—but if she ever hints at that at all I'll ask more questions about it. I don't really accept anything as just a rule, you know, I want her to show us.

I: *Do you find it brings more clarity?*

K: Yeah, definitely.

I: *Is there anything else that you would like to say about the course?*

K: I enjoyed it a lot more than regular math. And I learned a new method of doing math! So that was interesting.

One concrete sign of their increased interest in mathematics was their expressed intention to take more math courses in the future—even if they had already taken all the necessary mathematics credits for graduation.

R: *Are you planning to do some more math courses, either here, or others?*

K: Mrs. F.'s class, yeah.

R: *And after that?*

K: Yeah, I'll take a math course next year.

M: *I wanted to take the "math systems" course with Mr. D. It would please my mother if I took three math classes, but I have a class during the time they scheduled it. When Mr. D. subbed one week, he brought in all the kinds of systems, and we worked with p, q systems, and d, n, y, u and all those neat things, and . . . It was neat. And he said, "This is what I'm doing in my class, this is just the beginning," and that he felt that it would show another way of looking at math, as systems. And it was neat, I wanted to take that class, but . . . Do you think he'll be offering it again?*

Katya and Mary kept these promises only partially the following year, but this was due to scheduling conflicts rather than to a desire to avoid mathematics courses.

Evaluating the Teaching Experience | 10

I now abandon the narrative form assumed so far so that I can look at the teaching experience in a more analytic way. As a complement to the story I've reported, I wish to evaluate the results of the experience as a whole in this chapter and then, in Chapters 11 and 12, discuss explicitly the instructional approach that informed the experience.

The teaching experience reported in this book should be evaluated from a number of perspectives. First, it seems important to determine whether the unit encouraged any change in the students' conception, understanding, and use of mathematical definitions. Yet my objectives went far beyond a better understanding of mathematical definitions, since I hoped that in analyzing this topic, the students would reconceive their view of school mathematics and become better mathematicians. So I will examine whether the experience had any effect on the students' conceptions of mathematics as a discipline and on their approach toward learning mathematics. At the same time, the students are not the only ones who should gain from this kind of instructional experience: the instructor should grow along with them. Thus I will look at what I myself learned from it. Finally, the design of the unit itself should be critically examined in light of the results of the previous evaluations.

In this chapter I will therefore try to carry out such an articulated evaluation of the teaching experience, using as data my reconstruction of the instructional sessions (Chapters 2–7), the students' written work (their projects—see Chapter 8—and their responses to the two review sheets), and their own perceptions of the experience (Chapter 9). I think it will be helpful first to review briefly what we accomplished in the unit and to summarize my objectives.

Review of the instructional unit and its goals

In the traditional paradigm of education research, the evaluation of a novel curriculum unit or teaching strategy is approached essentially in terms of how well its outcome matches the instructional objectives set a priori. In the case of the teaching experience I have reported in such detail here, however, this approach is inadequate.

As I explained in Chapter 2, I began the mini-course with only a tentative overall plan and broad instructional goals. Since I knew that only a flexible instructional design could accommodate genuine student inquiry, I wanted to be ready to adjust the plan of specific sessions or activities in response to the students' reactions and input, on the spot if necessary. By presenting an overview and rationale at the beginning of each instructional episode, I have tried to show how the design of the unit evolved as the lessons progressed, occasionally even taking us in unexpected directions. Thus, the students' performance and learning outcomes in our experience should be evaluated on the basis of the *learning opportunities* actually offered to them in the mini-course, rather than according to a priori instructional objectives. To do that we need to determine what the students *could have learned* as a result of our instructional sessions.

In order to review what the students and I actually did in our unit on definitions, I have chosen to reproduce the complete text of the two review sheets (page breaks are indicated by asterisks). These review sheets, which Katya and Mary received after our fourth and eighth meetings, were intended to provide them with a summary of our activities and, more important, some clues about the significance of the learning tasks they had engaged in and the connections between them. These review sheets demonstrate, therefore, the overall design of the instruction that took place in most of our lessons and add an important piece of information to the data thus far, since they reveal what was explicitly communicated to the students about my expectations.

Review sheet #1

We started our unit on "mathematical definitions" by writing tentative definitions for nine chosen concepts from geometry, algebra, and "real-life" (they were: circle, square, polygon, variable, exponent, equation, cat, purple, crazy). We will come back later to those definitions to discuss the differences and similarities between definitions within mathematics and outside of mathematics.

Then we started to work on definitions of *circle*.

You were presented with eight incorrect definitions of circle (written on index cards), and asked to discuss them.

What were we looking for when trying to find a good definition for "circle"?

Do you remember how you decided whether a definition was correct or not?

* * * * *

From this preliminary analysis, we came up with two definitions of *circle* that seemed acceptable to us:

"A circle is the collection of all points on a plane equidistant from a given point."

"A circle is the collection of all points of coordinates (x, y) which satisfy the equation: $(x - h)^2 + (y - k)^2 = r^2$, where (h, k) are the coordinates of the center and r is the length of the radius."

We actually showed why the formula above does describe a circle.

This is not the only case in which we can have more than one correct definition for a concept. We also showed that an *isosceles triangle* can be defined in two alternative ways:

1: A triangle with two equal sides.
2: A triangle with two equal angles.

Can we have more than one definition for a concept?

How can we show that two definitions are equivalent?

What are the advantages of having more than one definition?

* * * * *

An interesting digression:

Katya observed that the formula that describes a circle with center in the origin and the formula in the Pythagorean theorem are very similar:

$x^2 + y^2 = r^2$ (circle formula)
$a^2 + b^2 = c^2$ (relation between the legs a, b and the hypothenuse c of a right triangle)

Can you comment on the difference between these two formulas?
(Hint: It is always important, when using letters, to distinguish between variables and constants.)

* * * * *

In order to explore the role of definitions in mathematics, we discussed some problems involving circles—to see when and how we really had to use a definition of *circle*.

We solved the following problems:

• How to determine the circle passing through three given points (and we did this in two alternative ways:
  1) by using the formula for circles and setting up a system of equations
  2) by using the fact that all the points in the circle are equidistant from the center).

- How to determine the angle of a regular polygon inscribed in a circle. (Actually, we solved this problem only in the case of a pentagon, but it should not be difficult to generalize our procedure to regular polygons with a different number of sides.)
- How to prove that all triangles inscribed in a semicircle are right triangles. (A first proof I suggested attempted to prove this by showing that the sides of the triangle satisfy the Pythagorean theorem equation $a^2 + b^2 = c^2$, but we recognized that this was not correct. We then proved this result in a different way, trying to show that the triangle has a 90 degree angle.)

*Can you remember when, in these proofs, we needed to use **definitions** and when instead we could simply use **properties** of a mathematical object? Why?*

Can you try to distinguish between a definition and a property?

*   *   *   *   *

Another interesting digression:

When trying to solve the problem of "finding the circle passing through three given points," Katya made a very interesting error. Since she only knew how to solve systems with two equations, she tried to work only with the equations generated by two of the given points, that is:

$$\begin{cases} (7 - h)^2 + (0 - k)^2 = r^2 \\ (5 - h)^2 + (4 - k)^2 = r^2 \end{cases}$$

and came up with an equation she still could not solve:

$$2k = h - 2.$$

However, this revealed an interesting new fact: that there are *infinitely many* circles that pass through *two* given points (while we can find only *one* circle passing through *three* given points). But the equation told us even more: that all those circles passing through the same two points have the center on a straight line.

Can you explain how we got these conclusions?

At the time, I did not notice it, but this result shows a close connection between the two alternative procedures we used to determine the circle passing through three given points.

Can you figure this out?

(Hint: Look back at my handout presenting both procedures and notice the role and meaning of the perpendicular bisector.)

*   *   *   *   *

After having worked so long with circles, we moved to a different geometric concept: polygon. I chose to work on the definition of this concept because in this case, unlike what happened with triangles and circles, we were not so sure from the start about what "polygons" should be.

So we started from the definition initially suggested by Mary—even if we expected it not to be totally satisfactory—and tried to modify it so that it would include all the figures we wanted to consider as polygons and exclude other figures we did not want to call polygons.

Another way to try to create a reasonable definition of polygon could be to start with a statement that we would like to be true—for instance "in all polygons, the sum of the interior angles is 180 times the number of sides of the polygon"—and try to make a definition of polygon that would "fit."

What do you think of these ways of creating a definition for "polygon"?

Do you think mathematical definitions are arbitrary? Give reasons for your answer.

How do you think mathematicians create the definitions you find in a mathematics textbook?

* * * * *

Review sheet #2

In our sessions, we have so far worked with many different definitions in mathematics. Let us now try to look at the similarities and differences among all those definitions.

First, we worked with circles, isosceles triangles, right triangles, etc. in geometry. We knew these concepts and we tried to come up with a suitable definition.

What was the definition trying to accomplish in this case?

We analyzed several definitions, some of which we thought were acceptable, and some of which we criticized and discarded. Let us try to think of how we made our decisions:

What elements did we NOT want a definition to have? Why?

What characteristics did we want a definition to have? Why?

* * * * *

With regard to *circle*, we sort of agreed that the following was a good definition:

> (1) A circle is the collection of all the points on a plane equidistant from a given point.

Later, when working in the context of "taxigeometry," we noticed that using this definition led us to quite a different looking object than the usual circle. This happened because in the case of a city like the one represented by the grid, you cannot go across buildings, so the distance cannot be measured "as the crow flies."

As a result of this experience, how would you now evaluate definition (1) as a definition of "circle"?

Do you think definition (1) is still an appropriate definition of "circle"? If yes, why? If no, what changes would you suggest to improve it?

Do you think that we must and can always be totally precise in mathematical definitions? Why?

What would be the value of having a more vague/wider meaning of "distance" in definition (1)?

* * * * *

When asked to give a definition for exponent, one of you suggested the following:

> (A) The exponent tells you how many times you have to multiply a number by itself. Example: $a^5 = a \times a \times a \times a \times a$

We realized that this definition makes sense only if the exponent is a positive whole number. In an analogy to what is done in multiplication, we tried to extend the meaning of "exponent" to negative whole numbers as well. We did this while trying to maintain as many properties of exponents as possible. As a result, we came up with the following "extended" definition:

> (B) If the exponent is a positive whole number, the exponent tells you how many times you have to multiply the number by itself. Example: $a^5 = a \times a \times a \times a \times a$.
> If the exponent is a negative whole number (say we have a^{-n}), it is the same as considering $1/a^n$.

How can you know if definition (B) is correct?

Would you still consider definition (A) correct? Explain your answer.

How would you compare (A) and (B) as definitions of "exponent"?

Do you think in the future you may want to further extend (B)? Why?

* * * * *

When trying to find a definition of *polygon*, we had some trouble to start with because we did not really know precisely what we wanted a *polygon* to be— except that it was going to be a concept generalizing triangles, squares, pentagons, etc. So we started with a tentative definition and "refined it" so that polygons would have some interesting properties.
We ended up with the following definition:

> (i) A polygon is a closed geometric figure, with straight edges that do not cross.

Are you satisfied with this definition? How could we ever know if it is correct? Explain your answer.

What are the main differences between this case and the definition of concepts such as "circle"?

It is possible that in the future we may want to further modify the definition of *polygon* or that of *exponent*.

What is the value, then, of a preliminary, tentative definition?

* * * * *

At the beginning of our experience, you were asked to write definitions of nonmathematical concepts as well—such as CAT, PURPLE, and CRAZY.

What were you trying to accomplish when writing a definition for these concepts? (Your answer may be different depending on the specific concept.)

What would be the use of a definition outside of mathematics?

How would you know if your definition is correct?

It may be very interesting to compare mathematical definitions with definitions of nonmathematical concepts such as these.

Are the uses of mathematical definitions different from those in any other field? If so, how? Why do you think so?

Are the criteria you would use to evaluate definitions in mathematics different from those you would use in other contexts?

These two review sheets give a thorough account of our activities in the first eight instructional sessions. In addition, we also completed the following activities:

- An analysis of *variable,* motivated by my desire to show the students that a rigorous definition is not needed for *all* mathematical concepts.
- A discussion of the problems caused by 0^0 and some fractional powers of negative bases, included to show the existence of unavoidable limitations even in the case of mathematical definitions.
- The final project, in which the students were expected to interpret given geometrical definitions in the context of both standard Euclidean plane geometry and taxicab geometry and to establish the equivalence of given definitions, designed mainly to determine what the students could do on their own.

In light of what actually happened in the mini-course and of the rationale behind my main instructional decisions, I can explicate a posteriori some of the specific dimensions along which I hoped the students would progress as a result of their inquiry.

1. With respect to the *specific mathematical content* addressed in the unit:
   A. To become aware of the special requirements (*noncontradiction, noncircularity, isolation of the concept, precision,* and *essentiality*) that are usually imposed on definitions in formal mathematics and to appreciate their rationale.
   B. To experience the possibility of "creating" good mathematical definitions through a process of successive refinements of tentative definitions, both in cases in which the concept to be defined is already established and familiar and in cases in which the concept is not.
   C. To realize the distinction between the *definition* and the *set of properties* of a given mathematical concept and to start questioning the relationship between the two.
   D. To appreciate the importance of context in the interpretation of a definition and also to recognize the power and the potential problems involved in extending a known definition to new contexts.
   E. To realize the existence, in some cases at least, of inherent limitations, which do not allow us to reach "perfection" in mathematical definitions.
   F. To recognize similarities as well as differences between mathematical definitions and definitions in other fields, and to realize that not all definitions in mathematics play the same role or respond to the same requirements.
2. With respect to acquiring a better *understanding of mathematics* and a better *approach to learning mathematics:*
   G. To appreciate the real nature of mathematics. More specifically, I hoped that the students would start to appreciate that mathematical results are neither arbitrary nor predetermined, but rather, that they result from a dynamic attempt to create meaning; that mathematics is not as "perfect" as it is often perceived to be, in the sense that there are some inherent limitations that mathematicians cannot overcome according to their wishes and areas and issues about which decisions have to be made.
   H. To approach mathematical tasks more actively by realizing the role and value of "thinking" creatively rather than relying simply on recalling; by taking a more critical stance with respect to mathematical results (whether their own work or somebody else's) and relying less on authority; and by taking more initiative in their mathematical activities both by pursuing the teacher's questions more actively and independently and by posing their own questions for inquiry.

These goals should not be interpreted as "behavioral objectives" against which students' performance should be measured at the end of a unit.

Rather, they are ideals to strive for and measure the students' achievement against, but with the clear realization that this achievement will be partial at best.

Students' achievement in understanding the nature of mathematical definitions

A. Appreciating the special requirements (noncontradiction, noncircularity, precision, isolation, essentiality) imposed on mathematical definitions and their rationale

By the end of the unit, both Katya and Mary were quite aware of the requirements usually imposed on mathematical definitions as their response on the second review sheet indicates.

> In our sessions . . . we worked with circles, isosceles triangles, right triangles, etc. in geometry. We knew these concepts and we tried to come up with a suitable definition.

> **What was the definition trying to accomplish in this case?**

> **M:** *Clear, concise, universal definition to identify a circle, isosceles triangle, etc. or to create one.*

> **K:** Create a better understanding of the concept by putting our ideas into words—apply our definitions to geometric proofs to see how they work.

> **What elements did we NOT want a definition to have? Why?**

> **M:** *Ambiguity → too vague or confusing. 1) Could only be → limited ← referred to or proven in a particular method and only used within the bounds of a "type" of problem. 2) We didn't want to have a definition that showed only one route or one direction to defining them.*

> **K:** Nothing vague or general that could be confused for something else—opinions are not necessarily in a definition.

> **What characteristics did we want a definition to have? Why?**

> **M:** *Clear, concise, able to be adapted to a situation—universal → so that we can use it as a general guideline in all work w/ these figures*

> **K:** Clear, explain what we mean using the least amount of words.

Notice that Mary and Katya both mention the criteria of *isolation*, *precision*, and *essentiality* in their responses. Since we never explicitly examined *noncircularity* and *noncontradiction* in the unit, it is not surprising that the students did not refer to those criteria here. Yet both students would probably have recognized them if they had been asked about them, since none of the definitions either of them produced presented any problem along these lines. It is also important to point out how the students were not only aware of these requirements but were also able to apply them (as shown especially in the student-generated activity of defining *diamond* reported in Episode 5.4).

From their behavior when they analyzed incorrect definitions of *circle* (see Episode 2.1), we can conclude that although the students (especially Mary) were probably vaguely aware of some of these criteria even before the unit started, their appreciation of the rationale and implications of these criteria was considerably improved as a result of the unit (especially as a result of the activities developed in Episodes 2.1, 2.2, and 2.3 dealing with the definition of circle).

B. Acquiring procedures to create good mathematical definitions in the case of both familiar and unfamiliar concepts

Prior to their participation in our mini-course, the students had probably never engaged in the actual "creation" of a mathematical definition. At best, they might have tried to reproduce a previously learned definition or to describe a notion intuitively. The process Katya and Mary followed in Episode 5.4 (when they set for themselves the task of creating a definition for *diamond*) is the best possible evidence of their progress in acquiring a method for defining a *familiar* concept. They started with a tentative definition of diamond that approximated their mental image of such a shape. Then they proceeded to refine this definition by verifying whether it allowed them to discriminate between what they wanted to consider as instances and noninstances of diamond. In this way, they mirrored the process we had followed together in Episode 2.1 when we examined incorrect definitions of circle.

During the unit, the students also had occasion to experience the limitations of this procedure in cases where the concept to be defined was not sufficiently familiar to them, such as polygon in Episode 3.1. I am not sure that in the end the students were able to predict in what circumstances this procedure would or would not work. But it is important to realize that it would have been quite unrealistic to expect them to be able to do so on the basis of their limited experience with this strategy in the mini-course.

In terms of acquiring a constructive strategy for dealing with the definition of an *unfamiliar* concept, Katya and Mary were certainly able to engage successfully in a process "à la Lakatos" under my guidance in Episode 3.2, where they tried to establish the validity of a theorem about polygons while at the same time working at refining tentative definitions of polygon. Yet I am not sure that this experience was sufficient for them to be able to "abstract" the principles and components of Lakatos's heuristic or to be able to apply them on their own in new situations.

C. Appreciating the distinction and complex relationship between "definition" and "set of properties" of a given concept

Prior to the unit, neither of the students had realized that there is a distinction between the *definition* and the *set of properties* of a mathematical concept and that such a distinction may be quite complex and "tricky," as their comments during the analysis of the list of incorrect definitions of circle in Episode 2.1 reveal. But as the unit progressed, their understanding of such a distinction and of the relationship between the two notions grew considerably. Our discussion of alternative definitions of isosceles triangle helped Mary reach some resolution about this issue, but at the time of the first review sheet Katya declared her confusion about the distinction between definition and property (although her explanation of her difficulties actually reveals a partial understanding of the crucial points of this complex issue):

> **Can you try to distinguish between a definition and a property?**
>
> **M:** *Definition → overall identifier. Properties → 2nd opinions, reaffirm.*
>
> **K:** I see them as mostly the same thing. Definitions can be a group of properties or one exact property, but a circle has properties that are also common to other geometric figures, so one property alone would not usually be an accurate definition, but most definitions are made up of properties. I guess I don't understand the difference.

Mary's conclusion, that the properties not stated in the definition of a concept should still be used to "double-check" the validity of the definition itself, created some potential conflict later on when she used this principle in her evaluation of the metric definition of circle after our experiences with "circles" in taxicab geometry in Episode 5.

It is interesting to observe that, even after working within taxicab geometry and with the extension of exponents to various numerical domains, neither student was yet able to appreciate that the same set of properties may no longer coexist when we move to a different mathematical context and that the relationship between a *concept*, its *definition*, and the *set of properties* shared by all its instances may be considerably affected by the domain in which one is operating. The relationship between the *definition* and the *set of properties* of a given concept is a very good example of an issue that helped the students to stretch their thinking, even if at the end of the unit they were still left with considerable doubt and no satisfactory resolution.

D. Realizing the influence of the context on mathematical definitions

At the beginning, it did not look as if the students had ever questioned that the meaning of mathematical definitions may depend on the context in which they are interpreted, and reasonably so, since no explicit attention is usually paid to this issue in the traditional mathematics curriculum. In Episode 1, when I asked the students to write definitions for nine concepts "out of context" (without having had the chance to work with the concepts previously or know what the definition would be used for), Katya and

Mary approached the task as if they believed that it was possible to write a "correct" definition—that definitions, in other words, could be "absolutely right or wrong."

Their first encounter with the importance of context occurred when the operation of exponentiation was extended beyond the whole numbers and thus lost the original meaning of "repeated multiplication" (Episode 4). But I believe the students came to see the role of context more clearly only when we looked at the definition of circle in taxicab geometry (Episode 5). As they realized that *distance* and *circle* could take on very different meanings in this new environment, they became aware of how the mathematical context in which one is operating affects the interpretation of a mathematical definition. Mary did not stop here. In Part 2 of her project she was able to solve the problems set in taxicab geometry by correctly transferring what she knew from Euclidean geometry (making all the necessary modifications). For example, in order to construct the taxiperpendicular bisector, she applied the usual procedure in Euclidean geometry for constructing the perpendicular bisector to a pair of points (by intersecting circles with center in the two points and equal radius), and made sure she was using taxicircles to do so.

E. Recognizing inherent limitations in mathematical definitions

In the course of the teaching experience, the students came to realize that there are limitations in what mathematicians can expect from mathematical definitions. I have already touched on most of these issues so I will just briefly recall them here. The students had to accept for instance, that the valuable process of "refining tentative definitions" against their image of the concept did not work so well in dealing with new and unfamiliar concepts (as in the case of polygon). In the case of variable, we confronted the difficulty of expressing precisely in a formal definition our intuitive understanding of the concept, even when this understanding was sufficient to allow us to use the concept successfully in most applications. The students also encountered some disturbing consequences when they extended a definition to new domains (such as the usual definition of circle in taxicab geometry). And they found "exceptions" when they tried to define fractional powers of negative bases and 0^0.

These realizations were valuable in themselves, even though they created a certain degree of frustration and uneasiness in the students. As Mary says in her interview:

> **M:** *Well, I guess . . . I'm glad I found out about the exceptions. But I think there should be someone out there that is going to perfect the definitions, because it would be nice to know that, in math at least, you can always go by it. Because if a definition is what you'll go by in all your work and then you find an exception*

and you can't do anything with it, I imagine that'll be frustrating. . . . It's like, where do you go when the definition written "in blood" isn't right?

The students might not have come out of the mini-course with a very clear idea of how to deal with these disturbing cases, but at least they became aware of their existence.

Another positive result of the students' encounter with these limitations was their new appreciation of the *tentative* and *dynamic* nature of definitions in mathematics. As a result of their own attempts to create definitions, they saw that further modifications were possible and learned to appreciate the value of tentative definitions. This is especially evident in the following responses in their final review sheet, when I asked them to evaluate the results they achieved in the definitions of polygon and exponent:

> **Do you think in the future you may want to further extend [the definition of exponent we have obtained]? Why?**
>
> **M:** *Yes. . . . It is unclear to me as it is written above.*
>
> **K:** Yes, when we come across other types of exponents.
>
> **Are you satisfied with this definition [of polygon]? How could we ever know if it is correct? Explain your answer.**
>
> **M:** *Not quite. Play w/ polygons. Test the theory. Use examples of figures that meet the requirements for the def. but don't meet properties. OR just T&E ["trial and error"].*
>
> **K:** I am satisfied with this for the time being but I think possibly as I start to use them more and more, I may desire something more exact.

> It is possible that in the future we may want to further modify the definition of *polygon* or that of *exponent*.

> **What is the value, then, of a preliminary, tentative definition?**
>
> **M:** *It's like a theory that hasn't been fully tested yet and therefore is open to modification.*
>
> **K:** Getting acquainted with a new concept—have something to base further defining on. You have to start with something.

Further, and even more concrete evidence of the students' appreciation of the dynamic nature of mathematical concepts and their definitions can be seen in Katya's suggestion to include complex numbers as possible results of the extended operation of exponentiation (Episode 4.4) and in Mary's questioning of what would happen if our number system were to be redefined by eliminating "zero" (again in Episode 4.4).

F. Appreciating similarities as well as differences between definitions in mathematics and definitions in other fields

Due mainly to lack of time toward the end of the course, this issue was not really addressed in our instructional sessions. But it is interesting to note Mary's attempt to approach the writing of an acceptable definition of cat just as we had previously done with circle and diamond—by attempting to isolate what characterizes cats and distinguishes them from all other animals.

When they were asked to compare the nature of definitions within and outside of mathematics on the final review sheet, the two students displayed interesting differences.

> *Are the uses of mathematical definitions different from those in any other field? If so, how? Why do you think so?*
>
> **M:** No. *Because definitions can be created for almost anything, though for a cat it may have to be more exacting while for infinity and other things often found in sciences it must remain ambiguous until the definition can be further discovered.*
>
> **K:** No. A definition is a definition ← just a tool to better understand what you are doing.
>
> *Are the criteria you would use to evaluate definitions in mathematics different from those you would use in other contexts?*
>
> **M:** No. Well, sometimes. *In mathematics you can work with properties of things that never change, and determining factors, while in the world things and determining factors rarely remain stable.*
>
> **K:** Yes. Especially math concepts when it is just a math "idea" not something solid like a cat.

As confirmed in other parts of the interviews and instructional sessions, Mary thought of the difference between mathematical definitions and definitions in real life more as a difference of degree rather than quality. On the contrary, Katya insisted that "you can't have opinions about mathematical definitions."

Some concluding remarks

As I hope my analysis makes clear, Katya and Mary achieved considerable growth in their conception of mathematical definitions as a result of our mini-course. The activities in the course highlighted several important aspects of mathematical definitions: the importance of requirements such as *essentiality* and *precision* in definitions; the difficulties involved in creating a definition for a "novel" notion; and the unexpected results that can occur when a definition is interpreted in a different context. The students occasionally surprised me by their ability to transfer principles and procedures learned in one specific activity to another. They became sensitive to the problems involved in working in new contexts and appreciated the need for tentative definitions.

At the end of the unit, however, it was still difficult for the students to decide which criteria would be most appropriate in evaluating particular definitions. Although they had been made aware of diversity in mathematical definitions, they were not yet able to generalize from the specific examples discussed in the course the appropriate criteria for distinguishing between different mathematical contexts or to set reasonable expectations about the necessary characteristics of a definition within a particular context. As a result, at the conclusion of the mini-course the students remained a bit confused and frustrated. I would suggest, however, that this confusion should be considered a positive achievement. It would have been unreasonable to expect the students to go much further within the limits of our sessions. Our goals were ambitious and could easily form the core of an entire mathematics curriculum. More important, a state of confusion may be a necessary step to a more sophisticated understanding of mathematical definitions by making students more cautious and reflective in their use of definitions and by drawing their attention to the context in which they are operating. At the same time, one of the greatest limitations of our unit was the few opportunities it offered to the students to organize, synthesize, and evaluate what they had learned—an important point to which I will return.

Effects of the experience on the students' conceptions of mathematics and their approach to learning mathematics

G. Moving toward an appreciation of the real nature of mathematics

Both their comments during the instructional sessions and the interviews and their behavior throughout the unit reveal how the students' conception of mathematics changed. Prior to the mini-course (see Chapter 2), when the students had tried to explain their dislike of mathematics, they used the following expressions: "Math homework . . . seems so silly and pointless; . . . mathematics is too impersonal, useless" (Katya) and "I wasn't meant for the subject" (Mary). However, their belief that mathematics is an absolute, meaningless, and predetermined domain, where there is no place for creativity and personal judgment, was increasingly challenged by the mathematical activities they experienced in the mini-course.

I have already shown that both students came to appreciate the role played by the context and by the presence of unavoidable limitations in mathematical results. Although we never discussed the implication of these discoveries, it was obvious from their reactions (see Episodes 4.4 and 5) that both students found them quite surprising and even a bit disturbing, since they did not agree with their previous experiences and expectations about mathematics. Their growing understanding of the real nature of mathematics also came out in their responses on the first review sheet:

> *How do you think mathematicians create the definitions you find in a*
> *mathematics textbook?*
> *M: Playing with theories like we have.*
> K: Gift from God—out of utter boredom—years of work and mental
>   strain—asking questions—working and coming across something
>   indefinite.

If we disregard the first two remarks in Katya's response (since they seem
dictated by an attempt at playfulness), we can see that both students had
come to appreciate that mathematical knowledge is the result of exploration
and inquiry. Commenting on the experience of encountering limitations in the
extension of exponentiation in one of the final interviews, Mary was even
more explicit about recognizing mathematics as the product of human activity:

> *M: When it just cannot be figured out by me, or by the next person, it just reminds*
> *me that this was all invented by people. It's not something like we are born and*
> *there is a tree and it has been there forever. It's like we invented this, out of our*
> *minds.*

The evidence brought up so far makes us appreciate that the students'
statements about their view of mathematics and the effects of the experience were not dictated by rhetoric or the desire to please the instructor but
reflected what they really thought. With these considerations in mind, I
would like to return to some of Katya's and Mary's comments (see Chapter
9) in an effort to determine the broader effects of our experience on the
students' conception of mathematics.

Katya's response to the question "Do you think that the course has
affected your perception of mathematics?" is especially revealing:

> K: Oh, yeah, definitely . . . our whole outlook on math has changed. I guess
>   it started changing last year, when I started to go to the School Without
>   Walls, seeing math as something interesting . . . seeing how it applies to
>   real things . . . seeing that it is something where you can discover things.
>   I thought . . . everything that was going to be discovered in math has
>   already been discovered and being a mathematician would be a really
>   stupid thing to do because everybody already knows everything there is
>   to know. But even the smallest thing is questionable.
> *I: Do you think that that's the case only with the mathematics that already*
> *exists or is there . . . or do you think new mathematics is being discovered*
> *in this way?*
> K: I think it is definitely being discovered this way or else people wouldn't
>   become mathematicians . . . I mean, if you get frustrated with something,
>   like accept the definition of circle, you know, with the taxigeometry, and
>   stuff. The same definition could get you something completely different.
>   There's all these questions.

The mini-course enabled Katya, too, to appreciate that mathematics is
the product of human activity and that mathematical discovery can provide

occasions for creative activity and be accessible—even to her! Although Katya herself recognized that her view of mathematics might have started to change even before the course, the specific example she refers to comes from one of our instructional sessions (Episode 5). I might add that I observed changes in her behavior throughout the unit that support the interpretation that she had not attained a full appreciation of the role of discovery in mathematics before our meetings. I will come back to this point a little later.

During her interview, Mary showed a similar awareness that a change had occurred in her view of mathematics, and she was able to articulate this realization quite well:

> **M:** *I can't really explain what mathematics is, but . . . It's kind of like an art, but it serve a purpose. . . . It's enabling us to see, just like reading a new novel enables you to see something. . . . I think the nature of [mathematics] is that it is well-patterned and there are exceptions just like in everything, as in languages. But it still . . . holds a definite shape and it does have a purpose and it can be figured out, even by me! I didn't think I could figure math out before.*

Mary's words are remarkable for many reasons. They shows a movement, of which the student herself was well aware, toward a more relativistic view of mathematics (as expressed in the words "there are exceptions just like in everything") and the realization that mathematics has meaning. Her comparison of mathematics with the arts is especially revealing of an appreciation of mathematics as a humanistic discipline. The strength of this view, and its effect on Mary's new realization that she *could* do mathematics, is further evidenced when she says, "I used to think that the material was to blame, but now I really think it is the way people were told to teach it. And I think that it is the way they were taught."

Mary also claims that our instructional sessions had a key role in changing her view of mathematics:

> **I:** *Does this experience now . . . encourage you to look at mathematics in a different way?*
>
> **M:** *I would say yes. I have never been in a class like this. I never had any kind of experience with anything beyond the clear-cut, out-of-the-book stuff. I look at [mathematics] differently just because we theorized a lot, a lot more than I'm used to.* .

Their realization that mathematics has a humanistic side was especially important to these girls, who had shown considerable ability in the arts and humanities, since it helped them see new opportunities for creative activities in mathematics. Their active participation in the unit activities and their enthusiasm were obvious. A few times, Mary reported having discussed what was happening in class with her boyfriend (even on a Friday night!).

H. Moving toward taking charge of their mathematical activity

One would hope that changes in the students' *view* of mathematics would eventually affect the way these students *do* mathematics. A shift in behavior toward a more creative approach to mathematics learning and a greater critical stance, however, does not automatically follow from the mere awareness that mathematics allows for such behavior. Thus, it is important to analyze the changes that actually occurred in the students' behavior as they engaged in various mathematical tasks.

Both students took advantage of almost every opportunity for creativity offered to them. Looking at the narrative of our instructional episodes, one is surprised by the quality as well as the amount of the students' insight, and also by their lively and focused participation (especially when compared with what usually happens in mathematics classes). Even when left on her own, Mary showed considerable creativity (especially in *Part 2* of her final project). Both her participation in the explorations initiated in our instructional sessions and her final project provide strong evidence of Mary's previously unrecognized mathematical ability. They also show her growing confidence in herself and in the possibility of using her "mind" to solve mathematical problems for which she had not been shown an answer. Though Mary often led the inquiry and showed more enthusiasm and initiative, Katya's more laid-back participation should not be misinterpreted as passivity or withdrawal. One can in fact point out several occasions during which Katya contributed crucial ideas and insights to the discussion: think for example of her valuable intuitions in proving informally the equivalence of the two definitions of isosceles triangle in Episode 2.3 or the theorem in Episode 3.2, and even her few but crucial remarks in the creation of a definition of diamond (Episode 5.4).

Yet Katya, unlike Mary, occasionally presented some resistance to a more open-ended approach to learning mathematics. Her initial tendency to rely on "remembering," especially at the beginning of the unit, is of particular interest in this respect. When we dealt with something that she had encountered in previous courses, her first attempt was often to remember what she had been taught there, rather than to think about the problem on her own or to use the opportunity to take a new look at the situation. Evidence of this can be found, for example, in Episode 2 when she was solving traditional geometric problems and again in Episode 4 when she was trying to remember facts about exponents. Trying to remember what she learned in the past is certainly a reasonable and worthwhile approach, especially for a student who, like Katya, has encountered some success in school mathematics. But giving a prominent role to remembering in mathematical activities also reveals an implicit conception of mathematics as a domain where things are static and determined forever, so that if you have done something once, it is not really worth going over it a second time to look at it with different eyes, nor is it reasonable to expect changes to occur. Katya's view of mathematics, however, seems to have changed as a result of later experiences. And this change found a match in her behavior, too, if we think of her spontaneous suggestion that we work with complex numbers in order to overcome some of the problems I raised over the exponentiation of negative bases in one of our last lessons.

Both students also displayed a more critical stance and greater initiative as a result of the course. It was evident as the unit developed that they were becoming more and more cautious about both the results of their own mathematical activity and the results suggested by Authority, consisting, in this case, of my input in the instructional sessions and what they had been taught in previous mathematics courses. Think, for example, of the students' lack of hesitation in choosing the results of their explorations over the "wrong" theorem I had initially suggested to them in Episode 3.2, the cautiousness they showed in presenting tentative solutions to the problem of extending exponents in Episode 4.2, and especially Mary's attitude in criticizing the traditional definition of circle after our experiences with taxicab geometry in Episode 5.3.

An increased critical stance is by itself evidence of reduced reliance on authority. The students showed further movement toward taking charge of their mathematical activity in yet another direction, as they increasingly took advantage of opportunities to shape their own mathematical explorations by generating new questions rather than by simply complying with the tasks imposed by the instructor—an unusual development considering the role that learners in general, and not just mathematics students, implicitly accept.

This shift is especially evident in Mary's behavior toward the end of the unit. For example, in Episode 5.3 she twice determined the direction the lesson was going to take. The first time, she decided that the definition of circle we had accepted until then could not be correct since it described figures that do not share the same properties; she then attempted to identify the mistake and correct it. It may be worthwhile to recall that my agenda, in contrast, had been to make the students appreciate the value of vague definitions by realizing that the standard definition of circle describes both Euclidean circles *and* taxicircles. Immediately after this, quite on her own Mary set out to create a definition for diamond and followed her first casual remark, "I wonder how we define diamond," by drawing examples and trying tentative definitions, never dreaming of asking the instructor's permission. Another remarkable proof of her initiative is in her project itself (Episode 8), in which she posed new questions, especially in *Part 2*.

The best example of their increased critical awareness and initiative, however, occurred when both Katya and Mary, with no qualms, expressed their disappointment in my original idea for their final project and helped me devise a better task (see the report of the genesis of the project at the beginning of Chapter 8). I find this event especially remarkable, since it involved the aspect of instruction that by definition is expected to be a privilege of authority—the evaluation of the students themselves.

Concluding observations

As I had hoped, the most remarkable effects of the experience were not limited to the students' improved understanding of mathematical definitions. It was evident that they found the material covered in our instructional sessions more interesting, complex, and challenging than they had ever thought possible in a mathematics class and that they appreciated the opportunity to explore mathematical issues on their own. Both Katya and Mary came to recognize aspects of mathematics that made this discipline closer to the arts and humanities (in which they had greater interest) and thus more appealing to them. The changes in their professed beliefs about mathematics were matched by changes in their behavior. It was evident, as the unit developed, that the students' independence increased, enabling them to assume more control of their mathematics learning and to consider it with a more critical eye.

The two students also revealed interesting differences in their experience of my instructional approach. While both participated actively in our mathematical inquiries, Mary seemed to take great satisfaction every time we challenged the given and discovered things that "did not work." Katya, instead, sometimes seemed a bit uncomfortable with our continuous challenging of what she had comfortably relied on so far. It seems worthwhile to discuss these different reactions, taking into account the students' prior experiences with mathematics.

While Katya had been reasonably (even if unevenly) successful with "regular" mathematics and seemed to enjoy its mechanical and organized nature, Mary had resented her previous mathematics course, refused to "memorize" when she thought she was expected to do so, and failed several other courses. It seems reasonable to suggest that sometimes our approach made Katya uncomfortable because it took away the source of her previous success in mathematics and thus some of her "security." Mary, on the other hand, had almost nothing to lose in terms of mathematical self-esteem. Furthermore, some of the reasons for her past failure seemed to have to do with precisely the mechanistic view of mathematics I was now challenging. I believe that there are many students like Mary whose success in mathematics has been hindered by an unrealistic view of the discipline. Mary's success makes me hope that an instructional approach that emphasizes students' inquiry could help other students to realize the more humanistic and contextualized aspects of mathematics and come to appreciate their own hidden mathematical potential.

What the instructor learned about definitions

At the end of the mini-course, I too had gained new insights into mathematical definitions, mathematics, learning, and teaching. In this section I will focus only on what I learned about the nature, role, and uses of definitions through our joint inquiry. The mathematical and pedagogical reflections stimulated by this experience will find expression in Chapters 11 and 12.

As a result of my own work on definitions before the course (see Chapter 2), I had already realized the need to challenge some of the requirements traditionally associated with mathematical definitions and had come to appreciate their dynamic nature and the important role played by context in their interpretation and development. Yet I did not feel that I had by any means reached a "complete" (or even satisfactory) understanding of definitions. Rather it seemed that my prior work had allowed me to identify a number of interesting issues worth further exploration. Thus, I approached the mini-course with the expectation that, at least to some extent, I would inquire and learn about definitions with the students. This, indeed, is what happened.

As I have noted, some of the students' observations triggered new insights for me, too. For example, in Episode 2.1 Mary's questions about whether she could draw a circle without knowing its radius made me realize that definitions cannot be expected to provide all the necessary instructions to "produce" an instance of the concept they characterize. In Episode 2.3, Katya's definition—"An isosceles triangle is a triangle with two equal sides or two equal angles"—made me consider for the first time the value of using disjunctions in mathematical definitions. In Episode 7, Mary's observations as she struggled with the definition of cat made me realize the overwhelming emphasis put on defining concepts *by abstraction* in mathematics and, in contrast, the alternative of defining some mathematical concepts by means of *family resemblances*.

Reflecting on the experience as a whole, however, made me reconsider my own conception of mathematical definition even more radically. More specifically, the inquiry on mathematical definitions conducted together with the students led me to a more refined understanding of the role played by *context* and *purposes* in the creation and evaluation of mathematical definitions and, consequently, of the standard requirements for mathematical definitions.

Toward a better appreciation of the role of context

When I began my own inquiry on mathematical definitions before the course, I was immediately struck by the importance of considering the mathematical context in which a specific definition is interpreted and used. In particular, I had realized that once familiar definitions are reinterpreted in new contexts they may identify objects that are different from those we are used to associating with them (as we saw in Episode 5 when the usual definition of circle was used in the context of a different metric space like taxicab geometry). When the course began, however, I had not yet realized several other important implications of the crucial role played by context.

My initial realization—that in a different context a definition can be interpreted differently and thus identify a different set of instances—had made me question the requirements of *precision in terminology* and *isolation of the concept* usually set for mathematical definitions. Though I had not thought much about it before, it now seemed clear to me that all mathematical definitions are quite *ambiguous,* at least until we specify the mathematical context in which they are to be interpreted. When I thought of the value usually placed on generality in mathematics—as shown, for example, in the attempt to determine properties that hold in any generic metric space instead of just the specific situation of the Euclidean plane—I concluded that this ambiguity was necessary and even valuable.

It was only later, after we had considered "or" definitions and new viewpoints about what would be the most appropriate definition of circle in Episode 5.3, that I realized that the role played by context could also help me better understand the mathematicians' decision to consider *essentiality* as a key property of mathematical definitions. As our experiences demonstrated, one of the first consequences of changing context is that some properties that were originally derivable from a given definition might no longer be derivable from it in the new context. This implies that definitions that were equivalent in the familiar context might now identify different sets of objects and thus no longer be equivalent. Even more important, properties that we were used to associating with a given concept might have become contradictory—in other words, they might not coexist—in the new context. Thus, whenever we include in a definition more properties than are strictly necessary we risk that these properties will turn out to be contradictory (and the definition meaningless) in the new context.

Mary's resistance to accepting both taxicircles and Euclidean circles as instances of the same concept also made me reconsider my initial assumption that a *more general* notion of circle would necessarily be *better*. Though many useful properties of circles can be maintained and generalized to other metric spaces if we are focusing only on the property that "all its points are at a given distance from the center," it is also true that much of the richness of the Euclidean circle (that is, most of the theorems we can derive about this figure in Euclidean geometry) is lost once the definition is interpreted in a generic metric space. This awareness has been implicitly recognized by mathematicians in their choice of a different name—that of *ball of radius r*—to distinguish the generalized metric concept of the "locus of points at a given distance from a given point" from that of the Euclidean *circle*.

The surprises we encountered in trying to define circle in a different context also made me revise my original distinction between familiar and unfamiliar concepts in creating and evaluating mathematical definitions. In fact, once we appreciate that even familiar notions need to be reviewed— and perhaps even reconceived—when new contexts are considered, it becomes even more obvious that every mathematical concept is to a certain extent tentative and that its definition should be approached in a dynamic spirit. In other words, all mathematical definitions—even those found in mathematics textbooks!—are good only *for the time being*. We cannot know beforehand all the situations in which a concept might be used and the meaning the definition will assume in all of those contexts. Each new situation may lead us to refine both the concept and its definition, thus contributing positively to the growth of mathematical knowledge.

Toward a better appreciation of the role of purpose

If mathematical concepts are not predetermined and we cannot even say that more general is always better, then there is no "sure" way to choose between alternative interpretations of a given mathematical concept, and hence, no predetermined way to decide what would be its *best* definition when alternative ones have been proposed. Similarly, definitions that are equivalent in the system we are used to working with may not be equivalent in the new context. When this happens, we need to reconsider which properties best identify the concept in question.

Every time such a dilemma presents itself, mathematicians have to judge the advantages of the available alternatives. To do so, they must consider how they plan to use the notion—in other words, their *purposes* in trying to shape the mathematical concept the definition in question is trying to characterize in the first place. Such a decision is by no means arbitrary. Rather, it is based on an evaluation of the mathematical consequences of the available options, which may be different at different times and perhaps even in different branches of mathematics. The history of the concept of infinity (Borasi, 1985) and polyhedron (Lakatos, 1976) provides good evidence in this regard. This serves to underline the need to look at definitions in a dynamic way—as good for the time being but always open to revision.

The standard requirements for mathematical definitions revisited

When I was planning the unit on mathematical definitions, I was quite excited by my discovery of the limitations in the standard requirements for evaluating them listed in most mathematics texts—*isolation of the concept, noncontradiction, precision in terminology, noncircularity,* and *essentiality.* My initial intention was to share this awareness with the students by encouraging them to challenge the validity of the standard criteria in a number of specific circumstances. Although I still think it is important to challenge the belief that these five requirements are absolute, I now think that it is also important to come to a more positive, constructive appreciation of *when and how* they should be used in mathematics.

When the mathematical context in which we are operating is clearly stated and we are trying to solve a specific problem or derive a theorem, we can and should use a mathematical definition that is sufficiently precise to single out the concept in question and to allow us to derive its properties efficiently and unambiguously. In these circumstances, the five criteria established by the mathematics community not only make a lot of sense, but they are quite necessary to guarantee shared meaning as well as consistency in mathematical results. At the same time, it is important for students to understand that we can assume a definition is "fixed" in this way only at a specific time and within a specific mathematical context. As these variables change, we need to reconsider the meaning and implications of a definition and perhaps modify it to better serve our expanded purposes. A metaphor that comes to mind as I try to grapple with this need for "double standards" is that of definitions as "wax objects." In order to "handle" (or "use") definitions, we need to act as if they were solid and immutable. But this is only for the time being: if a slightly different shape seems more appropriate, we know that we can always modify the original object in a process of continuous refinement.

Indeed, mathematicians frequently switch between these two modes—accepting things as given or challenging them—in their research. Most of the time, they assume as a given the axioms, rules, and definitions of a specific system in order to work deductively within it and derive all its possible properties and implications. Occasionally, however, they may question and challenge the premises of the system itself and consider the possibility of alternatives. Notable historical examples are the creation of non-Euclidean geometries (Kline, 1980) and the evolution of the concept and definition of polyhedron discussed by Lakatos (1976) (see Chapter 4). This pattern also supports the thesis proposed by Kuhn (1970) that scientific knowledge has been achieved through the alternation of traditional scientific research conducted within an existing paradigm, and scientific revolutions that challenge the status quo and cause a total change in perspectives and assumptions.

A first critique of the instructional design: What can be learned about teaching definitions

Overall, the activities designed for the unit were quite successful in helping students understand mathematical definitions. The mini-course provided ample opportunity for the students to explore the various aspects, uses, and roles of mathematical definitions. The reports of each instructional episode (Chapters 3–8) also illustrate the richness of the students' mathematical discussions and the extent of their active involvement throughout the unit. As can be expected, however, there is still room for improvement in the instructional design of the unit in order to make the teaching of mathematical definitions more effective in school mathematics. Throughout my reports on specific episodes I have tried to point out what I perceived as shortcomings in specific activities and suggest ways in which these activities could be improved. Here I will comment on the strengths and weaknesses of the unit's overall design.

An important principle informing the unit was that students need to engage in *concrete activities* that require them to analyze specific definitions and use them in a variety of mathematical situations, rather than in *abstract discussions* on the nature of mathematical definitions. Three instructional heuristics seem to have been especially successful in designing such activities in the mini-course:

1. The in-depth analysis of a list of incorrect definitions of a given concept.
2. The use of definitions in specific mathematical problems and proofs.
3. The exploration of what happens when a familiar definition is interpreted in a different context.

The first of these strategies proved especially valuable in helping the students understand the rationale behind some of the standard criteria imposed on definitions by the mathematics community and recognize important properties of the concepts they were trying to define. This seems to be the case especially when students are already intuitively familiar with the concept to be defined and when the list of definitions analyzed is sufficiently *rich*—as was the case with circle in Episode 2.1 but not with the other concepts. It is also important, however, that the students realize the limitations of this approach.

Looking at definitions "in action"—analyzing their use in typical mathematical activities such as solving a problem, proving a theorem, or exploring

ing a new mathematical area—seems to me crucial to understanding the *purpose* and *role* of definitions in mathematics. Students can thus be enabled to see more clearly the rationale for the standard requirements imposed on mathematical definitions, their limitations, and their appropriate domain of application. I employed this strategy extensively in Episodes 2 and 3, but I am not sure the students were always able to appreciate the significance of what they were doing in terms of their understanding of the notion of definition. In any future implementation, I think I would encourage students to reflect on how definitions are used in solving problems or deducing proofs, and what this means for creating "good" mathematical definitions.

Finally, analyzing what happens to specific definitions in different contexts (Episodes 4 and 5) proved to be an especially successful strategy for generating surprise and doubt, thus challenging some of the students' previous conceptions about mathematical definitions. Once again, however, more explicit reflection on the consequences of a shift in context might have helped the students relate what they were doing with their growing understanding of the nature, roles, and uses of definitions.

One important shortcoming of the unit is the fact that the students often had too little time or opportunity to reflect upon, assimilate, and integrate with their everyday mathematical activities the new insights their learning experiences in the unit produced. Thus, some activities might not have had the impact they could have. My attempts at synthesis using review sheets, though helpful, were not really enough; in Chapter 12 I will propose some alternative ways for helping students synthesize what they learn from nontraditional learning activities. Some of these problems could also be overcome if, instead of discussing the nature of mathematical definitions as an isolated unit, one could disperse and integrate the activities we tried out in the mini-course throughout a whole mathematics course and, possibly, throughout the whole mathematics curriculum. This would give students more time to organize and elaborate on their discoveries, reflect on them, and apply what they learned to the definitions they encounter in their regular mathematical experience. If the activities Katya and Mary experienced in the mini-course were embedded in a regular mathematics course, they could also be used to encourage traditional school mathematics activities such as solving problems or proving theorems. In our mini-course such opportunities frequently arose, but unfortunately, I could not exploit all of them as I would have wished to because of the constraints of our unit topic and our schedule.

Beyond the Story: Articulating the Assumptions of a Humanistic Inquiry Approach to School Mathematics

11

I would now like to move beyond the particulars of the mini-course on definitions to discuss more generally the *humanistic inquiry* approach to mathematics instruction this experience exemplifies. Let me remind the reader that my intention in telling the story of our inquiry was not to present a "model unit" to be reproduced by other teachers or to suggest activities for teaching definitions in mathematics more effectively. Rather, I hoped that our experience would illustrate what can happen when mathematics instruction is organized around students' genuine inquiries and would inspire mathematics educators to examine the potential contributions of this approach to a rethinking of mathematics instruction.

Teachers' instructional decisions about curriculum choices, teaching strategies, and classroom organization and management are informed by the system of beliefs about school mathematics each of them holds (Brown and Cooney, 1988; Cooney, 1985; Thompson, 1988). A real change in instructional practices, therefore, is likely to require a shift in beliefs as well. In this chapter I want to articulate the set of pedagogical assumptions that characterize a humanistic inquiry approach and contrast it with the set of assumptions that inform most current mathematics instruction. I am well aware that these two approaches do not present a dichotomy, and that there are a number of alternative approaches—such as a "guided discovery" or a "problem-solving" approach—worthy of discussion. But an extended comparison of alternative approaches to mathematics education is beyond the scope of this discussion.

As I hope to show, the assumptions behind a humanistic inquiry approach are in sharp contrast with the transmission model dominating current instructional practices. I will also point out how a humanistic inquiry approach is in line with current recommendations about improving mathematics instruction (e.g., NCTM, 1989a, 1991; NRC, 1989), although it also highlights some aspects that have so far been neglected in the debate about school mathematics reform.

I will start by questioning what the nature of mathematics and mathematical activity is. In light of this discussion, I will then critique the current goals of school mathematics and identify how I think they should be redefined. I will then discuss what theoretical models of learning and teaching seem most consistent with the reconceived view of mathematical knowledge and the educational goals proposed. I will also briefly address how issues of equity may assume a new meaning when we approach mathematics education as humanistic inquiry.

Rethinking the nature of mathematics

For many people, mathematics can be reduced to a collection of preestablished facts, rules, and techniques essentially having to do with numbers and (at best) geometric shapes. This is not surprising if we consider the content of current precollege school mathematics curricula. Unfortunately, the following description captures well the kind of mathematics that many students experience as a result of their schooling:

> Arithmetic computation is entrenched as the basis of the mathematics curriculum, with the "four" rules gradually being developed to handle more and more complicated "numbers"—natural, integer, fractions, decimal, complex and, later, matrices and vectors. Algebraic work develops the skills of solving more and more complicated "equations" and of rearranging complicated expressions so that they can be "solved". Geometry, if taken seriously at all, is developed as an area to which one can apply arithmetical and algebraic techniques, be it thereby trigonometry or coordinate geometry. And for those who have succeeded at, or survived, that diet, the gateway to further delight is the calculus, with its myriad of integrals and differential equations waiting to be recognized, classified, and of course, "solved". (Bishop, 1988, p. 7)

As a result of their experience of mathematics in school, most people (not just young students) conceive of mathematics as "the discipline of certainty" par excellence, consisting only of indisputable facts and techniques:

> Educators and cognitive scientists commonly think of mathematics as the paradigmatic "well-structured discipline." Mathematics is regarded as a field in which statements have unambiguous meanings, there is a clear hierarchy of knowledge, and the range of possible actions in response to any problem is both restricted and well defined in advance. (Resnick, 1988, p. 32)

However reasonable such a conception of mathematics may at first seem, many mathematicians and mathematics educators have argued that it does not reflect the real nature of mathematics. I agree with this contention and want to propose an alternative view of mathematics as a *humanistic* discipline.

The activity of applied mathematicians today challenges the perception of mathematics as a well-structured domain (Pollak, 1970). Whether they are asked to deal with real-life situations, such as improving the public transportation of a certain city, or to propose models that can help us predict complex phenomena, such as the weather, these mathematicians face problems that are very different from those encountered in mathematics textbooks, even those at the college level. These professionals are rarely, if ever, presented with a well-defined problem and expected to apply known mathematical methods to come up with an objective solution. Rather, the task is more often presented to them in the more vague and open-ended form of a "problematic situation"—a situation the client is not satisfied with and would like to improve, such as the perceived inefficiency in a city's public transportation. The first and most crucial step for an applied mathematician is to define more specific problems that can be approached with mathematical tools and whose solution can help achieve the original goal. Obviously, a good understanding of the context—the whole complexity of the problematic situation presented to them as well as the goals and values of the client who proposed it—is essential at this stage. Since the way problems are framed will determine the type of solutions sought for, the evaluation of the solutions obtained cannot be made solely on the basis of the appropriate choice and execution of algorithms. It will have to take into account other factors as well, such as the client's satisfaction with the proposed solution, the relationship between the costs and the benefits of its implementation, and even the acceptability of its potential consequences in light of the mathematician's own values and beliefs.

The complexity and nonlinearity of mathematical applications is a reality that affects not only the work of professional mathematicians but also the activity of most business employees and even the daily lives of people. Recent studies by anthropologists interested in everyday cognition have revealed that people's spontaneous use of mathematics in their daily lives has more in common with the activity of professional mathematicians as I have described it than with the tasks traditionally assigned in school mathematics (Rogoff and Lave, 1984). Consider, for example, the following description of how shoppers use arithmetic in the routine task of selecting grocery items in a supermarket:

> Although arithmetic problem-solving plays various roles in grocery shopping, its preponderant use is for price comparison. This kind of calculation occurs at the end of largely qualitative decision-making processes which

smoothly reduce numerous possibilities on the shelf to single items in the cart. A snag occurs when the elimination of alternatives comes to a halt before a choice has been made. Arithmetic problem-solving is both an expression of and a medium for dealing with these stalled decision processes. It is, among other things, a move outside the qualitative characteristics of a product to its characterization in terms of a standard of value, money. . . .

Shoppers are not comparing prices merely to gain information that will then be weighted appropriately with respect to other information, such as other features of competing brands. Rather, shoppers explicitly compare prices only when they have no strong preference among brands. . . .

The routine nature of grocery-shopping activity and the location of price arithmetic at the end of decision-making processes suggest that the shopper must already assign rich content and shape to a problem solution by the time arithmetic becomes an obvious next step. Problem solving under these circumstances is an iterative process. It involves, on the one hand, what the shopper knows and what the setting holds that might help and, on the other hand, what the solution looks like. The activity of finding some-thing problematic subsumes a good deal of knowledge about what would constitute a solution. In the course of grocery shopping many of a problem solution's parameters are marshalled into place as part of the process of deciding, up to a point, what to purchase. (Lave, Murtaugh, and de la Roche, 1984, pp. 81–83)

As this discussion makes clear, mathematical applications require not only good technical knowledge but also the ability to take into account the context in which one is operating, the purpose of the activity, the possibility of alternative solutions, and also personal values and opinions that can affect one's decisions. Unfortunately, none of these elements is usually recognized as relevant to mathematical activity by people who have gone through traditional schooling.

I am well aware of the objection that some may want to raise at this point: "But this has nothing to do with *mathematics*, it has to do only with its *applications!*" The debate on the distinction between "pure" and "applied" mathematics, and on the legitimacy of the latter to be considered *mathematics* proper, has indeed a long history in the field (Halmos, 1981; Poston, 1981). Although I do not wish to get into it here, I would like to point out that conceptually separating mathematical knowledge from its uses can have dangerous repercussions when discussing the learning and teaching of mathematics, as recent research on situated learning has suggested (Lave, 1988). For the scope of this discussion, let it suffice to say that, since one of the major goals of school mathematics is to empower students to use mathematics appropriately, schools have the responsibility to make stu-dents aware of the ambiguous and contextualized nature of "real-life" mathematical problems.

Regardless of one's conclusions about whether the application of mathe-matics constitutes proper mathematical activity or not, it is important to realize that the realm of "pure" mathematics, too, is far from achieving the ideals of objectivity, certainty, absolute truth, and rigor usually associated with this discipline. The way mathematics has developed historically challenges these common expectations.

Perhaps because textbooks and lectures tend to present mathematical results in a "neat" and organized way, few people realize that those results have not always been achieved in a straightforward manner. On the contrary, historical accounts like those of Morris Kline (1980, 1985) reveal the centuries of intellectual struggle that were needed to produce even the most fundamental mathematical results, such as the number systems middle school students work with today. The development of certain topics, such as infinity, was punctuated by debates and controversies as alternative (and often incompatible) solutions were proposed by different mathematicians (Borasi, 1985). Even the logical-deductive method for deriving results, perceived by many as the most "solid" feature of mathematics, has encountered a number of criticisms throughout the centuries, some of which have remained unresolved (Kline, 1980).

We cannot hope that uncertainties and controversies are only a thing of the past or that future mathematicians will eventually be able to resolve all of them. Rather, mathematicians have had to accept the existence of some unavoidable limitations within the structure of mathematics itself. Starting with the creation of the first non-Euclidean geometries, mathematicians had to abandon their confidence in the absolute "truth" of even the most rigorously developed branch of their discipline and recognize, instead, that mathematics can house logically sound, yet conflicting, axiomatic systems. Even the ultimate belief that one would someday be able to verify the internal coherence and consistency of mathematics itself had to be relinquished after Gödel's proof that any formal system of a certain complexity contains some undecidable propositions (Kline, 1980; Hofstadter, 1980). Most important, Lakatos's interpretation (see Chapter 4) of the construction of mathematical knowledge as an iterative process of "proofs and refutations" that produces increasingly refined results, finally makes us doubt the finality of any of the mathematical results we are currently working with.

Far from affecting only the work of a small elite of professional mathematicians and philosophers, uncertainty and ambiguity pervade even the most elementary areas of mathematics, although we often do not perceive them because of the way mathematics is presented in schools and the traditional expectations about the nature of this discipline. The inquiry into the notion of mathematical definition recorded here provides ample evidence. In Episode 4, for example, as Katya and Mary attempted to extend the familiar operation of exponentiation, they realized that the definition of exponentiation they had previously learned—"repeated multiplication"—was no longer appropriate and needed to be modified. They had to construct new rules as well as an entirely new meaning in order to operate with negative or fractional exponents. The creation of these rules was neither predetermined nor arbitrary; rather, it took into account the new mathematical context for the operation (the nature of the new numbers one was working with) and the purposes behind the extension of exponentiation to new numbers (such as the desire to maintain coherence with how the operation worked with whole numbers). Finally, although we achieved extension in a satisfactory way, it was not free of problems, since we encountered unavoidable contradictions in trying to define 0^0 and fractional exponents of negative bases, and finally had to accept the need to make some exceptions.

As a result of all these considerations, mathematicians concluded that mathematical knowledge is neither absolutely true nor fully verifiable but, just as in any other science, only falsifiable and open to continuous revision:

> History supports the view that there is no fixed, objective, unique body of mathematics. Moreover, if history is any guide, there will be new additions to mathematics that will call for new foundations. In this respect, mathematics is like any one of the physical sciences. Theories must be modified as new observations or new experimental results conflict with previous established theories and compel formulation of new ones. No timeless account of mathematical truth is possible. (Kline, 1980, p. 320)

Once we realize that mathematical results are neither predetermined nor absolute, we also have to accept the fact that mathematics as we know it now is as fallible as any other product of human activity. Both mathematical results and their truth are socially constructed—they are sanctioned by a community of practice (the mathematical community of the time) on the basis of agreed on criteria, which may change over time and in different contexts (Lerman, 1989; Schoenfeld, in press). Thus, mathematical results and procedures are not totally objective. They can be influenced by cultural values, political agendas, or even just the desire to solve specific problems deemed important by the contemporary mathematics community. Alternatives to the axioms and rules that characterize accepted mathematical systems can always be devised, and the decision to accept them as part of mathematics needs to be evaluated on the basis of a number of criteria. Various non-Euclidean geometries, for example, have now been accepted as a legitimate part of mathematics along with Euclidean geometry, partly because mathematicians and physicists have realized that each geometry can be used to represent alternative models of physical space and thus can help solve problems within each context.

The following excerpts highlight some of the fundamental challenges to the common view of mathematics as the "discipline of certainty" and the ultimate example of a well-structured domain:

> The history of mathematics is not one of the gradual revelation of absolute truths, but, as with all knowledge, the consequence of people's ideas, interest,

conflicts and patronage, and is culturally and temporally relative. Mathematical knowledge is a social construction, the meaning of a concept such as 'polyhedron' for example, following Lakatos, is negotiated and adapted according to convention and agreement, through proofs as explanations, leading to basic refutable statements. (Lerman, 1990a, p. 27)

Mathematics is an inherently social activity, in which a community of trained practitioners (mathematical scientists) engages in the science of patterns—systematic attempts, based on observation, study, and experimentation, to determine the nature or principles of regularities in systems defined axiomatically or theoretically ("pure math") or models of systems abstracted from real world objects ("applied math"). . . .

Truth in mathematics is that for which the majority of the community believes it has compelling arguments. In mathematics truth is socially negotiated, as it is in science. (Schoenfeld, in press, p. 9)

I have used the term *humanistic* to try to convey the complexity of this view of mathematics—that is, mathematics as a fallible, socially constructed, contextualized, and culture-dependent discipline driven by the human desire to reduce uncertainty but without the expectation of ever totally eliminating it. Other terms have been used to express essentially the same idea: mathematics as an *ill-structured domain*, mathematics as *social construct*, mathematics as a *contextualized discipline*. There is also a *constructivist* view of mathematics (referring to the philosophical sense of the word; see Lerman, 1989). My choice of the term *humanistic* has been motivated by the current usage of this term within the mathematics and mathematics education community[1] and by my belief that emphasizing its human and humane elements can help us realize that mathematics is closer to other fields, and thus more approachable, than is usually perceived.

For many of those holding a logical positivist view of mathematics and science, the pervasiveness of this "loss of certainty" in mathematics, as Kline (1980) has characterized it, may appear quite disappointing and even somewhat disturbing. On the contrary, I would suggest that a humanistic view of mathematics not only comes closer to describing the real nature of mathematics and mathematical activity, it may also have some important benefits for mathematics students.

The recognition of limitations and "human" elements in the discipline could make it more attractive to those who have been intimidated by the absolute and authoritarian image of mathematics currently presented in schools, an issue I will return to later in this chapter in discussing issues of gender in mathematics education. If we agree that mathematics as a discipline is not totally objective and predetermined but is influenced by economic, cultural, and even political agendas, just like any other human domain, we should question the choices made thus far about how mathematics should be covered in the precollege curriculum. We may, for example, start to look critically at the kinds of situations used to create word problems in most textbooks and see a need for alternatives:

Look at the kinds of examples we draw on in the teaching of mathematics at the moment: percentage increases in pay; simple and compound interest; hire purchase; exchange rates and angle of missile projection to hit a target. Why shouldn't we use examples to reveal prejudice and injustice, and raise children's awareness of social issues? (Lerman, 1990b, p. 29)

Once we accept the idea that mathematics is a social construct, the philosophical view of knowledge proposed by John Dewey and C. S. Peirce can help us appreciate the uncertainty that permeates the discipline as a positive element rather than a limitation. As Siegel and Carey (1989) point out, in Peirce's definition of *knowledge* as a dynamic process of inquiry, uncertainty plays a generative role:

Peirce does not set up "truth" as the goal [of knowledge]. Unlike practitioners of conventional logic, Peirce understands that we have to abandon any hope of knowing that something is true once and for all and be satisfied with the idea that *we can only be certain about something for the time being*. In fact he claims that the pragmatic stance towards truth and certainty improves on traditional logic; for *it is this uncertainty that sets the process of knowledge-making in process*. (My italics) (Siegel and Carey, 1989, pp. 21–22)

Dewey expresses a similar view of the motivating power of uncertainty and doubt within a discipline when he defines "reflective thought" as involving "(1) a state of doubt, hesitation, perplexity, mental difficulty, in which thinking originates, and (2) an act of searching, hunting, inquiring, to find material that will resolve the doubt, settle and dispose of the perplexity" (Dewey, 1933, p. 12). The presence of ambiguity and limitations in mathematics and in its applications is thus a major force for inquiry, and consequently for the production of mathematical knowledge, as mathematics researchers, users, and students should recognize.

Rethinking the goals of school mathematics

This analysis of the nature of mathematics fundamentally challenges the adequacy of current curricula and teaching practices. The first element requiring reexamination is the set of overall goals that are assumed for mathematics education. Despite rhetoric to the contrary, current textbooks and evaluation measures leave no doubt that the goals set for mathematics students today can be reduced to the acquisition of a few fundamental facts and techniques in arithmetic, geometry, elementary algebra. More recently, they have also come to include basics of probability and statistics, and the ability to apply such "knowledge" efficiently in simplified textbook problems (the "infamous" word problems). Such goals are obviously informed by an oversimplified view of what it means to do mathematics. They should be replaced by a set of goals that would provide students with both the mathematical expertise required of them by our technological world and an appreciation of mathematics as a "way of knowing" (Bishop, 1988).

Indeed, the mathematics education community has begun to realize the inadequacy of the current goals of school mathematics in preparing future citizens for jobs and responsibilities in today's society. The two most influential documents among those calling for reform, the NCTM Curriculum and Evaluation Standards (NCTM, 1989a) and *Everybody Counts* (NRC, 1989), begin their critique of the current situation in mathematics instruction by acknowledging these changing needs.

> All industrial countries have experienced a shift from an industrial to an information society, a shift that has transformed both the aspects of mathematics that need to be transmitted to students and the concepts and procedures they must master if they are to be self-fulfilled, productive citizens in the next century. (NCTM, 1989a, p. 3)

> Jobs that contribute to this world economy require workers who ... are prepared to *absorb new ideas, to adapt to change, to cope with ambiguity, to perceive patterns, and to solve unconventional problems*. It is these needs, not just the need for calculation (which is now done mostly by machines), that make mathematics a prerequisite to so many jobs. (My italics) (NRC, 1989, p. 1)

In addition to the "economical" reasons emphasized in these reports, the current goals of school mathematics should also be challenged on the grounds that they communicate a view of mathematics that is *dysfunctional* to students' success in the discipline. I have already mentioned that the perception of mathematics as a "cut-and-dried" and authoritarian domain may turn away even capable individuals (such as Katya and Mary). Even more important, the view of mathematics that informs current curricular goals can interfere with students' learning by inducing expectations and behavior that are not conducive to success in the long run—such as focusing on memorization rather than conceptual understanding or engaging in the meaningless practice of many routine exercises instead of examining a few complex problems in depth (see Borasi, 1990). If these are *not* the guidelines we want students to adopt in learning and using mathematics, then we must begin to rethink school mathematics in order to achieve a new set of goals.

In what follows I have attempted to identify and articulate the new overall goals for mathematics instruction that are assumed by a humanistic inquiry approach. For the sake of exposition, I have chosen to present them in four separate categories, although these categories obviously overlap and connect with one another.

1. Students should come to appreciate the nature of mathematics as a discipline

Conveying an appropriate image of the nature of mathematics was already recognized as an important curriculum goal by the authors of many of the

"New Math" projects of the post-Sputnik era, such as the School Mathematics Study Group project (SMSG) and the Comprehensive School Mathematics Project (CSMP). They strove to make students aware of some of the *unique* characteristics of mathematics—the deductive method, which is used to derive and justify results, and the axiomatic structures that allow for the organization and presentation of mathematical facts in an elegant and efficient way. The importance of communicating to students ways of thinking that are characteristic of mathematics is also recognized in the NCTM Standards (NCTM, 1989a) and *Everybody Counts* (NRC, 1989). The latter, for example, identifies the following as "mathematical modes of thought" that students should feel competent in using:

> *Modeling*—Representing worldly phenomena by mental constructs, often visual or symbolic, that capture important and useful features.
> *Optimization*—Finding the best solution (least expensive or most efficient) by asking "what if" and exploring all possibilities.
> *Symbolism*—Extending natural language to symbolic representation of abstract concepts in an economical form that makes possible both communication and computation.
> *Inference*—Reasoning from data, from premises, from graphs, from incomplete and inconsistent sources.
> *Logical Analysis*—Seeking implications of premises and searching for first principles to explain observed phenomena.
> *Abstraction*—Singling out for special study certain properties common to many different phenomena. (NRC, 1989, p. 31)

It is certainly important for mathematics students to be familiar with these "modes of thought" as well as with the deductive method and axiomatic structures, since all of these elements are characteristic of mathematics as a "way of knowing." Yet these elements alone do not represent all the ways of thinking relevant to mathematics and its applications and may tend to set mathematics apart from everyday activities and from other disciplines traditionally perceived as humanistic. I believe that it is also important to highlight aspects of mathematical thinking—such as intuition, proceeding by "proofs and refutations" (Lakatos, 1976), and thinking through a problem—that may help students to see mathematics as closer to the domains of human activity they are more familiar with and thus to dispel the feeling that it is "not for them."

As I would like to suggest, to understand the nature of mathematics as a discipline is to appreciate its more humanistic aspects. Thus, school mathematics should strive to make students aware of the presence of uncertainty and ambiguity in pure mathematics and mathematical applications, and of the role played by personal judgment, cultural values, purpose, and context in shaping mathematical knowledge.

This goal was uppermost in my mind as I approached the design of our unit on definitions. It was one of my main instructional objectives (see

Chapter 10, goal G), and it guided my choices of content and activities as I tried to provide the students with experiences to help them realize that mathematical definitions are not as rigorous, context-free, and value-free as people believe. My hope that Katya and Mary would begin to reconceive their conception of mathematics also motivated what I said about the significance of our exploration of the nature of mathematics (Episode 4.4) and the explicit discussion of the students' views of mathematics in the final interviews (Chapter 9).

2. Students should be prepared to approach a wide variety of mathematics-related problems

The NCTM (1980) called a "focus on problem solving" in school mathematics the key goal of mathematics instruction for the 1980s. Indeed, the mathematics education community has accepted for quite some time that the acquisition of specific mathematical facts and techniques is of little use unless students are able to use them to solve novel problems. This ability does not come automatically (at least for most students), it needs to be nurtured in mathematics instruction (Charles and Silver, 1988; Krulik and Reys, 1980; Schoenfeld, 1985; Silver, 1985).

At the same time, the term "mathematical problem" has often been interpreted too restrictively by mathematics educators and teachers alike. Almost all of the mathematical tasks or "word problems" assigned in school are well formulated, present no ambiguity, admit a few objective solutions, and can be solved by the application of a suitable combination of learned algorithms. But as I have tried to show, experiences with only this type of problem will not be sufficient to prepare students to use their mathematical expertise outside of school. Rather, throughout their schooling, students should encounter a wide variety of mathematical problems—including complex and ill-defined problems and problematic situations—in pure mathematics and in applied situations in various domains (Borasi, 1986c; Charles and Silver, 1988).

In our mini-course on definitions, I consciously tried to present the students with tasks that moved from well-defined technical problems, such as "Find the circle passing through three given points" (Episode 2.2), to more open-ended problematic situations, such as "How can we extend exponentiation beyond the whole numbers?" (Episode 4). The students also worked with unsolvable problems, such as defining 0^0 (Episode 4.4), and with questions that allowed for genuinely different answers and required value judgments, such as "What *is* a circle and how can we characterize this mathematical concept?" (Episode 5.3).

In order to approach more open-ended and ill-defined mathematical problems, students will need to become familiar with problem-solving heuristics (Polya, 1957) and metacognitive strategies for monitoring one's activity (Schoenfeld, 1985), to master strategies for *framing* and *redefining* the problems they approach, to search for and identify relevant information in the context where the problem occurs, and to evaluate alternative solutions that take into account the values and purposes of all the constituencies with a stake in the problem (Brown and Walter, 1990; Kilpatrick, 1987b). Developing a set of functional expectations about the nature of mathematical problems and of mathematical problem solving should also become a stated goal of school mathematics, since most students today do not appreciate the fact that the solution of mathematical problems may take considerable time and effort, that most "real" mathematical problems are ill-defined, and that some mathematical problems admit genuinely different solutions (Schoenfeld, 1985; Borasi, 1990).

3. Students should become critical thinkers within the field of mathematics

Critical thinking has been identified by many educators as the new "basic" of the future and thus the ultimate goal for school education generally. This, in turn, has important implications for mathematics education in particular. But the term *critical thinking* itself is the subject of considerable debate within the field of education. One commonly held definition is based on the work of Ennis (1962), who argued that critical thinking is a matter of correctly assessing the truth value of statements. Drawing heavily on the rules of informal logic, Ennis identified a list of twelve "aspects" of critical thinking, which he claimed could serve as ways to "avoid pitfalls" in assessing statements. This interpretation has led to the identification of a set of content-free and context-free procedures that can be used to evaluate the form of an argument, and has consequently informed the creation of a number of instructional programs for fostering critical thinking that are merely the teaching of isolated skills (Beyer, 1984). The characterization of critical thinking as a particular set of "skills" has been criticized by several scholars, since it fails to capture adequately the actual practice of critical thinking in context. Drawing on the work of John Dewey to work out a perspective on critical thinking that captures its complex and fluid nature, these scholars have proposed an alternative definition of critical thinking as an attitude of "informed skepticism" (Cornbleth, 1983) or "reflective skepticism" (McPeck, 1981) requiring knowledge of the relevant domain.

Thus, let me be clear that I am not identifying critical thinking with a set of content- and context-free skills for evaluating the logical validity of given statements. Rather, I will use the term to indicate an attitude of inquiry and the ability to generate as well as evaluate hypotheses—that is, tentative explanations of puzzling phenomena or "educated guesses" about potential solutions to a problem. In this framework, critical thinking involves first of all the posing of specific questions or problems to be investigated. What often stimulates this process is the realization of an anomaly—something unexpected that does not make sense in light of what we already know. Once a question or a problem has been identified or framed, a tentative explanation or solution can be proposed by means of the creative combination of observation, prior knowledge, and judgment. The evaluation of a hypothesis involves the analysis of its logical soundness, its potential consequences and implications, and even the worthiness of spending the effort to explore it in the first place (see Siegel and Carey, 1989).

In light of these considerations, setting critical thinking as a key goal of mathematics education adds some important elements to the goal of preparing students to be problem solvers. Embedded in a critical thinking perspective is an emphasis on making students independent learners, able to generate questions and problems worth pursuing and to decide on the potential benefits and costs of engaging in their pursuit. Thus, in order to become critical thinkers in mathematics, students should not only engage in the solution of problems (however complex and ill-defined) assigned by the teacher, they must also make mathematical conjectures and work to justify and refine them.

In our unit on definitions, one of my first concerns was the development of the students' initiative and independence as mathematics learners. One way I tried to achieve this goal was to present the students, whenever possible, with problematic situations rather than well-defined problems— for example, by asking questions such as "What could 2^{-2} mean?" instead of "Why is $2^{-2} = 1/4$?" (Episode 4). I also tried to encourage the students to pursue questions they had themselves generated, even when this meant deviating from my original plan for the lesson, as happened, for example, in Episode 5.4, when the students got interested in creating a good definition for diamond.

In a critical thinking perspective, ambiguity and anomalies within mathematics also come to play a new and crucial role. Such elements can provide the seed of doubt that may lead students to question what they already know and move them to refine their mathematical knowledge. Hence, making students aware of the existence of contradictions, limitations, and controversy within mathematics comes to assume an even greater importance, since it is an important prerequisite for engaging in genuine inquiry.

Throughout the course design I tried to uncover and exploit the uncertainty and ambiguity in the specific mathematical concepts we were examining and within the notion of mathematical definition itself. The students' responses to the activities developed around the problems created by 0^0 and negative bases (Episode 4.4) and around the unexpected outcomes of interpreting familiar definitions in taxicab geometry (Episode 5) are both good evidence of the power of anomalies to stimulate critical thinking within school mathematics.

The generation and evaluation of hypotheses rarely occur in isolation. In order to encourage students to act as critical thinkers in school mathematics and to become more confident and proficient in their ability to do so, it is important that mathematics classrooms become "communities of learners and thinkers" who are working together to create *original* mathematical knowledge (Lampert, 1986, 1990; Schoenfeld, 1985, in press). I saw creating and sustaining such a learning environment as my major role as the teacher in our mini-course. As we analyzed definitions of circle, polygon, and exponentiation, or solved more specific problems, I wanted the students to feel responsible *to all of us* for the results they were producing. These results were new to them (and occasionally to me too), regardless of whether they coincided with rules and properties already established within the mathematical community. And I would not exclude the possibility that original results could be generated by this kind of classroom interaction—as one could argue happened to a certain extent when the students coined the definition of diamond, a shape that is not among the ones traditionally studied in geometry, although it is a legitimate geometric figure with interesting mathematical properties.

Within a community of learners engaged in the creation of knowledge, mathematical communication becomes an essential way of sharing guesses and ideas, providing and using feedback constructively, and ultimately building the consensus that sanctions new knowledge. Thus, while the ability to "talk mathematically" can certainly contribute to one's problem-solving skills (especially when working with others at solving a complex problem), acquiring this ability is a crucial prerequisite if students are to act as critical thinkers in school mathematics. A good example is the key role played by our conversations throughout the mini-course.

4. Students should come to think of themselves as mathematicians

Within a humanistic inquiry approach, thinking of oneself as a mathematician should be considered the ultimate goal of mathematics education. It is only when students stop distinguishing between what "real" mathematicians do and their own activity in learning mathematics that they can see engaging in genuine mathematical inquiries as the *essence* of that activity. Thinking of oneself as a mathematician also includes interiorizing the set of beliefs and values that belong to mathematics as a "culture" (Bishop, 1988; Schoenfeld, 1988, in press) and feeling part of a community of practice (Greeno, 1988; Lave and Wenger, 1989). As Schoenfeld articulates it, "Becoming a mathematician involves a process of acculturation in which initiates become members of, and accept the values of, a particular community" (Schoenfeld, 1988, pp. 86–87).

Students need to see themselves as mathematicians in order to fully achieve the goals of thinking mathematically, valuing mathematics, and being confident and ready to use their mathematical expertise whenever appropriate. Feeling like an "insider" in the mathematics community is also crucial if students are to stop being intimidated and marginalized by school mathematics, "victims" of the decrees of "experts" in the field and of the myths that surround it (Atwell, 1987).

As an important prerequisite for achieving this goal, each student needs to recognize and exploit his or her mathematical ability. An appreciation of the actual nature of mathematics and its applications is an important step in this direction, since students often underestimate their mathematical potential as a result of their unrealistic perception of what mathematics is all about. This was certainly the case with Katya and Mary at the beginning of our mini-course. Becoming good problem solvers and critical thinkers will also contribute to students' confidence in their ability to use their mathematical expertise in novel situations within the classroom and in their everyday lives.

Unfortunately, the attainment of this goal is far from reality in today's schools. Recently, when secondary school students in four different courses and schools were asked to think of a good mathematician they knew, not one of them identified him or herself or a classmate![2] A quite different attitude is revealed by Mary's comment, "We are the Discovery Channel today!" as the students were exploring what for them was a novel theorem about polygons (Episode 3.2), and her responding to the question "How do you think mathematicians create . . . definitions?" with "Playing with theories like we have" (Review sheet #1). Thus, we can only hope that the situation will change in mathematics classrooms informed by a humanistic inquiry approach.

The four major goals articulated here clearly resonate with the overall goals set by the NCTM Standards (NCTM, 1989a) for school mathematics—valuing mathematics, gaining confidence in one's mathematical ability, becoming problem solvers, learning to reason and to communicate mathematically—and the similar goals proposed in *Everybody Counts* (NRC, 1989). At the same time, a humanistic inquiry approach further emphasizes elements such as the role of *ambiguity* and *uncertainty* in mathematical knowledge and learning and the importance of attending to students' conceptions of mathematics, elements that these reports do not address sufficiently.

Goals for school mathematics that emphasize problem solving, critical thinking, confidence in one's mathematical ability, and an understanding of the nature of mathematics cannot simply be "added" to the current ones.

Rather, they will require a radical change in priorities within the mathematics curriculum as well as a shift in focus from product to process. This, in turn, has practical consequences for curriculum choices and evaluation, which I will discuss fully in Chapter 12.

The goals I have articulated here, in fact, not only influenced my *teaching method* but also the *content* I addressed in the mini-course as a result. This is clear first of all in the way I defined what I hoped the students would learn about mathematical definitions in Chapter 10 (see p. 138). Elements such as the students' appreciation of the role played by the context, the existence of limitations in mathematical definitions, and the resulting similarity between definitions in mathematics and in other domains received prominence in my formulation of the "content" goals of the mini-course. My decision to focus on these elements, in turn, translated into the decision to look at the definition of concepts such as circle (since I thought the students could easily see the effect that changing context had on the interpretation of the familiar metric definition of this concept), exponentiation (since in extending the original definition of this operation beyond the whole numbers one encounters some unavoidable problems and limitations), and variable (since students may not be able to define this concept, although they consistently use it in secondary school mathematics).

The ambitious goals for mathematics education I am calling for may naturally raise some concerns about feasibility. One might seriously question whether most precollege students, who already have a hard time meeting the demands of a "techniques" curriculum, would ever be able to cope with solving novel problems, initiating mathematical inquiries, or pursuing a philosophical analysis of the nature of mathematics as a discipline. Mary's success in our mini-course should give us both hope and food for thought, since she was a student who had previously failed in more "traditional" school mathematics. Indeed, the question of what can or cannot be achieved in school does not make sense unless we also consider what *learning opportunities* are offered to students. This, in turn, will be greatly influenced by the way we conceive of learning and teaching mathematics.

Rethinking the nature of learning mathematics

The goals for school mathematics I have discussed redefine the desired *outcomes* of learning mathematics within a humanistic inquiry approach. Consequently, what it means to learn mathematics—as a *process*—and how it can be fostered also need to be reexamined.

For most students today, "*doing* mathematics means following the rules laid out by the teacher [and] *knowing* mathematics means remembering and applying the correct rule when the teacher asks a question" (Lampert, 1990, p. 32). Consequently, *learning* mathematics is often equated with paying attention to the teacher's explanations and worked-out examples (making sure that one has put down the correct sequence of steps of the algorithm being taught), memorizing the algorithm at home, and, finally, practicing it on a number of exercises (similar to the examples given by the teacher) until one consistently obtains correct answers. This interpretation of what is required in learning mathematics is consistent with a behavioristic view of learning as the successive accumulation of bits of information, achieved by means of listening, memorizing, and practicing.

This theoretical model of learning may seem a reasonable way to explain the acquisition of simple, unrelated skills. But it falls short as soon as we try to apply it to more complex phenomena such as the creation of new mathematical knowledge, the solution of mathematical problems of a certain degree of complexity (see, for example, Schoenfeld, 1985, 1987; Charles and Silver, 1988), the acquisition of the mathematical expertise needed in the workplace (Borman and Reisman, 1986), preschool children's attempts to solve mathematical problems (Ginsberg, 1977), and the kind of mathematical experiences Katya and Mary engaged in in the mini-course. Thus, students who try to "learn mathematics" merely through listening, memorizing, and practicing may have little hope of ever succeeding in becoming good problem solvers and critical thinkers. The following critique of a popular metaphor of learning mathematics, "building a brick wall," points out the shortcomings of the behaviorist assumptions at the core of the view of mathematics learning commonly held in today's instruction:

> Courses for teachers used to stress how important it is to break the teaching of a subject like mathematics into discrete pieces organized in a logical hierarchy, like the bricks in the wall of a building. The student begins at the bottom, with the simplest possible tasks, and works his or her way up the wall—the complex task having as prerequisites all the simpler tasks below it. Unfortunately, this metaphor for organizing instruction has two flaws: it ignores how people learn, and it distorts what they are learning. . . .
>
> Many decades of research on human learning of complex subjects suggests that people do not always learn things bit by bit from the ground up. . . . They often jump into any situation with some knowledge, however rudimentary or inaccurate, and, even before they have mastered specific techniques, they begin fitting their knowledge into a larger picture. Students bring their own interpretation of tasks and concepts to the instructional process. Forcing them to master all the so-called pre-requisites in a hierarchy before moving on dooms many of them to trivialized, repetitious instruction and keeps them from seeing where they are headed. They cannot see the building for the bricks. (Silver, Kilpatrick, and Schlesinger, 1990, p. 6)

Indeed, Katya and Mary showed us that students can succeed in complex tasks even when they have some gaps in their mathematical background. For example, their obvious uneasiness with radicals and Mary's acknowledged weakness in algebraic manipulations did not prevent them from developing new rules for negative and fractional exponents. Within traditional schooling, these students would have been prevented from engaging in the high-level thinking task of extending exponentiation until they had mastered all the "prerequisites" (rules of exponents, rules to operate with fractions, radicals, and complex numbers, and so on). In contrast, in Episode 4 we saw how the challenge posed by the task of extending exponentiation provided a motivating factor for recalling rules that had been forgotten and for engaging in computations. Errors (such as Mary's $(3 \times 4)^{-1} = 3/4$) and things that did not make sense (such as having two conflicting results for 0^0) were valuable as they made the students reexamine what they already knew and expand upon it.

The careful analysis of what people do when they engage in challenging mathematical tasks and of the explanations they provide for their actions (see, for example, Schoenfeld, 1985, 1987; Silver, 1985) has caused many mathematics education researchers to challenge the assumption, implicit in behaviorist theories, that students can be treated as "empty vessels" to be filled with information and "knowledge." These studies suggest that in order to understand and use mathematical concepts and techniques, students need to elaborate and reconstruct the information proposed to them until it makes sense and fits in with their preexisting knowledge. A *constructivist* interpretation of learning as "a process of interpretation, justification and meaning construction" (Resnick, 1988, p. 33) has indeed found great support in the mathematics education community (see, for example, Bergeron, Herscovics, and Kieran, 1987; Davis, Maher, and Noddings, 1990). Such a view of learning seems to describe more appropriately than a behavioristic one the cognitive processes Katya and Mary engaged in as they tried to refine their understanding of mathematical concepts (whether complex, such as the notion of *definition*, or simple, as *circle*).

A *constructivist* interpretation of learning has allowed researchers to provide convincing explanations for the systematic errors many mathematics students make (Maurer, 1987) and to approach the study of complex cognitive processes such as memory (Silver, 1987), representation (Janvier, 1987), and problem solving (Charles and Silver, 1988; Schoenfeld, 1985; Silver, 1985). The knowledge about learning revealed by these studies has important implications for the kinds of activities mathematics students should engage in in order to promote their problem-solving skills and their understanding of technical content. Some of these studies (Schoenfeld, 1985) have refined the problem-solving heuristics initially identified by Polya (1957), such as thinking of a related problem one has already solved, working first on a specific instance or a simplified version of the original problem, or making tables and diagrams in order to appreciate the significance of the available information. This represents an important step toward helping students acquire these heuristic techniques, either by discussing them in class or by designing problem situations and activities that illustrate their value. Studies on metacognition have also helped to identify important functions that enable successful problem solvers to monitor their activity and make constructive use of their mistakes (Campione, Brown, and Connell, 1988; Schoenfeld, 1983).

Studies conducted from a constructivist perspective have also suggested how important it is that students engage in solving complex problems, as a whole class as well as in small groups, and reflect on both the process and the product of this activity in order to identify successful strategies, potential pitfalls, and possible generalizations. Using a variety of media to represent what one knows has been recommended as another way to gain insight and discover new connections. Examining the bases and justifications of mathematical results and applying these results in a variety of situations has also been proposed as an activity that can help students appreciate the significance and implications of what they learn. Further recommendations about encouraging argument and interpretation of mathematical facts have been made as well:

> We need to take seriously, with and for young learners, the propositions that mathematical statements have more than one interpretation, that interpretation is the responsibility of every individual using mathematical expressions, and that argument and debate about interpretations and their implications are as natural in mathematics as they are in politics and literature. (Resnick, 1988, p. 33)

These new insights about mathematics learning are of particular interest for a humanistic inquiry approach. Since these results have been produced by research involving students engaged in mathematical tasks of a certain complexity, they are more relevant than results of studies based on the observation of students' behavior when performing computations or routine exercises (as was the case in most studies informed by a behavioristic framework). In addition, the fundamental premises of constructivism are consistent with the view of knowledge as a dynamic process of inquiry. This is especially clear in the case of what has been called radical constructivism, a position characterized by the following assumptions:

1. Knowledge is actively constructed by the cognizing subject, not passively received from the environment.
2. Coming to know is an adaptive process that organizes one's experiential world; it does not discover an independent, pre-existing world outside the mind of the knower. (Kilpatrick, 1987a, p. 7)

Indeed, I would argue that the pedagogical significance of a constructivist perspective on learning cannot be fully appreciated unless we also recognize the socially constructed nature of mathematical knowledge. Students' mathematical interpretation and construction of meaning will only feel *authentic* if teachers and students share the belief that mathematics *is* an ill-structured domain—that is, a field in which alternative interpretations and debate are all integral elements, as described in the previous comment by Resnick.

Another important contribution to our rethinking of learning in mathematics is provided by L. S. Vygotsky's perspectives on learning (Vygotsky, 1962, 1978). Vygotsky's research on learning, too, examines not the acquisition of simple and specific skills but rather the more complex activities leading to higher-level learning products (Wertsch, 1985). Instead of looking at learning as a phenomenon occurring purely at the individual level, Vygotsky has pointed out the importance of also looking at the *social* aspects of learning. In this framework, language and communication take on a key role, since they are seen not merely as vehicles for expressing and receiving already formed ideas but as "tools for thinking"—for helping individuals clarify and refine their tentative interpretations and explanations even as they try to articulate them in an effort to share them with others.

This view of learning—as a social as well as an individual phenomenon informed by language—is especially interesting for mathematics, since it mirrors at the individual level Lakatos's thesis about the construction of mathematical knowledge as an iterative process of "proofs and refutations" carried on within the mathematics community (Lakatos, 1976). It also suggests that even in the context of schooling, learning mathematics should include activities such as articulating and sharing results and interpretations, providing and receiving feedback, examining collectively the soundness of arguments and explanations, and trying to reach consensus—all activities in which Katya and Mary engaged consistently and successfully throughout the mini-course.

In all the activities described above, language plays a key role. Unfortunately, mathematics is usually perceived as the area of the curriculum most independent of natural language, so that students have not been empowered to use language as a means for learning mathematics in school. Yet one can find notable examples of how students can productively engage in mathematical discussions (Fawcett, 1938; Lampert, 1986, 1990; and, indeed, this book), writing (Borasi and Rose, 1989; Connolly and Vilardi, 1989), and reading (Siegel, Borasi, and Smith, 1989). In all these examples, we find ample evidence of how both language and social interaction can help students develop a deeper understanding of mathematics.

Recognizing the social dimensions of learning also suggests that mathematics should not always be studied in isolation, as is usually the case when students listen to teachers' lectures, fill in worksheets at their desks, or do their homework at home. Working together with peers, whether or not with the support of an "expert," can provide mathematics students with valuable opportunities for feedback, models of successful behavior, and shared values about what mathematical activity should entail—all sources of intellectual and affective support that can help students make the best of their mathematical ability:

> Something about *performing* in social settings seems to be crucial to acquiring problem solving habits and skills. "Thinking aloud" in a social setting makes it possible for others—peers or an instructor—to *critique and shape* a person's performance, something that cannot be done effectively when only the results, but not the process, of thought are visible. It also seems likely that the social setting provides a kind of *scaffolding* (Wood, Bruner and Ross, 1976) for an individual learner's initial limited performance. Instead of practicing bits of thinking in isolation so that the significance of each bit is not visible, a group solves a problem, writes a composition, or analyzes an argument together. In this process, extreme novices can participate in solving a problem that would be beyond their individual capacities. If the process goes well, the novices can eventually take over all or most of the work themselves, with a developed appreciation of how individual elements in the process contribute to the whole.
>
> Yet another function of the social setting for practicing thinking skills may be what many would call *motivational*. Encouraged to try new, more active approaches, and given social support even for partially successful efforts, students come to think of themselves as capable of engaging in interpretation. The public setting also lends social status and validation to what may best be called the *disposition* to meaning construction activities. (Resnick, 1988, p. 40)

Our experience in the mini-course appears to support all Resnick's hypotheses as expressed above. Since in our instructional setting the two students and I were constantly working together to solve problems or resolve mathematical issues, the students were sharing thoughts and opinions all the time. This forced them to articulate more precisely their ideas and also to justify or correct them in response to each other's and/or the teacher's comments. Learning mathematics was indeed a joint enterprise for Katya and Mary, and they supported each other in the process, thus achieving results that probably neither of them would have been able to produce on her own. The central role assigned to group problem solving and discussions in our lessons also clearly conveyed the message that student initiative, exploration, risk taking and original thinking were highly valued. The two students thus felt encouraged to approach more and more challenging mathematical tasks and became increasingly confident in their mathematical ability.

The importance of socialization and the power of learning within a community of practice have been further confirmed by recent studies on how people learn and use mathematics in everyday situations. These studies have also revealed new dimensions of learning in context, that is, taking into account where a learning event is generated and how one uses what one has learned. Cognitive anthropologists such as Lave (1988) have criticized the common expectation that one can learn mathematical facts, rules, procedures, and even problem-solving heuristics "out-of-context" in school and then "transfer" such learning to other applications, something most students fail to do anyway. They have argued that learning and problem solving—intended both as process and product—can only be understood once we consider the specific context in which they take place and the reasons and goals that made the learner engage in them in the first place. Furthermore, studies of apprenticeship have shown that learning presents different characteristics in situations where "master practitioners . . . are also in the process of doing what they do . . . [and where] knowing, thinking, and indeed, problem solving activity, are generated in practice" (Lave, Smith, and Butler, 1988, p. 64).

These considerations should make us acknowledge the influence of the learning context in which mathematics activity occurs in schools. If students approach their learning in school mathematics as an activity that should allow them to pass the test at the end of each chapter, they will try to develop study habits and techniques to assure them of such an outcome most efficiently, regardless of whether their teacher has stressed the importance of general problem-solving abilities or conceptual understanding. What students do in learning mathematics, what they learn as a result of these efforts, and how they evaluate their success will be greatly influenced by the "cultural climate" of the classroom and by the expectations created by the daily activities in which the class engages. It seems crucial, therefore, that classrooms become "microcosms" (Schoenfeld, 1988) or "communities of practice" (Lave and Wenger, 1990) that *live* these values and practices— something that I attempted to achieve, I think with considerable success, in our mini-course.

The role played by context and purpose in learning mathematics, as studies on everyday cognition have demonstrated, suggests an interesting parallel between what happens when an individual learns mathematics and what happens when professional mathematicians engage in the construction of mathematical knowledge. Together with the results of constructivist and Vygotskian studies, the everyday cognition approach challenges the behaviorist interpretation of learning mathematics (acquiring bits of information by memorization and imitation) by showing that it is too simplistic to explain the complexity of what occurs when students try to solve novel mathematics problems, engage in mathematical inquiries, or apply mathematics in real-life situations. Furthermore, an everyday cognition approach helps us appreciate that the isolated learning of skills cannot be perceived even as a "first step" toward becoming proficient at more complex mathematical tasks. Rather, such isolated learning may give students the wrong expectations about what outcomes can contribute to their success in mathematics and, consequently, what kind of activities they should engage in in order to learn mathematics.

The view of learning that has traditionally informed mathematics teaching practices has been radically challenged by research on learning in contexts that are closer to the essence of mathematical activity than those most typical of school mathematics. These studies demonstrate that learning mathematics is a very complex process involving the subject in the active construction of meaning, that it does not occur in a vacuum but is shaped by considerations of purpose and context, and that it requires the stimulus and support of a community. These considerations also suggest that students will need to engage in activities quite different from those that characterize school mathematics today.

Rethinking mathematics teaching

The way we conceive of a discipline and of its learning greatly influences the way we *teach* that discipline, since it determines what we want students to achieve as a result of instruction, what kind of experiences we try to organize in class (and, thus, what learning opportunities we offer students), and what we value in students' performance. Consider, for example, the consistent structure that characterizes most mathematics classes throughout the country:

> Mathematics instruction begins with checking the previous day's assignment. Troublesome problems are worked by the teacher or a student. Then the teacher briefly explains or demonstrates the next piece of material, and the remainder of the time is spent at seat-work on the next assignment. (NCTM, 1989b, p. 2)

This routine is the ultimate consequence of a particular pedagogical model, which conceives of knowledge as a static body of facts and techniques that can be broken down and "passed along" by an expert using direct methods (such as lectures and demonstrations) and in turn "captured" by novices in a similar fashion. This model, which is prevalent in several areas of schooling, although perhaps most evident in mathematics instruction, has been characterized by several educators as the *transmission* model (Barnes and Shemilt, 1974; NRC, 1989). Neilsen (1989) has described its essence as follows:

> Our current educational system has been largely shaped by . . . mechanistic assumptions . . . [that] equate knowledge with facts, skills and procedures. . . . Having subscribed (however unconsciously) to a view that sees knowledge as objective, atomistic, and hence portable, educators have developed a system dominated by a pedagogy which places overwhelming emphasis on teaching and considerable faith in direct instruction (lectures, readings, and drill exercises) as the chief means of transmitting the facts and skills that students will need to understand in order to operate in the world. This transmission pedagogy assumes that knowledge can be passed along from one person to another. (Neilsen, 1989, pp. 3–4)

The view that mathematical knowledge is socially constructed and contextualized on one hand, and that learning mathematics is a personal construction of meaning, shaped by context and purpose as well as social interaction, on the other, challenges the very foundations of a transmission model of teaching. Thus, they also require us to rethink our notion of what teaching mathematics is all about.

In the teaching experience I have described here, there was very little direct instruction on my part. Rather, the students and I together engaged in a variety of learning experiences, ranging from their solution of mathematical problems I had posed, under my guidance (Episode 2.3), to the student-led solution of problems they had generated themselves (Episode 5.4), to our collaborative exploration of open-ended questions and situations (Episodes 4 and 5) and our joint reflections on the processes followed, the results obtained, and their implications.

These inquiries were not intended as quests for preestablished "truths" and solutions, which I hoped the students would "discover" under my careful guidance, as is characteristic of the *guided discovery* approach to mathematics instruction introduced in some of the New Math projects. Rather, my aim was to engage the students in genuine attempts to "make sense" of mathematics phenomena (just as mathematicians do); I also hoped they would realize the tentativeness of the results thus obtained because they depend on the context and could be continuously improved. This is why I like to characterize our inquiry in the mini-course as *humanistic inquiry*.

An emphasis on humanistic inquiry in mathematics education requires a radically different approach to mathematics teaching, a paradigmatic shift from the transmission model informing today's school mathematics. To better appreciate what such a shift implies, I have found it helpful to examine how educators in the areas of reading and writing have analyzed the change in pedagogical beliefs and teaching practices implied by a "whole language" approach (Barnes, 1985; Rowe and Harste, 1986; Neilsen, 1989; Siegel and Carey, 1989). Barnes's distinction between the beliefs held by what he calls a *Transmission* teacher and an *Interpretation* teacher in terms of (1) knowledge; (2) students' performance; (3) the teacher's role; and (4) students' evaluation, seems to me especially relevant to a discussion of what characterizes a humanistic inquiry approach to mathematics instruction:

(1)	*The Transmission teacher . . .* Believes knowledge to exist in the form of public disciplines which include content and criteria of performance.	*The Interpretation teacher . . .* Believes knowledge to exist in the knower's ability to organize thought and action.
(2)	Values the learner's performances insofar as they conform to the criteria of the discipline.	Values the learner's commitment to interpreting reality, so that criteria arise as much from the learner as from the teacher.

(3)	Perceives the teacher's task to be the evaluation and correction of the learner's performance, according to criteria of which he is the guardian.	Perceives the teacher's task to be the setting up of a dialogue in which the learner can reshape his knowledge through interaction with others.
(4)	Perceives the learner as an uninformed acolyte for whom access to knowledge will be difficult since he must qualify himself through tests of appropriate performance.	Perceives the learner as already possessing systematic and relevant knowledge, and the means of reshaping that knowledge.

(Barnes, 1985, pp. 144–155.)

The beliefs of an *Interpretation* teacher, as Barnes describes them, seem quite compatible with the set of assumptions about the nature of mathematics, the goals of school mathematics, and the interpretation of learning in mathematics that I have outlined. I would thus characterize a humanistic inquiry approach to mathematics instruction as follows.

Good mathematics teaching should be conceived not as the "clear and efficient" transmission of established mathematical results but as the creation of a community of learners engaged collaboratively in the construction of mathematical knowledge in order to increase their understanding of the world, to solve specific problems, and to come to appreciate and expand their mathematical ability. This, in turn, will involve the development of a "rich" classroom environment, which can stimulate students to engage in humanistic inquiries about mathematics and provide the necessary support for pursuing such inquiries. Such an alternative paradigm shaped the mini-course, but it is also illustrated by a number of other important examples: Magdalene Lampert's elementary classes (Lampert, 1986, 1990); Judi Fonzi's secondary mathematics courses at the School Without Walls in Rochester, New York; Alan Schoenfeld's problem-solving courses with college mathematics students (Schoenfeld, 1985); and Stephen Brown's graduate courses for preservice and in-service mathematics teachers (Brown and Walter, 1990; Borasi and Brown, in preparation).

In Chapter 12 I will examine how such learning environments can be created in a mathematics classroom. As a preliminary, I would like to consider the changes in student and teacher roles that a humanistic inquiry approach to school mathematics involves. Once we appreciate that knowledge is a dynamic process rather than a finished product, the teacher can no longer be seen as the ultimate source of knowledge and truth. As students engage in their own personal inquiries, the teacher will no longer know all the answers or be able to establish the "right result" in case of controversy. This change can be a difficult one for both the students (who may misinterpret this as a lack of competence on the part of the teacher) and the teacher (who may start feeling more insecure, especially if his or her knowledge of the subject matter is not very deep) to accept. My own reaction when I chose not to follow Mary's inclination to explore whether any triangle satisfying the Pythagorean relation ($a^2 + b^2 = c^2$) is a right triangle (Episode 2.4) is a good example.

Another common assumption of the transmission model of teaching is the expectation that good mathematics teachers should always provide very *clear* explanations. A humanistic inquiry approach instead values uncertainty, even a certain degree of confusion (see Brown, in preparation), as a positive element in a mathematics lesson, since it can generate doubt and thus stimulate students' thinking. As Neilsen has pointed out in the case of reading instruction, "schools can actually make students functionally blind to anomalous situations by doing all their seeing for them" (1989, p. 17) and thus rob students of important learning opportunities. Absolute clarity on the part of the teacher may in fact turn out to be counterproductive in the long run for students' mathematical learning.

Another important consequence of these alternative assumptions about knowledge, teaching, and learning is a shift in control and authority from teacher to students. If we truly accept the premise that learning is a personal and open-ended process of inquiry stimulated by doubt and ambiguity, we can no longer expect the teacher to be in absolute control of the class agenda. Engaging in genuine inquiry means, in fact, that the students should be able to make certain decisions on their own about what they consider worth pursuing, by what means, when to stop, and how to evaluate the results, something Katya and Mary started doing in our exploration of exponentiation (Episode 4) and taxicab geometry (Episode 5), and in their own final projects (Episode 8).

All these changes are going to require students, too, to redefine their expectations of the teacher's role and of their own role as learners in a mathematics classroom. Most mathematics students expect that as long as they pay attention to the teacher's explanations and are able to apply, with success, this information in solving sets of well-defined problems or exercises, either prepared by the teacher or found in the textbook, they have fulfilled their duties as learners. By demanding more of students in terms of initiative and responsibility for their own learning, a humanistic inquiry approach asks them to take greater risks. As Lampert has pointed out, generating and evaluating hypotheses within a learning community involves more risk taking, both intellectually and emotionally, than merely reproducing "learned" answers:

> From the standpoint of the person doing mathematics, making a conjecture . . . is taking a risk; it requires the admission that one's assumptions are open

to revision, that one's insights may have been limited, that one's conclusions may have been inappropriate. Although possibly gaining recognition for inventiveness, letting other interested persons in on one's conjectures increases personal vulnerability. . . . Examining one's assumptions is an emotionally risky matter, but . . . essential to doing good mathematics. (Lampert, 1990, p. 31)

This change in expectations may be difficult for many students to achieve. An important precondition is that students come to understand the educational values of the alternative pedagogical model. This was easy to achieve in our mini-course on definitions because these values were already shared by the school the students attended (see Chapter 2); this situation, however, is unfortunately quite unusual. At the same time, we cannot expect students to comply with these new and more demanding expectations unless they perceive that their efforts are going to be rewarded. As I will discuss in more depth in the next chapter, we will need to pay attention to evaluation standards, criteria, and procedures to be sure that they are supportive of the kind of mathematical learning we expect from students.

Although more demanding, the new role assumed by the learner within a humanistic inquiry approach to mathematics instruction has the potential to resolve the problem of students' motivation in learning mathematics— one that has been foremost in the minds of many mathematics teachers. Recent research on students' motivation and self-systems (Connell and Wellborn, in press; Deci and Ryan, 1985; Skinner, in press) has in fact suggested that students' decision to engage in a specific enterprise will depend on their expectation about the extent to which such an action will help them meet such fundamental psychological needs as *competence, autonomy,* and *relatedness,* defined as:

> The need for *competence* . . . [is] the need to experience oneself as capable of producing desired outcomes and avoiding negative outcomes. . . . The need for *autonomy* is . . . the experience of choice in the initiation, maintenance and regulation of activity and the experience of connectedness between one's actions and personal goals and values. . . . The need for *relatedness* . . . encompasses the need to feel securely connected to the social surround and the need to experience oneself as worthy and capable of love and respect. (Connell and Wellborn, in press, p. 59)

In a humanistic inquiry approach, the emphasis on students' initiative on the one hand, and on creating classrooms that are supportive communities of learners on the other, reinforces autonomy and relatedness. Similarly, the higher degree of control that students assume over the scope, direction, and evaluation of their own activities is likely to increase their sense of perceived competence (the feeling that they can "control" the outcome of their actions) and thus their engagement in academic activities. These elements certainly seemed to play an important role in Katya and Mary's level of engagement in the mini-course.

In becoming facilitators of students' inquiry and learning rather than transmitters of established knowledge, mathematics teachers are by no means less important in the classroom. In fact, teachers are likely to encounter greater demands in terms of their mathematical knowledge and ability, their understanding of individual students' needs and personalities as well as of group dynamics, and their instructional creativity. Far from becoming passive observers of their students' efforts, mathematics teachers will be active participants in demonstrating this new approach, and in helping their students to experience and come to value it (Rowe and Harste, 1986; Schoenfeld, 1988). This, in turn, will require that teachers set up rich mathematical situations and tasks, devise strategies to stimulate student inquiry and share individual results, create a classroom environment and evaluation procedures that support risk taking, and orchestrate genuine discussions and classroom explorations.

Rethinking gender issues in mathematics education

Because my teaching experiment involved two bright young women, neither of whom liked mathematics, I decided to examine more closely my position on the problem of "women in mathematics" in light of the preceding mathematical and educational assumptions. The fact that, usually starting in junior high school, female students worldwide take fewer mathematics courses and achieve lower results in mathematics than their male schoolmates is a well-known and well-documented reality (NRC, 1989; Fennema and Carpenter, 1981; Hanna, Kundiger, and Larouche, 1988). Among the possible causes of this disturbing phenomenon most researchers have identified social pressures and stereotypes that tend to orient women toward less technological and quantitative (and less lucrative) careers (Isaacson, 1989) and toward somewhat less successful learning styles—such as the tendency to be less autonomous and to look to the teacher for reassurance identified by Elizabeth Fennema's research (Fennema and Peterson, 1985).

These results have already provided important insights into the problem and inspired interventions that have increased the success of female students in school mathematics. Yet these studies continue to approach the problems experienced by women in school mathematics by accepting as a given the way *mathematics* is taught in schools and the measures currently used to evaluate academic success in the discipline. In the spirit of the most recent tradition of feminist studies and the arguments I have developed here about the nature of mathematics and its teaching and learning, I would question whether sufficient attention has been paid to the way the problem has thus far been framed, and whether there are other ways to define it besides "How can women become more successful in current school mathematics?"

Dorothy Buerk's case studies of math-avoidant women (1981, 1985), together with the information Katya and Mary provided at the beginning and end of the mini-course, reveal that the image of mathematics as a cold, cut-and-dried, impersonal discipline is often at the bottom of many women's dislike of the discipline, and, consequently, of their decision to abandon their study of it as soon as possible. This image has been powerfully expressed by one of Buerk's subjects who, when asked to create a metaphor that would illustrate her image of mathematics, wrote:

> Math does make me think of a stainless steel wall—hard, cold, smooth, offering no handhold, all it does is glint back at me. Edge up to it, put your nose against it, it doesn't give anything back, you can't put a dent in it, it doesn't take your shape, it doesn't have any smell, all it does is make your nose cold. I like the shine of it—it does look smart, intelligent in an icy way. But I resent its cold impenetrability, its supercilious glare. (Buerk, 1981)

When I have mentioned this metaphor to students, many of them (not necessarily only females) have found it close to their own experiences and perceptions of the discipline (Borasi, 1986d). And indeed, when we consider the way mathematics is usually presented in the schools, this should not come as a big surprise. A humanistic view of mathematics, in contrast, challenges the appropriateness of such an image of mathematics for *any* student and makes us question whether the problem is with what female students do or think, with the nature of mathematics itself, or rather, with the way mathematics is currently experienced in schools.

These considerations may, in turn, promote a different way of thinking about gender issues within mathematics education, since they suggest that research and intervention be informed by an alternative question: "How could school mathematics be changed in order to become more appealing to women and better accommodate their thinking and learning styles?" Interesting parallels can indeed be identified between female ways of thinking, as analyzed by Carol Gilligan (1982) in her studies of women's moral development and Mary Belenky, et al. (1986) in their studies of women's conceptions of knowledge, and the humanistic and contextualized dimensions of mathematics that have so far been neglected in the mathematics curriculum. Suzanne Damarin has pointed out the heritage of the many centuries in which essentially only men worked in mathematics in the language used today in mathematics education, showing for example the abundant references to *aggressiveness*—a typical male trait—in expressions such as "*mastery* of a topic, mathematical *power*, or *hierarchies* of objectives" (1990, p. 148). She also notes that the emphasis on formal and abstract activities that characterizes much of current mathematics instruction may not be conducive to women's preferred ways of thinking:

Belenky and colleagues . . . have identified stages of women's cognition. In this analysis women learn abstractions (such as mathematical principles) best if statements of rules are preceded by quiet observation, by listening to others, and by personal experiences that women can relate to the abstractions. The personal mathematical experiences through which females understand abstractions often differ from those of males. (1990, p. 148)

Gilligan's distinction between "separatist" and "connectivist" modes of moral thinking has also formed a basis for Paul Ernest's argument against the tradition of training students to approach mathematical problems in total abstraction from the social context in which they originated, a procedure that "allows social decision-makers to consider and adjudicate social issues without feeling the human consequences of their decisions" (1989, p. 201). By pointing out that the "connectivist approach explores the full social context surrounding a moral situation" (1989, p. 202), Ernest has brought further evidence to the contention that the mathematics we teach today, although apparently culture- and value-free, may in reality be sexist.

In his critique of the traditional way in which problem solving has been approached in mathematics education, Stephen Brown highlights similar parallels between gender differences in moral thinking and in approaches to mathematics. After having identified "(1) context-boundedness, (2) a disinclination to set general principles to be used in future cases, (3) a concern with connectedness among people" (1984, p. 12) as the key elements identified by Gilligan in female moral thinking, he comments that

The set of problems to be solved as well as the axioms and definitions woven into proofs are part of the "given"—the taken-for-granted reality upon which students are to operate. It is not only that the curriculum is "de-peopled" in that contexts and concepts are for the most part presented ahistorically and unproblematically, but as it is presently constituted the curriculum offers little encouragement for students to move beyond merely accepting the non-purposeful tasks.

Furthermore, rather than being encouraged to try to capture what may be unique and unrelated to previously established precedents in a given mathematical activity (the legalistic mode of thought we referred to as the second characteristic behind Gilligan's analysis of morality as responsibility and caring), much of the curriculum is presented as an "unfolding" so that one is "supposed" to see similarity rather than difference with past experience. It is commonplace surely in word problems to tell people to *ignore* rather than embellish matters of detail on the ground that one is after the underlying structure and not the "noise" that inheres in the problem.

In so focussing on essential isomorphic features of structures, the curriculum tends not only to threaten a Gilligan perspective, but as importantly, it supports only one half of what I perceive much of mathematics to be about. That is, mathematics not only is a search for what is essentially common among ostensibly different structures, but is as much an effort to reveal essential differences among structures that appear to be similar. With regard to context-boundedness, there is essentially no curriculum that would encourage students to explicitly ask questions like:

What purpose is served by my solving this problem or set of problems?

Why am I being asked to engage in this activity at this time?

What am I finding out about myself and others as a result of participating in this task?

How is the relationship of mathematics to society and culture illuminated by my studying how I or other people in the history of the discipline have viewed this phenomenon? (1984, pp. 12–13)

Evidence supporting the claim that women could be more attracted to mathematical studies and achieve better if they could experience the more humanistic and contextualized aspects of the discipline is already available. In addition to Katya and Mary's success story, several teaching experiences by Buerk (1981, 1985) with math-avoidant women have shown that a change in mathematical content and activities, such as the introduction of problem-posing experiences, reading about the history of mathematics, and discussions of the nature of mathematics, led the women to appreciate the more relativistic aspects of mathematics and, consequently, to revise their negative images of it. Once they had achieved this, their attitudes toward the discipline became more positive, and they were able to begin to realize their unexplored mathematical abilities. The introduction into the Dutch secondary school system of an alternative mathematics curriculum, which focuses more on "social" applications of mathematics than the traditional ones, has also led a greater number of girls to take higher-level mathematics courses in that country, showing once again that a change in the mathematics curriculum itself can affect women's attitudes toward mathematics and their success as mathematicians (Isaacson, Rogers, and Dekker, 1986).

What I am proposing is that the changes in curriculum content and emphasis, and in teaching practices suggested by the alternative theoretical framework I have articulated here may contribute to the resolution of the problems with mathematics currently experienced by many women. Furthermore, introducing neglected components of mathematics into the school curriculum, along with less direct instruction, could contribute to a resolution of the gender-equity problem in mathematics education that would benefit not only females but all mathematics students.

This discussion also has larger implications for the problems experienced in school mathematics by other "minorities" (students who are not middle-class, white, Western). There is in fact increasing evidence that the cultural background and social pressures within particular ethnic groups and social classes could influence how mathematics is perceived and, thus, how interested individuals are in engaging in it. In turn, as I have argued in the case of women, we can expect that each group could contribute valuable new perspectives to mathematics, to the benefit of everyone involved in its study and use.

At the very least, a view of mathematics as a social construction and of its learning as an individual as well as a social process of meaning-making and inquiry, is likely to make school mathematics less oppressive to the students who have traditionally been left behind. It is important to be reminded of Paolo Freire's (1986) argument that the traditional transmission model of teaching (what he calls "the banking concept of education") is authoritarian in that the teacher is in total control of the learning agenda, and that it can be oppressive insofar as students are encouraged to be passive receivers of knowledge. A pedagogical approach based on inquiry and problem posing, in contrast, is likely to "empower" students as they take on greater responsibility for their own learning and begin to approach knowledge as a tool over which they have control and which they can use for their own ends.

Toward Implementing a 12
Humanistic Inquiry
Approach in Everyday
Mathematics Instruction

Making a humanistic inquiry approach to mathematics instruction a reality in today's schools is obviously no easy task. The mathematical experiences provided by prior schooling are likely to make most students react with disbelief at the very suggestion of their ability to engage in mathematical inquiry. In order to help students overcome this response and the many difficulties intrinsic to engaging in open-ended explorations, mathematics educators will need to create an environment supportive of student inquiry in the mathematics classroom. In addition, the attempt to put into action the educational beliefs I have articulated in Chapter 11 may bring some surprises to even the most innovative mathematics teacher. Indeed, coming to grips with all the practical and theoretical implications of this educational framework is a life-long process that can only be achieved gradually as each teacher examines his or her own practice. Last, but not least, we must be prepared for the fact that the current structure of schooling is likely to create considerable resistance to any attempt at implementing instructional practices that radically challenge the status quo.

In this chapter, I would like to look at the significance of the fundamental beliefs I have advocated—that mathematics is a humanistic discipline, that learning mathematics results from personal inquiry and the construction of meaning within a community of learners, and that teaching mathematics involves creating a stimulating and supportive environment for students' own mathematical inquiries—for the future of mathematics instruction. More specifically, I will reexamine what happened in our mini-course on mathematical definitions in order to suggest some specific strategies for dealing constructively with anticipated obstacles. This will involve, first, identifiying the instructional strategies I employed (or could have employed) to stimulate and support student inquiry; second, discussing the fundamental implications of these strategies and my theoretical assumptions in terms of curriculum choices, student evaluation, and classroom organization and management; third, considering the obstacles that students' conflicting beliefs about school mathematics are likely to create and suggesting ways for dealing with them constructively; and finally, discussing other obstacles to implementing a humanistic inquiry approach.

Before proceeding, however, I would like to clarify the spirit in which these recommendations are being made. The foregoing discussion has, among other things, attempted to highlight the complex and problematic nature of mathematics teaching, particularly when approached in an interpretative or inquiry mode. It is thus impossible and even inappropriate to expect that any general prescription about how to implement a humanistic inquiry approach can ever be provided. Rather, we all need to personally work through the practical consequences of this theoretical framework in terms of our specific instructional setting, our students' background, and even our individual personalities, and to engage in a continuous reexamination of our own pedagogical beliefs and practices. At the same time, in undertaking such a demanding task, it will be helpful for each of us to take advantage of the experiences and insights provided by other teachers engaged in the same enterprise. It is in this cooperative spirit that I offer the results of my thinking about the significance of my work with Katya and Mary.

Creating a conducive mathematical environment: Strategies to initiate and support students' mathematical inquiry

The first group of strategies described here will focus on helping students appreciate "what there is to inquire about in mathematics." In the previous chapter I argued that anomalies are the seed for generating doubt and, thus, genuine inquiry. The first six strategies (A to F) will propose complementary ways of making students aware of the presence of ambiguity, conflict, and limitation in mathematics and also suggest how such elements can be exploited to stimulate questions for reflection and exploration. The remaining three strategies (G to I) will suggest a number of instructional activities that can support students while they engage in mathematical inquiries and make them more meaningful and productive. Given the broad scope of this chapter, I will only be able to sketch the characterizing principles and potential contributions of each strategy briefly. Since several of the strategies are discussed in greater depth elsewhere, whenever possible I will provide bibliographic information for readers who want more detailed discussion, further examples, or the results of implementations other than the story I have told here.

A. Exploiting the complexity of real-life problematic situations

The educational value of engaging students in real-life mathematics-related problems is clear. By approaching such problematic situations, students can experience firsthand the need to frame problems in real life, the role played by values in mathematical applications, and the importance of elements such as context. If students propose contrasting solutions, these differences may act as an anomaly and trigger curiosity about how people interpret and solve a problem and their justifications for doing so, which may lead students to both evaluate different ways of approaching a given problem and generate new questions.

Mathematics teachers will be surprised by the number of real-life problems that are accessible to their students' limited mathematical background and yet rich enough to provide opportunities for interesting mathematical explorations. Once one is on the look-out for them, instances of such problems can easily be found in newspaper articles, television programs, and even in one's everyday life. For example, elsewhere (Borasi, 1989b) I have developed an illustration dealing with the ranking of national performances in the 1988 Olympic Games and involving mathematical content accessible even to elementary school students. My own interest in this problem was sparked by the realization that the rankings reported by Italian and American newspapers were different; this anomaly made me look more closely at the criteria used to rank nations on the basis of the different types of medals won and to discover several alternative (and fully justifiable) ways of doing so.

Though I did not take advantage of this strategy in the mini-course, I believe that Katya and Mary's understanding of mathematical definitions, especially their appreciation of the role played by context and purpose, could have been enhanced had they engaged in a real-life problem requiring the creation and use of appropriate definitions for specific concepts (mathematical or otherwise).

B. Focusing on nontraditional mathematical topics where uncertainty and limitations are most evident

Once students appreciate the role played by anomalies in mathematical applications, it is important to make sure that they do not attribute this only to the "messiness" of the domain of application. Uncovering the presence of conflicts and alternatives within what is perceived as "pure" mathematics will then be essential in order to enable students to "see" and exploit such anomalies in their everyday school mathematics. One way to accomplish this goal is to introduce into the mathematics curriculum the study of mathematical topics where contradictions, limitations, alternative approaches, or results that are neither absolute nor "exact" are easily recognized. My choice of the notion of mathematical definition as the theme of our unit was guided by considerations of this kind. A similar role, however, could be played by many other technical concepts, general mathematical notions, or even whole branches of mathematics.

Consider, for example, the notion of mathematical proof. A critical analysis of how mathematical results have been justified at different times and in different branches of mathematics may raise serious doubts about the absolute rigor of mathematicians' practices and highlight the key role played by the mathematics community in establishing criteria for an acceptable "proof" (Hanna and Winchester, 1990; Kline, 1980). A controversial concept such as infinity is also an ideal topic, since the conflicting intuitions we hold about infinity have led mathematicians to propose alternative (and incompatible) definitions and procedures for working with infinite sets, with no predetermined way of deciding which is "better" (Borasi, 1985). Introducing students to branches of mathematics, such as probability or numerical analysis, may also be very valuable per se, since it shows how mathematicians have dealt head-on with uncertainty and approximation and how this required them to establish new criteria for evaluating and using the mathematical results developed within these branches. The study of probability, in particular, presents an additional advantage, since people's intuitions about chance and random events are often misleading and at odds with the results derived in probability theory, thus causing surprise and curiosity (Borasi, 1991).

C. Uncovering humanistic elements within the traditional mathematics curriculum

While focusing on unusual topics may highlight the presence of uncertainty in mathematics, it is also important that students realize the presence of humanistic elements within the most "traditional" areas of the mathematics curriculum—arithmetic, elementary algebra, and Euclidean geometry—since these areas are often perceived as the most representative of "real mathematics."

A historical analysis of how some of the most basic mathematical results have come about may provide a valuable first strategy for helping students see humanistic elements within the mathematics they study in school. Such an analysis may even uncover some of the problems encountered by mathematicians in creating the most fundamental and taken-for-granted concepts or show the possibility of alternatives. Becoming aware of the intellectual struggles that have accompanied the development of what they are now studying can influence students to look at mathematics as the cumulative product of human inquiry and challenge the belief that mathematical results are absolute and predetermined, a belief often fostered by the way mathematical results are presented in textbooks and lectures.

For instance, the study of how number systems have been progressively expanded through the centuries can provide a very good example of the tentativeness of mathematical results and also alert students to the resistance that is likely to accompany the proposal of new "additions" to the current system. In geometry, considering the implications of non-Euclidean geometries could have an impact on students' approach to the traditional results derived in most precollege curricula. A historical view of these two topics could certainly have contributed to Katya's and Mary's appreciation of the significance of their own work with exponentiation (Episode 4) and taxicab geometry (Episode 5).

The benefits of being aware of how mathematical knowledge has developed, however, will be even more powerful if the students also realize that even today mathematics includes unresolved issues, unavoidable contradictions, and intrinsic limitations. In other words, we do not want students to acknowledge uncertainty in the development of mathematics yet continue to believe that such uncertainty is only a "thing of the past," something that has to do only with the "discovery" of a mathematical result.

An open-minded examination of arithmetic, algebra, and geometry can uncover a number of "exceptions to the rules," even in those areas. As evidence, I would mention Episode 4, in which the students realized that 0^0 and the power of certain negative bases cannot be determined without introducing complications or even contradictions, and Episode 6, when they were unable to create a formal definition of *variable*. As happened in our experience, these anomalies are bound to generate surprise and invite inquiry about their potential causes and consequences. In addition, our analysis of definitions has also shown the value of encouraging students to question the rationale behind traditional definitions and concepts within arithmetic and geometry, and to appreciate the possibility of alternatives.

D. Using errors as "springboards for inquiry"

Another occasion for challenging taken-for-granted assumptions within the traditional mathematics curriculum is offered by errors, provided that we see their potential as *springboards for inquiry* (see, for example, Borasi, 1986b, 1987, 1988b, 1989a, in preparation.) Indeed, since errors are by definition results that do not meet the original expectations, they can be considered prototypical instances of an anomaly, and therefore a natural force for promoting questions for reflection and exploration on the part of the students themselves. This interpretation of the educational role of errors, however, also requires a change of approach from that which has so far characterized much of the educational literature on errors.

Although mathematics educators have long been interested in student errors, their focus has essentially been on how these errors can be eradicated. Thus, researchers as well as teachers have used errors as a tool for diagnosing learning difficulties and directing their remediation. However valuable for mathematics education, this approach does not invite students to view errors as learning opportunities or to engage in their own analysis of errors.

In the mini-course, in contrast, Katya and Mary were often invited to examine specific errors: for example, the list of incorrect definitions of circle in Episode 2.1, the error Katya made on her homework assignment in Episode 2.3, my incomplete proof of a known theorem in Episode 2.4, and the initial proposal of the contradictory results "$0^0 = 1$" and "$0^0 = 0$" in Episode 4.4. Later in the unit, Mary occasionally initiated an analysis of perceived errors by herself, as when she made some incorrect guesses while attempting to extend exponentiation (Episode 4.2) and when she decided to find out what was wrong with the traditional metric definition of circle (Episode 5.3).

In all these cases, a mathematical error provided the stimulus for the students to ask "What went wrong?" "How can it be fixed?" "What are the implications of what we have done?" By pursuing these questions, the students not only were able to eliminate the original mistake and reach the desired solution, they also gained unexpected insights and made new discoveries (as is well illustrated by what happened in Episodes 2.3 and 4.4 in particular). Occasionally, however, they approached the error not with the ultimate goal of eliminating it but, in the spirit of a challenge, by asking questions such as "What if this were indeed the right result?" and "What would be the implications of accepting this instead of the traditional result/ definition?" This happened especially when working within the context of taxicab geometry.

Errors can be used as *springboards for inquiry* at various levels of mathematical discourse. Within Episode 2.1, for example, the students' analysis of the list of incorrect definitions of circle inspired them to propose solutions to a specific problem (since we produced an acceptable definition of circle), gain a better understanding of mathematical content (since we learned more about circles, especially the relationship of some of the properties of this geometric figure), and better appreciate the nature of mathematics (since we gained general insights on the nature, role, and use of a fundamental meta-mathematical notion).

TABLE 12–1   A Taxonomy of Constructive Uses of Errors

LEVEL OF MATH DISCOURSE STANCE OF LEARNING	*Performing a Math Task*	*Learning Technical Content*	*Learning ABOUT Nature of Mathematics*
Remediation	Analysis of recognized errors to understand what went wrong and fix it in order to perform the set task successfully	Analysis of recognized errors to clarify misunderstanding of technical mathmatical content	Analysis of recognized errors to clarify misunderstandings about the nature of mathematics or general mathematical issues
Genuine Learning — Discovery	Errors are used constructively in the process of solving a novel problem or task	Errors are used constructively for learning a new concept, rule, topic, etc.	Errors are used constructively for learning about the nature of mathematics or some general mathematical issues
Openness to Challenging the Given— New Directions	Errors motivate questions that may generate inquiry in new directions and new mathematical tasks to be performed	Errors motivate questions that may provide new perspectives and insights on a concept, rule, topic, etc.	Errors motivate questions that may provide new perspectives and insights on the nature of mathematics or some general mathematics issues

These complementary ways in which errors can stimulate students' mathematical explorations and reflections are summarized in Table 12–1 (Borasi, 1989a).

E. Exploiting the surprises elicited by working in new domains

We can stimulate student inquiry within the traditional mathematics curriculum not only by uncovering and exploiting existing anomalies but also by occasionally setting up instructional situations that can *create* such anomalies. The strategy described here, together with the one described next (F), proposes some ways to create such situations in the mathematics classroom.

Katya's and Mary's curiosity when they were asked to work in new domains—when they looked at circles in taxicab geometry (Episode 5) and when they tried to extend exponentiation beyond the whole numbers (Episode 4)—suggests that a change of mathematical context can often provide valuable stimuli for inquiry. When working in an unfamiliar domain, in fact, we are likely to carry with us (more or less consciously) a number of expectations that have been built in by our prior experiences in more familiar situations. Often, however, these expectations may not be warranted by the peculiarities of the new domain, and thus may easily lead to surprises, errors, and, more generally, anomalies. Trying to explain these anomalies will require that we explore the new domain in order to become better aware of its specific characteristics and their implications. At the same time, the anomalies may also invite us to "revisit" the old domain and reconsider our previous knowledge of it, since what we had previously been taking for granted may be seen in a different light once we discover possible alternatives.

As our experiences with circle in the mini-course clearly illustrate, when the definition of a familiar concept is interpreted in a new domain we may realize that it identifies objects that do not have some of the properties we are used to associating with it. Thus, we may need to reexamine our rationale for the original concept and definition and decide whether to resolve the conflict by changing the definition (to add a previously implied property to those characterizing the concept) or changing our image of the concept itself (which could make it more general, and thus applicable to a wider range of situations but at the cost of relinquishing some of our original intuitions and expectations).

As we discovered in the mini-course, there are at least two different ways to introduce new mathematical contexts. First, one can change some attributes in the standard one to create an alternative—taxicab geometry, for example, was proposed by imposing different kinds of constraints (and thus a different way of measuring distances) on the familiar plane. Less obvious but even more common in mathematics is the change of context that occurs whenever a familiar domain is extended into a more inclusive one. This second setup is particularly likely to generate anomalies and errors, because one tends to assume that all the relationships and properties that worked in the original system should continue to do so in the extended one, though this is often not the case (as shown by our study of exponentiation).

F. Creating ambiguity and conflict by proposing alternatives to the status quo

Ambiguity, by definition, refers to the possibility of interpreting something in more than one way. In the previous two strategies, the possibility of alternatives to established mathematical systems and results was suggested either by presenting students with a different context (strategy E) or by making them appreciate that the content of an error proposes the consideration of a solution different from the accepted one, which may be worth evaluating on its own grounds (strategy D).

It also seems worthwhile, however, to encourage students to create alternative situations to the status quo on their own as a way of taking the initiative in generating inquiry and also of coming to a better understanding of the "standard" content of the mathematics curriculum. In other words, we would like students to ask the question "What would happen if things were different?" or "What would happen if we changed some of the traditional assumptions, definitions, goals, in mathematics?", to pursue such a question, and to have a sense of the significance of the results of their inquiry.

Brown and Walter have proposed a systematic way to enable students to ask, pursue, and evaluate alternatives to the status quo in what they have called the *What-If-Not* strategy (Brown and Walter, 1970, 1990; Walter and Brown, 1969). Starting from a known mathematical result, theorem, problem, or concept, students are encouraged first to identify all the attributes of this mathematical situation they can think of. The list of attributes thus generated is recorded, and then the whole class is asked to suggest possible modifications, which are recorded next to the original attributes. The next step involves generating questions and hypotheses about each alternative without worrying at this point about their "mathematical" interest. It is only after a rich set of questions is produced that the students are asked to choose the most worthwhile ones to be explored. This process is obviously not linear, but rather involves a lot of going "back and forth," since some of the questions for inquiry may suggest further alternatives to the original situation or highlight interesting attributes in the original situation that were initially overlooked.

One can notice some interesting similarities between the *What-If-Not* strategy and Mary's and Katya's suggestions for considering alternative ways of measuring distances in a city (Episode 5.1). It is indeed a pity that at the time I was not able to take advantage of this opening for introducing a full fledged *What-If-Not* activity around the definition of distance.

G. Generative reading activities as a means of sustaining inquiry

In most mathematics classrooms today, the teacher is the ultimate source and authority when it comes to providing answers, evaluating results, settling doubts, and deciding among possible alternatives. A humanistic inquiry approach rejects this position and proposes, instead, that students learn to use sources of information other than the teacher in order to become independent learners, problem solvers, and critical thinkers.

In the instructional strategies proposed thus far, the major means for framing questions and proposing and evaluating solutions is provided by the students' own mathematical activity. *Reading* could provide students with another crucial tool for sustaining independent inquiry by presenting new data and new perspectives that can both invite new questions and supply valuable information for settling existing questions.

The role of reading as a "mode of learning and inquiry" is certainly exploited in most academic disciplines, though unfortunately this is not usually the case in school mathematics. Elsewhere (Siegel, Borasi, and Smith, 1989; Borasi and Siegel, 1989a, in press; Borasi, Sheedy, and Siegel, 1990), I have provided theoretical and empirical support for the claim that, contrary to what most mathematics students currently believe, reading can provide a very valuable strategy for critical thinking within mathematics, once a *transactional* approach to reading (Carey and Harste, 1985; Eco, 1979; Rosenblatt, 1979) is assumed and "rich" mathematical texts are employed as reading material.

It is obvious that nontraditional mathematical texts could contribute to students' learning. Historical and philosophical essays, reports describing specific mathematical applications, or biographies of famous mathematicians could provide students with different perspectives and help them better appreciate the value of mathematics. Reading about different ways of resolving a mathematical problem or an issue the students themselves have approached could suggest new interpretations, methodologies, and solutions, and even require a reevaluation of previous results. Introducing "nonmathematical" readings in order to learn more about the context of a real-life "mathematical problem" could also be very important in considering alternative ways of framing the problem in question and evaluating proposed solutions.

This kind of reading material can be even more supportive of students' mathematical inquiries, however, if it is not approached merely as a receptacle of information. Rather, students should approach reading as an active and generative event, realizing that different interpretations are not only possible but valuable and that the specific purpose that brought the reader to the text will shape what he or she is going to look for and get out of its reading. This interpretation of reading as a "transaction" involving text, reader, and context translates into reading strategies that call on the reader to invent and transform meaning, make connections, exploit the ambiguity inherent in a text, and share his or her interpretations with other readers.

The importance of organizing creative reading activities to help students exploit the potential of a mathematical text was demonstrated in Episode 5. To introduce the students to the nonstandard situation of taxicab geometry, I assigned them a thought-provoking "mathematical story" for homework. Left on their own, however, Katya and Mary did not get much from reading the story. In contrast, the same story stimulated valuable reflections and discussion in a different instructional situation, when the students read the story in class and divided up into pairs with the task of reading a paragraph silently and then "saying something" to their partner before proceeding to the next (see Borasi and Siegel, in press; similar results were obtained by Judi Fonzi in a course on "Alternative Geometries," spring 1990, at the School Without Walls in Rochester, New York).

H. Providing occasions for reflecting on the significance of one's inquiry

Students may not recognize or may downplay the learning that occurs during nontraditional instructional activities, unless they are helped to recognize and value the outcomes of their work in these situations[1]. This calls for devising occasions to encourage students to reflect on the results of their mathematical inquiries. This could include:

- Identifying the mathematical insights they have gained from their inquiries (not only in terms of technical mathematical results but also in terms of their increased understanding of certain mathematical notions, situations, or procedures, and of the nature of mathematics in general).
- Making connections with other learning activities or background knowledge.
- Recognizing the discoveries they may have made about themselves in the process.
- More generally, stating and appreciating what they have "learned" from their activity and discussing its significance.

A first and necessary step in this direction is to make sure that results, reflections, and insights are somehow explicitly stated and recorded *while the inquiry is in progress.* In our experience, this happened spontaneously to a certain extent, since during the lessons I often paused and pointed out the significance of what we had just done, or the value of specific questions or insights voiced by the students. In a regular classroom, especially when the students engage in different inquiries on their own, it would be very difficult for the teacher to play this role, and it should be up to the students themselves to take on the responsibility of recording the outcomes of their inquiry. Indeed, there are good pedagogical as well as logistical reasons for students to do this as soon as possible, since evaluating the results of one's inquiry is a crucial element to becoming independent learners and critical thinkers. They should be helped in this difficult task, however, by being provided with some structure—for example, keeping a written log as part of any inquiry or using index cards to write down anything they find out about the topic, about mathematics, and about the process of inquiry itself (to be organized and sorted out later). The teacher will also need to demonstrate the activity and discuss it with the whole class before the students can productively engage in it on their own.

As a complement to what I have just described, it is also valuable for students to reflect on what they have learned and on its significance *after* they have completed an extensive exploration or comprehensive project. The ultimate goal in this case would be an overall evaluation of the significance of one's inquiry, and it could include:

- Examining the results and insights obtained.
- Categorizing and organizing them, in order to better appreciate their connections, relevance, and relative importance.
- Recognizing and recording the most important results for future reference.
- Relating these results and insights with other learning events or background knowledge.

Once again, students should be actively involved in this evaluative activity and be provided models to guide them. The review sheets I prepared were an attempt in this direction. I tried to point out some of the main elements of what we had been doing, while at the same time encouraging the students to participate by responding to some open questions. It would be even more valuable, however, to have the students themselves prepare summaries of this kind, so that they could exercise their own judgment about what was most important in what they had done and why. Indeed, I feel that one of the weakest aspects of the mini-course was the lack of a structured way for the students to synthesize and organize what they had learned. In a later informal conversation, Mary reported that she and Katya sometimes left our meetings aware that something worthwhile had happened but unsure about what they had done "to make [the instructor] so excited."

I. Promoting exchanges among students

The results of one's inquiry (or even a group inquiry) always become much more significant and valuable when they are shared with others. Having a prospective audience immediately makes the tasks of identifying, evaluating, and organizing what one has learned (described in strategy H) more meaningful. Such communication is also likely to generate requests for more clarification from the audience, which may lead the presenter to spot limitations and identify issues worthy of further exploration.

Even more important, sharing the results of one's inquiry can become a powerful heuristic when it is interpreted as more than a one-way report of a finished product, when it is part of an exchange that can be helpful to both author and audience. This may involve proposing alternative solutions or interpretations that (as in strategy A) are likely to create anomalies spurring discussion and further exploration until consensus is reached on a common solution or an explanation is provided for the existence of acceptable alternatives. Positive as well as negative feedback on one's ideas can also affect the direction of one's inquiry and eventually lead to more valuable results. The ideas and results of others might also provide new perspectives and new avenues for inquiry.

While oral presentations and discussions seem the most obvious way to realize these exchanges, it is also important to realize the potential of writing as a complementary vehicle for doing so, especially in the context of classroom instruction. Writing and sharing diaries and logs, preparing and presenting posters that summarize one's questions and results, writing a report and having it "reviewed" by peers for publication in a class journal, are all valuable ways to engage individual students in the collaborative exchange of ideas, questions, and results (Borasi and Rose, 1989; Connolly and Vilardi, 1989).

Creating a supportive learning environment for students' inquiry

These instructional strategies cannot be successfully implemented unless the mathematics classroom becomes a learning environment more supportive of students' inquiry than is the case in most schools today. This, in turn, has important implications for curriculum choices, evaluation standards and procedures, and classroom organization and management. The National Council of Teachers of Mathematics has recently proposed a comprehensive set of recommendations in each of these areas (NCTM, 1989a, 1991). In what follows, I will add to these efforts by highlighting some crucial issues suggested by the experience I have described and especially relevant to the implementation of a humanistic inquiry approach to mathematics instruction.

Implications for curriculum choices

A teaching approach that is based on supporting students' own construction of meaning rather than on the direct transmission of information will require considerable modification of the current content of the precollege mathematics curriculum. It would obviously be impossible, for example, to expect students to solve complex real-life problems, read about the history of mathematics, or study extracurricular topics where uncertainty and contradiction are especially evident (as suggested by strategies A to C) in addition to covering all the topics already included in the overcrowded state-mandated curricula for precollege school mathematics.

No fixed and established curriculum, however well constructed, could really respond to the needs of an instructional approach that stresses students' independent learning. The open-endedness that characterizes inquiry requires extreme flexibility in terms of curriculum content and choices. A teacher will often need to deviate from the original lesson plan in order to follow a new lead, pursue valuable questions raised by the students, or let the class fully engage in a debate stimulated by a difference in opinion or different solutions. Indeed, the best discussions and explorations are most often those that have not been preplanned, or even conceived as possible, by the teacher—as often happened in our minicourse. Think, for example, of Mary's unexpected decision to analyze the problem related to the usual metric definition of circle (after the surprises of taxicab geometry in Episode 4.3) and her consequent insight that the Euclidean plane is a "plane with no obstacles"; or, in the same episode, the students' decision to create a mathematical definition for diamond.

If we want students to become critical thinkers, they will need to experience the freedom of directing and focusing their own inquiries. As I have argued, an essential component of critical thinking is the ability to pose questions and evaluate their worthiness. But we cannot expect mathematics students to acquire this ability if they always depend on an external authority to sanction their choices. Encouraging students to participate in setting the class agenda, however, is unlikely to be an easy or straightforward matter. It will require continuous negotiation to insure that the overall objectives of the course are fulfilled and valuable learning opportunities exploited on the one hand and that students are genuinely involved in making decisions on the other.

The radical changes I am proposing here in how curriculum choices are made will affect the mathematical content covered in a particular mathematics course. This does not necessarily imply, however, that students should only be exposed to nonstandard branches of mathematics such as taxicab geometry. On the contrary, it is likely that most students' inquiries will be conducted within the areas currently included in most precollege curriculums (arithmetic, elementary algebra, geometry, and probability). What will be different in a mathematics course informed by an inquiry approach, however, will be the extent, purpose, emphasis, and sequence in which traditional mathematical content would be "covered."

The episode on exponents in our mini-course on mathematical definitions provides a good illustration. Negative and fractional exponents are included in most high school mathematics curricula, and a few class periods are usually devoted to this topic. It is usually introduced by giving students the new "rules" for operating with negative and fractional exponents

($a^{-n} = 1/a^n$ and $a^{n/m} = \sqrt[m]{a^n}$) and occasionally also providing some explanation (for example, the rule for negative exponents could be justified with an example such as $3^{-2} = 3^{2-4} = \frac{3^2}{3^4} = \frac{1}{3^2}$). Troublesome cases, such as 0^0 or fractional powers of negative bases, are taken care of upfront by stating that "by definition" these values are undefined and thus excluded from the domain of the operation. Students are then expected to practice the new rules on a number of exercises, in order to be able to compute the result of exponentiations involving different types of numbers correctly.

In Episode 4, in contrast, Katya and Mary spent the equivalent of three class periods trying to *create* new rules that would allow them to operate with exponents other than whole numbers. They looked for inspiration for hypotheses about what these rules could be in what they already knew—the extension of multiplication to negative integers—and by trying to identify the general heuristics used by mathematicians to extend familiar operations to new domains. We did not deal with troublesome cases a priori but examined them when we encountered them. In this way, Katya and Mary understood the limitations of the proposed extension and, more important, were challenged to reexamine their original belief in the absolute perfection of mathematical results. Although they were never asked to perform operations according to the rules they finally created in teacher-assigned exercises, throughout Episode 4 they had plenty of practice with the operation of exponentiation as they engaged in several computations involving various types of exponents in their effort to discover patterns and test hypotheses.

Implications for student evaluation

A novel teaching approach is doomed to failure unless student evaluation is made compatible with its goals. In order words, we cannot ask students to comply with new academic expectations unless we show that we really value those expectations by shaping student evaluation accordingly. Considerations of efficiency and (mistaken) objectivity have so far privileged standardized tests as a means of evaluating students' learning and determining who has access to educational opportunities, especially in mathematics. Unfortunately, these tools only value the production of exact answers in response to rather mechanical tasks, and they are therefore quite inappropriate for measuring learning that results from student inquiries. Even most of the existing teacher-generated tests, which may add to simple multiple-choice questions a request to write the answer to given questions and to "show one's work" in the solution of the assigned problems, do not get much closer to supporting humanistic inquiry. Mathematical tests—with their time constraints, teacher-assigned problems, and well-defined tasks that admit only one correct solution—simply do not allow students to show what they may have learned in their inquiries and may send the wrong message about what is considered "successful learning" in the context of school mathematics.

In planning evaluation within a humanistic inquiry approach, one should first of all examine what it means in practice to value process over product, risk taking over correct answers, and student initiative over compliance with tasks assigned by the teacher. An important implication of the first two points is that students' performance and learning should be evaluated not by looking at the worthiness of their mathematical results but by considering *how* the students engaged in the inquiry (in terms of their risk taking, inventiveness, initiative, and so on) and by identifying what *insights* they gained as a result (not only in terms of their technical knowledge but also with respect to the larger mathematical context in which they were working, the nature of mathematics, and even the process of inquiry itself). Valuing students' initiative, in turn, calls for involving students more actively in defining what data can be used for evaluation and what tasks can produce such data. In this spirit, teachers should accept and even encourage students to challenge or modify assigned tasks. Katya and Mary's contribution to the development of their final project (Episode 8) is an example of the value of student input in the definition of an evaluative task.

When I discussed the final project in Chapter 8, I identified an important limitation that should be kept in mind in evaluating student work within a humanistic inquiry approach. I pointed out that my concern about using the final project to evaluate what the students had learned had actually gotten in the way of the learning opportunities this activity could have offered. Indeed, evaluation and learning should not be considered separate events. On the one hand, evaluation can only occur while learning is taking place; on the other, every evaluation activity can contribute to student learning. Once evaluation is regarded as an integral part of the learning process, however, it cannot remain the teacher's prerogative; it should also involve the student and his or her peers. In other words, evaluation should become the shared responsibility of the whole class.

Evaluation should not be perceived as something having to do only with the performance of individual students. Rather, evaluation (that is, reflecting on what has been learned and judging its worthiness) should be an integral part of every class and group activity, and its results should shape the future agenda of the class.

In light of these considerations, it seems obvious that independent projects would provide a better vehicle than in-class tests for evaluating students' learning within a humanistic inquiry approach, since they enable the teacher to observe students' behavior and achievement when engaged in inquiry and at the same time provide valuable learning opportunities.

Expecting students to synthesize what they have learned as a result of their inquiries—in the spirit of the review sheets prepared in our mini-course on definitions—could also be a valuable means of encouraging students to make sense of what they have done and would allow the teacher to assess what students have learned. Summaries of this kind could be prepared by individual students or by the whole class in collaboration. Opportunities for the ongoing informal evaluation of collective and individual performances should be built into most class activities, if only in the form of brief discussions at the end of each class or a few moments for writing in student journals.

Implications for classroom organization and management

If inquiry is supposed to inform the learning approach of mathematics students, it is crucial that it becomes an integral part of their classroom experience. Students are very quick to realize which activities the teacher considers really important. If they are always asked to explore mathematical questions as part of their homework assignments or in class only after other matters (such as homework review, teacher explanations, or student practice on sample exercises) are fully taken care of, they will quickly realize where to put most of their time and effort.

Devoting ample time to students' inquiry within classroom instruction, however, will require considerable modifications in classroom organization and in teacher and student behavior. Working as a whole class may be effective for certain activities, but it cannot be the prevailing mode of inquiry. As supporters of a problem-solving approach also suggest, working in small groups may be a more appropriate format. This arrangement, in fact, is more likely to encourage individual students to think and question, since they cannot easily "sit back" and let those classmates who are perceived to be "brighter" do all the work (as often happens in whole-class activities). At the same time, students may feel more willing to take risks when they enjoy the intellectual and affective support of their peers.

Coordinating and organizing group work obviously requires a different kind of teacher expertise than direct instruction. The growing literature on "cooperative learning" has already provided valuable suggestions about how to make groups "work" effectively in a classroom. Here I would just like to point out that working together as a group in genuine inquiry will be significantly different from group work on well-defined mathematical tasks assigned by the teacher. Groups engaging in inquiry will have to negotiate (among themselves and with the teacher) not only the sharing of tasks (who is going to do what), but also elements such as the direction that the inquiry is going to take, how results are going to be monitored and evaluated, and even criteria for deciding when the task can be considered to be completed.

Group work should by no means take up classroom instruction entirely, since activities in which the whole class works together will still play a crucial role. It will still be important, for example, for the class to get together to brainstorm at the beginning of an investigation, to share and discuss their ideas and results at various stages, and finally to synthesize what they have learned from the experience. The roles of teacher and students in these discussions, however, will be quite different from those in direct instruction and even in the "guided discovery" or Socratic approach, in which the teacher tries to "move" students toward some predetermined goal and orchestrates their input in order to achieve it. In an inquiry, the teacher does not necessarily know beforehand where the discussion should lead. Even more important, the students themselves need to take an active role in deciding on issues such as which ideas should be pursued in more depth, which conclusions need more justification, and what questions should be posed. This will require new skills and strategies from both teacher and students as they negotiate goals and procedures and discover new ways to communicate.

These changes in classroom organization and in student and teacher roles are obviously going to influence classroom management. In a classroom where direct teaching is the prevailing mode of instruction, the familiar structure of homework review, teacher explanation, and seatwork gives the teacher a great deal of control over the class and makes "managing" classroom dynamics relatively easy. Even within a "guided discovery" or a problem-solving approach, the teacher still assigns the tasks on which students are going to work and thus retains a good deal of control. It is the teacher who always knows "where the class is supposed to go" and thus can concentrate on making sure that it "gets there" in an efficient way. The dynamics are very different, however, in a humanistic inquiry approach. Here the teacher not only may not know the answers but may not know the questions either. The term "management" itself does not seem appropriate for describing the teacher's nondirective role in the continuous negotiation of goals, activities, and responsibilities when the whole class becomes a learning community.

Dealing with students' conflicting beliefs

In introducing a humanistic inquiry approach in a mathematics class for the first time, we need to be prepared for a less than enthusiastic reaction. Students are likely to have quite different expectations of what school mathematics is all about. Research studies on this subject (Buerk, 1981, 1985; Oaks, 1987; Schoenfeld, 1985, 1989) have revealed that most mathematics students share the following beliefs:

- *The scope of mathematical activity:* Providing the correct answer to given problems, which are always well defined and have exact and predetermined solutions. This applies to the activity of both mathematicians and mathematics students, though the complexity of the problems approached would obviously differ.

- *The nature of mathematical activity:* Appropriately recalling and applying learned procedures to solve given problems.

- *The nature of mathematical knowledge:* In mathematics, everything is either right or wrong; there are no gray areas where personal judgment, taste, or values can play a role. This applies both to the facts and procedures that constitute the body of mathematics and to the results of each individual's mathematical activity.

- *The origin of mathematical knowledge:* Mathematics always existed as a finished product; at best, mathematicians at times discover and reveal some new parts of it, while each generation of students "absorb" the finished products as they are transmitted to them. (Borasi, 1990, p. 176)

The view of mathematics characterized by these beliefs leads in turn to the following "dangerous" corollaries:

- **Learning mathematics is a straightforward matter and practice *alone* should "make perfect."**
  If mathematical activity is equated with applying the appropriate algorithms to given problems, then learning mathematics should only involve taking down notes of the procedures that the teacher gives out, memorizing all the steps in their correct sequence, and practicing on a sufficient number of exercises to become able to perform the procedures quickly and without mistakes; if the results are not satisfactory, all you can do is practice more.

- **It is no good trying to reason things out on your own.**
  If you learned successfully, you should be able to do the problem quickly; if instead you did not pay sufficient attention to the teacher in class or did not practice enough, "thinking" alone cannot help remediate these deficiencies; furthermore, since for any problem there is a correct procedure to be applied and you do not know it, you cannot hope to come up with another one on your own.

- **Staying too much on a problem is a waste of time.**
  It is difficult to appreciate that by looking closely at *one* problem you can learn something more general and transferable when "reasoning it out" is not conceived as appropriate, and furthermore there is the perception that mathematical results are disjointed.

- **You cannot learn from your mistakes.**
  If there is no connection between a right and a wrong way of doing mathematics, trying to analyze and understand your mistakes is just a waste of time; therefore, if you do something wrong, you should forget about it and start from scratch to do it right.

- **Formal mathematics is just a frill.**
  Proofs, deductions, formal definitions, are not really helpful when it comes to finding and correctly applying the appropriate algorithm to solve a problem; therefore, formal mathematics becomes a ritual that can be performed on the teacher's request but that can be ignored in the context of solving problems.

- **History and philosophy of mathematics are irrelevant to learning mathematics.**
  A reasonable conclusion, if mathematics learning is defined in terms of mastering procedures to solve specific problems and such procedures are believed to exist independently of the way they were discovered; consequently, readings and teachers' lectures in these areas are likely to be perceived as a digression and a "luxury," which a student struggling with mathematics cannot afford.

- **A good teacher should never confuse you.**
  From the assumption that ambiguity does not exist in mathematics, it follows that the origin of confusion must be a poor presentation; this expectation can easily justify "blaming the teacher" for the learning difficulties experienced and also make students resistant to innovative teaching approaches based on discovery, problem solving, and explorations. (Borasi, 1990, p. 178)

This set of beliefs is unfortunately quite justified by the mathematical experiences students are likely to have had during their years of schooling and cannot be ignored nor disregarded. Rather, teachers interested in introducing a humanistic inquiry approach should not only take these beliefs (and the negative reactions they are likely to cause) into account when they evaluate their attempts to implement the proposed strategy but try to deal explicitly and constructively with the problems they present.

Indeed, even if at first students' conflicting expectations are likely to lead them to misunderstand the nature and scope of the learning tasks the teacher is proposing or to resent the new responsibilities assigned, this does not mean that the approach is doomed to failure. The mini-course on definitions stands as proof of this claim. Katya's and Mary's initial conception of mathematics (see Chapter 2) did not differ much from that of most of their schoolmates. Yet these students succeeded in taking full advantage of the opportunities for inquiry offered to them and found that it led them to change their views and attitudes about school mathematics considerably (Chapter 10).

The positive experience reported here, however, should not detract from the fact that such a shift in beliefs is neither automatic nor easy to achieve. Katya and Mary had a great advantage, in that they attended a school that valued student initiative in learning and risk taking. These values were not only explicitly stated by the faculty and administration, they were practiced in daily instruction and evaluation (see the description of the School Without Walls in Chapter 2). When institutional values do not support the instructional beliefs embodied in a humanistic inquiry approach, any change may be more difficult to achieve.

The chances of success of a *humanistic inquiry* approach will thus depend to some extent on the way students are helped to examine their preexisting beliefs about school mathematics. In what follows, I would like to share some strategies for doing so.

A first important point is that the more unconscious these beliefs are, the more powerful they will be. Thus, making students aware of what their expectations are is a crucial step in solving the problem. Precollege students often never realize they even hold a view of mathematics (Oaks, 1987) let alone consider the possibility of alternatives to it.

In order to encourage students to reflect on their beliefs, it may be helpful, especially at the beginning of a course, to engage them in activities that require them to state what they think and feel about mathematics. In the mathematics course Katya and Mary took with me the semester before our mini-course, in the very first class I asked the students to complete a questionnaire which included, among other things, the following items:

Please complete each of the following sentences by writing whatever comes to mind first:

Doing mathematics makes me feel . . .
The problem with mathematics is . . .
Mathematics is totally different from . . .
When I make a mistake in mathematics I . . .
What I especially like in mathematics is . . .

For each of the following statements, say whether you think it is:

- *DEFINITELY TRUE (by writing 4)*
- *SORT OF TRUE (by writing 3)*
- *NOT VERY TRUE (by writing 2)*
- *NOT TRUE AT ALL (by writing 1)*

__ There is always a rule to follow in solving mathematical problems.
__ Mathematics is a very good field for creative people to enter.
__ Every mathematical question has only one right answer.
__ There is little place for originality in mathematics.
__ Only people with a very special talent can learn mathematics.
__ There are usually several equally correct ways to work math problems.
__ If I understood x then I could do algebra.
__ Everything in mathematics is either right or wrong.

Later in the same course, I asked the students to think of a metaphor that captured their image of mathematics. I presented the "stainless steel" metaphor (see Chapter 11) as an example of what I meant. This activity proved to be a powerful tool in helping the students express their views in a way that avoids answers informed by rhetoric or by the desire to please the teacher.

Students could be encouraged to express their views of mathematics more indirectly in a journal, in which they report and comment upon aspects of their previous experiences with mathematics. Here is an example of this type of assignment.

> For the first three entries in your journal, write about any three mathematical experiences you have had. The narratives should be told as stories, with as much detail and description as possible. Include your thoughts, reactions, and feelings about the entire experience, not just about the mathematical parts. (Rose, 1989, p. 367)

These activities are not meant to be used as diagnostic tools but as opportunities for reflecting on one's experiences and sharing them with others. When students start to hear their classmates' ideas and compare them with their own they begin to realize that alternative views of school mathematics are possible.

Other ways of encouraging students to start questioning their own preexisting beliefs about mathematics are suggested by some of the instructional strategies I described earlier (see strategies A to F). By uncovering or creating uncertainty within mathematics, these strategies are likely to cause students to question their assumptions of absolute truth and rigor. In fact, the very realization that students like themselves can engage productively in mathematical inquiry has the potential to call their preexisting beliefs into question.

For this to occur, however, students should recognize that what they are doing is generating mathematical knowledge and working like a mathematician. Helping students realize the significance of what they are doing (see strategy H) is thus particularly important. Especially at the beginning time should be set aside to discuss the rationale of the new instructional approach.[2] Later, the class can occasionally return to a consideration of the instructional approach. If students keep journals to record their results and reflections, they can reread their entries or exchange journals with classmates. By reviewing the initial responses in their journals as well as to questionnaires and metaphors, students will be able to see how their views have begun to change as a result of new learning approaches.

Some concluding thoughts on putting a humanistic inquiry approach into action

The limited success of the New Math movement and of other more recent attempts at instructional innovation has made educators aware of the great challenge involved in implementing educational reform on a large scale. However sound its mathematical and philosophical foundations, however well developed its implications in terms of curriculum content and instructional strategies, these elements alone are no guarantee that a novel approach to mathematics instruction will be endorsed, put into practice, and succeed in today's schools. And this is especially true when the proposed innovation requires radical change. Not surprisingly, studies on teachers' practice reveal that teachers have been "most receptive to proposals for change that fit with current classroom procedures and [do] not cause major disruptions" (Feinman-Nemser and Loden, 1986, p. 516).

Despite the favorable climate for instructional change created by the national call for reform in education in general and mathematics education in particular in the 1980s, current practices pose many obstacles to implementing a humanistic inquiry approach in mathematics instruction. Surely we cannot underestimate the resistance on the part of students, parents, and school administrators, who still hold a conception of school mathematics as the efficient transmission of a specified set of results. Many states, districts, and even individual schools are mandating the mathematics content to be covered in specific courses, and in many cases (especially at the high school level), such content is prescribed to such a degree of specificity that it leaves little room for inquiry. The need to cover all the prescribed material is often further emphasized because of the importance attributed to student scores on standardized tests, whose scope and format tend to undermine the new goals and values proposed by a humanistic inquiry approach.

In addition to these *external* obstacles, there are also a number of *internal* obstacles that arise from each teacher's own set of beliefs and practices. Even if one theoretically shares the mathematical and pedagogical assumptions discussed in Chapter 11, it may be difficult to live with their practical implications in one's everyday teaching. I was often surprised in the minicourse at my own resistance to deviating from the original lesson plan or engaging with the students in unexpected explorations whose potential value I could not immediately evaluate. Indeed, only when we become involved in instructional innovation do we appreciate what an alternative pedagogical model really means in practice and realize the nature and strength of our own pedagogical beliefs.

These potential external and internal obstacles suggest that making a humanistic inquiry approach a reality in mathematics classes of the future will require a concerted effort in two directions:

- *Top-down:* initiating movements that can lead to a global change in the current structure and conditions of teaching and learning in schools, as the National Council of Teachers of Mathematics, among others, is doing with the comprehensive project that started with the *Curriculum and Evaluation Standards for School Mathematics* (NCTM, 1989a) and *Professional Standards for Teaching Mathematics* (NCTM, 1991).
- *Bottom-up:* engaging in the introduction of instructional innovation in specific classrooms in order to begin reexamining our own beliefs and practices and refining our new ways of thinking. These initiatives would be even more valuable if we took advantage of the support of peers engaged in the same enterprise, who can act as a sounding board for problems and new ideas, and as a support group with whom we can share all the surprises, difficulties, and satisfactions of our experiment in innovation.

Participating with Katya and Mary in a joint inquiry on mathematical definitions and then reflecting on our experience as I told its story have made an important difference in my own teaching. It is my hope that this story, and the theoretical framework it has helped to define and illustrate, will provide an eloquent demonstration of what it means to value the humanistic aspects of mathematics, critical thinking, and mathematical communication in mathematics education. I want to encourage other educators at all levels to implement some of these innovative practices in their own classrooms and to share in the demanding but rewarding enterprise of making learning and teaching mathematics an act of inquiry.

Appendix: Methodological Considerations

The narrative format of Chapters 1–9 did not allow me to go into much detail about the research methodology I employed to conduct and analyze the mini-course reported in this book. In this Appendix, I would like to provide some additional information about important methodological choices regarding the format of the teaching experience, the collection and analysis of data, and the writing of a "story" to communicate the results.

Let me preface these technical notes with some brief comments on the overall research paradigm underlying my work. The view of knowledge described in Chapter 11—as a dynamic process of inquiry, motivated by doubt and anomaly, that aims not to discover absolute truths but rather to generate and refine hypotheses in order to make sense of the world—has informed my approach not only toward the learning and teaching of mathematics, but also toward educational research. Thus, my study of a humanistic inquiry approach to mathematics instruction has itself been conducted within the framework of a *naturalistic inquiry* paradigm of educational research (Lincoln and Guba, 1985).

The overall goal of my research could be briefly stated as "reaching a better understanding of how students can be encouraged to engage in humanistic inquiry in school mathematics, what happens when they do so, what the potential educational gains and implications of such learning activities are (for both the students, the teacher, and the larger education community), and how teachers and students can interpret their experience of such an approach in the context of mathematics instruction." These research questions require the in-depth study of situations in which a humanistic inquiry approach to mathematics instruction can be observed "in action" in order to produce an interpretation of this phenomenon grounded in empirical data. As a result, one cannot expect the identification of general principles or "teaching prescriptions" that can be applied in any instructional context. Rather, the analysis of specific situations is intended to provide working hypotheses about the potential costs and benefits of the proposed innovation as well as valuable insights to guide its implementation and evaluation in other instructional contexts.

On the choice of the "teaching experiment" format

The setup of a *teaching experiment* is in many respects ideal for conducting research on the potential of a proposed educational innovation in a spirit of naturalistic inquiry, especially when the proposed innovation is far removed from established teaching practices. I am employing the term *teaching experiment* here (consistent with its use in the current mathematics education literature) to mean an instructional experience, usually involving the implementation of some new mode of teaching, which is conducted with a very small number of students and under careful monitoring in order to capture the learning process "in action" and the changes that take place as a result.

One of the main advantages of a teaching experiment format is the fact that it allows the freedom from curricular constraints necessary to try out truly new curriculum content and teaching approaches. Experimental units conducted within a regular classroom unfortunately tend to be influenced too much by state-imposed or schoolwide curricula, either in the form of mandated syllabi or final standardized exams. More subtly, the expectations of students, teachers, and parents about what kind of content, activities, student and teacher roles, and so on are suitable in the mathematics classroom are very difficult to overcome, partly because they are mostly unconscious and partly because they are the result of years of traditional schooling. Thus, both students and teachers are likely to be more willing to try out novel things in an instructional context that is new to them.

A small number of students is essential if we want to capture "learning in action." Even with the most sophisticated technology and a great number of observers, it is virtually impossible to follow each individual student's thought processes and reactions in a large group. When instruction is conducted with a very small group of students (usually from one to five), it is possible not only to reconstruct what each single student is doing, but also to question the students on what they are doing and why, and what they think about the learning activity they are engaging in. This kind of data is very important for researchers studying the process of learning mathematics and for those evaluating new teaching methods.

At the same time this type of educational research also has some draw-backs. Although the results of such an experiment can provide valuable indications of the educational potential of a learning activity or of a specific teaching approach in an "ideal" situation, they may not predict the outcome of using such an activity or approach in the "real-life" situation of today's mathematics classrooms. We are all aware of the role played by classroom dynamics and good classroom management in determining the success or failure of a teaching experience. When current teaching practices, teachers' beliefs, and students' expectations run counter to a proposed innovation, they can pose formidable obstacles that can make even the most pedagogically sound ideas fail. The failure of most of the New Math projects and of many other similar curricular innovations has confirmed that the transfer to everyday instruction of what "worked" in an experimental setting is by no means guaranteed. A teaching experiment, however, can at least help us decide whether it is worthwhile to attempt to include a proposed innovation in our regular instruction, and it can also provide some indication of the kind of obstacles we are likely to encounter in introducing it in a mathematics class.

I took all these advantages and drawbacks into consideration when Katya and Mary asked me if they could do some extra work to make up for their absences in one of my courses. As I mentioned in Chapter 2, their request provided me with some ideal elements for conducting a teaching experiment: a small number of students who were in many respects representative of the population I was interested in; the possibility of working outside of regular classroom instruction yet granting academic credit; a previously established relationship between the instructor and the participating students based on mutual respect. In addition, it was important to me to be working with more than one student, since this would make it possible to organize activities built on discussion and collaboration among peers—an essential aspect of the approach to mathematics learning I was interested in putting into practice.

On monitoring and recording the results of the mini-course

Given my interest in studying a humanistic inquiry approach "in action" and in gathering information about student and teacher reactions to this instructional approach, I could not just look at the outcomes at the end of the teaching experiment. I needed to collect a rich set of data on *what happened* in the instructional sessions and on the *participants' perceptions* of the experience (see Lincoln and Guba, 1985; Eisenhart, 1988).

To monitor what was happening during instruction, each lesson was tape-recorded and transcribed, field notes were kept by a nonparticipant observer, and all the written material produced by the students in class and at home was collected. A narrative report of each lesson was then prepared by selecting and integrating all these data (often on the very same day the lesson had taken place). These narrative reports should not be confused with the "story" of the experience reported in Chapters 2 to 8. Rather, they consisted of a detailed chronological account, essentially devoid of commentary, of what happened in each lesson. They included a large part of the verbatim transcripts of the dialogues that occurred during our instructional sessions integrated with a description of the activities during which they occurred and relevant figures. They also included the students' responses to the two review sheets they were assigned and their final projects.

Information about the students' background as well as their impressions of the experience were gathered mainly through a series of interviews— one conducted by me (the researcher/instructor) with both students, and two by the nonparticipant observer with Katya and Mary individually after the instructional unit was concluded. The students' academic advisers and other teachers also contributed by sharing additional information about the two students. In addition, I used some autobiographical writing that the students had done at the beginning of the course they had taken with me the prior semester. This consisted of an autobiographical essay on their previous experiences with mathematics, their reactions to the "stainless steel" metaphor for mathematics (see Chapter 11), and their responses to a brief questionnaire on their views about mathematics.

All the data described thus far were then used to evaluate what the students' gained as a result of participating in the teaching experiment and the effectiveness of some of the instructional strategies adopted. A narrative report of this analysis, detailing the major conclusions of this evaluation and the evidence supporting them, was then written.

The raw data (the transcripts of the ten lessons, the students' responses to the two review sheets, the complete text of the students' project, and the transcript of the final interviews) and the other documents (the narrative reports and my evaluation of the teaching experiment) were then collected in a preliminary research report (Borasi, 1988a).

On writing the story

The daunting size and complexity of my preliminary research report made me search for alternative formats that would allow me to communicate all the interrelated components of the teaching experiment, along with the results of my analysis, in a more readable way. The idea of writing the "story" of our joint inquiry into the nature of mathematical definitions seemed very appealing, since I thought that a narrative format would allow me to capture the complex, holistic nature of the teaching experiment while also sharing the insights I gained about teaching and learning mathematics as a result of living the experience and then analyzing it.

Stories about instructional experiences written by practitioners and researchers are not new to the education literature. It is only recently, however, that *narrative inquiry*—the collection and recording of stories—has been accepted as a legitimate research approach in the field of education (see Rosen, 1984; Van Maanen, 1988). "Telling the story" of a specific educational experience is now recognized as a way to make sense of the experience itself and of its larger implications for education. It is also a way to recreate a complex experience in its entirety so that others can "relive" it and draw their own interpretations, mediated by their specific interests and experiences, just as we all do when we read good stories in literature.

Using stories in educational research, however, is not the same as writing a good work of fiction, and, as with any other research approach, it requires the consideration of a number of methodological issues. The educational research community has therefore developed a set of guidelines for "good educational stories." A comprehensive review of these guidelines is provided in a recent article by Connelly and Clandinin (1990). Although I wrote the story of the mini-course before this article was published, the guidelines proposed by these authors were very useful in reviewing the major methodological decisions that went into its writing, and I will refer to this article frequently in what follows.

When stories are used as a tool in educational research, a fundamental concern is that of recreating a faithful account of what happened. This does not mean that we should strive for an objective report, since any two observers of the same event are likely to tell a different story about it. What it does mean is that the author must make a conscious attempt to ground the story in empirical data, while being aware of personal biases and interpretations that he or she brings to the story. According to Connelly and Clandinin,

> Narrative inquiry in the social sciences is a form of empirical narrative in which empirical data is central to the work. The inevitable interpretation that occurs, something that is embedded even in the data collection process, does not make narrative into fiction. . . . Data can be in the form of field notes of shared experience, journal records, interview transcripts, others' observations, story telling, letter writing, autobiographical writing, documents such as class plans and newsletters, and writing such as rules, principles, pictures, metaphors, and personal philosophies. . . . The sense of the [narrative] whole is built from a rich data source with a focus on the concrete particularities of life that create powerful narrative tellings. (1990, p. 5)

I indeed used many of the sources these authors suggest, and these data form the base for my reconstruction of the experience and for the creation of the *scene* and *plot* of the story (Connelly and Clandinin, 1990, pp. 8–9). Thus, in Chapter 2 I tried to "set the stage" by providing some initial information about the major characters (the two students and myself) and the context (the "cultural" environment of the school the students attended). My attention to the *scene*, however, continued throughout the story, as I tried to describe the instructional context and the feelings that accompanied specific learning activities and dialogues. I realize now, however, that I never paid much attention—either during our meetings or in my writing of the story—to the physical setting. All our instructional sessions took place in a small spare room in the school, where we all sat around a table with some sheets of paper and the tape recorder in front of us; I did not think that this element played any role in our experience, yet I now wonder about the significance of this omission from my narrative.

My efforts in writing the story were certainly more focused on the *plot* as I consciously attempted to reconstruct our instructional experience faithfully and at the same time to do so in a way that would make the account not only more interesting than a chronological report but also more significant with respect to a number of mathematical and pedagogical themes. I think that the distinction between *chronologies* and *narratives* in history may help clarify this difference:

> Although it is clear that the events in a chronology are linked, the meaning of the events, and the plot which gives the explanatory structure for linking the events is unstated. It is these matters which, when added to the chronology, make it a narrative. (Connelly and Clandinin, 1990, p. 9)

After playing with a number of alternative ways of organizing my narrative, I finally decided not to provide a lesson by lesson account of the teaching experience but rather to group together the events that related to the same mathematical topic or theme (such as "the analysis of the definition of circle in the standard context of Euclidean geometry" or "the analysis of the definition of variable"), and to report each group of events as separate instructional episodes. Depending on the complexity of the topic and the time constraints, some episodes were initiated and concluded within a lesson, while others developed over a few meetings. Occasionally, the same topic was revisited at a later time because one of the students requested it (see Episode 2.2) or because I had come to realize the value of further pursuing some neglected aspect it (see Episode 4.4); thus, reporting together all the learning events pertaining to the same episode required a few deviations from a strictly chronological order. This minor disadvantage, however, was more than compensated for by the fact that this method of organization allowed me to provide a good explanation of the rationale of the planned instructional activities at the beginning of each episode and to discuss some of the larger implications of the specific episode at the end, without disturbing the development of the "story" itself. To account for the necessary deviations in my narrative and to demonstrate the minimal extent to which this occurred, I want to give a brief overview of what happened in each instructional session, highlighting how specific events were subdivided into instructional episodes:

Lesson 1 (20 minutes)

The students were asked to write a definition for the concepts of circle, square, polygon, variable, exponent, equation, cat, purple, and crazy to provide information on their notion of *mathematical definition* before instruction and to generate a few concrete examples of definitions to come back to in the rest of the unit (**Episode 1**).

Lesson 2 (40 minutes)

Eight erroneous definitions of circle (including the two generated by Mary and Katya in Lesson 1) were examined by the students with the dual purpose of creating a "good" definition of circle and of identifying important characteristics of mathematical definitions (**Episode 2.1**).

Lesson 3 (30 minutes)

Definitions of the familiar notions of *circle* and *isosceles triangle* were used for the solution of two simple mathematical problems: "Finding the circle passing through three given points" (**Episode 2.2,** part 1) and "Determining the measure of the interior angle of a regular pentagon" (**Episode 2.3**). This exercise was intended to further clarify the rationale behind the requirements of a "good" mathematical definition identified in Lesson 2.

Lesson 4 (40 minutes)

The problem of "Finding the circle passing through three given points" was revisited in response to the students' request (**Episode 2.2,** part 2). Then, to further illustrate the distinction between *set of properties* and *definition* of a mathematical concept, the students analyzed an "erroneous" proof for the theorem *All angles inscribed in a semicircle are right* (where the statement: "a triangle with sides a, b, c, satisfying the condition $a^2 + b^2 = c^2$" was used as a definition of right triangle) (**Episode 2.4**). The lesson concluded with the open-ended task of creating an acceptable definition of polygon, a concept for which the students had previously declared they did not know the "standard" definition (**Episode 3.1**).

Lesson 5 (40 minutes)

To help the students in their search for a "good" definition of *polygon*, I proposed to follow an approach "à la Lakatos," that is, to refine a tentative definition of polygon while simultaneously attempting to prove the tentative theorem: *In an n-sided polygon, the sum of the interior angles is (n − 2) ×* 180° (**Episode 3.2**). The first review sheet, prepared to help the students review and synthesize what they had learned up to this point, was assigned as homework at the end of this session.

Lesson 6 (30 minutes)

The notion of variable and the problems created by its definition were briefly discussed, taking advantage of an issue raised by one of the students in Lesson 2 (**Episode 6**). Toward the end of the lesson, the students were asked to start thinking about how the operation of exponentiation could be extended beyond the whole numbers.

Lesson 7 (40 minutes)

Since the students experienced substantial difficulties in approaching the task of extending exponentiation, a similar yet more familiar case, extending multiplication beyond the whole numbers, was first discussed at the beginning of the lesson (**Episode 4.1**). With this help, the students were then able to extend the original definition of exponentiation to include negative integer exponents and to explore some properties of the extended operation (**Episode 4.2**).

Lesson 8 (40 minutes)

In the first part of the lesson, the students undertook the extension of exponentiation to fractional exponents (**Episode 4.3**). Most of the session was then devoted to an analysis of what happens when the metric definition of circle is interpreted in taxicab geometry (**Episode 5**). The second review sheet was assigned as homework at the end of this session.

Lesson 9 (30 minutes)

Some inherent limitations encountered when extending the definition of exponentiation—the fact that contradictions are generated when trying to define 0^0 and that fractional exponents might not be used with a negative base—were identified and analyzed (**Episode 4.4**).

Lesson 10 (30 minutes)—conducted with Mary only

The unit ended by revisiting the activity of writing an appropriate definition for the nine concepts of circle, square, polygon, variable, exponent, equation, cat, purple, and crazy with the goal of discussing the difference between mathematical definitions and definitions in other fields (**Episode 7**). The final project (**Episode 8**) was assigned as a take-home activity after this last instructional session.

Now that the subdivision of my narrative into instructional episodes has been clarified, I would like to address how I attempted to reconstruct our experiences and to discuss their significance within each episode. First, I attempted to provide an overview of what I, as the teacher, had hoped to accomplish along with a description and the rationale behind the main learning activities.

The sequence of events that took place in each episode was carefully reconstructed by describing in detail what happened in each instructional activity. This was achieved not only by reporting the most relevant excerpts from our dialogue but by describing the feelings that accompanied our activities and the students' reactions as well. The dialogue all comes from the verbatim transcripts of our conversations during the instructional sessions, although it has occasionally been edited slightly to make it more readable (by eliminating expressions such as "hmm" and "like," repetition and broken sentences, and incorrect grammar). I did this (with some qualms) in response to some reviewers of the manuscript and to the students themselves, who felt that the verbatim dialogue did not always succeed in conveying the intended meaning because the repetitions and false starts characteristic of oral language were distracting. Finally, to better indicate the significance of specific events, I incorporated a running commentary on our activities to provide the reader with the reasons behind some of my decisions and my reflections on the activity.

Finally, I added overall observations on the episode. This allowed me to highlight the major insights I had gained and to point out some of the limitations in the instructional design or in my decisions. Thus I could show how the unit on definitions could be further improved and at the same time avoid the common danger of the "Hollywood plot . . . where everything works out well in the end" (Connelly and Clandinin, 1990, p. 10).

Since I was both the researcher-writer of the story and the instructor in the teaching experiment, I did not have to worry about how well I was representing the point of view of the teacher-practitioner, something that other researchers must consider carefully (Connelly and Clandinin, 1990, p. 4). But I did pay careful attention to the way I represented the other major participants—the two students. I relied as much as possible on the actual dialogue that occurred during instruction and the reflections and viewpoints expressed by the students during the final interviews, but I also asked the two students to review a draft of the narrative and to tell me if there were any points they disagreed with or any places where they thought I had misinterpreted their activities or reactions. Though I would have liked to involve the students even more deeply in the reconstruction of our common experience, I think their final decision to have their real names appear in the story speaks for their feeling of trust in my reconstruction.

Notes

Chapter 1

1. My use of the term *humanistic* in conjunction with mathematics is consonant with the use made of this term in the recent mathematics education literature (especially by a number of mathematicians and mathematics educators belonging to the Humanistic Mathematics Network recently organized by Alvin White). This usage differs in many respects from the meaning attributed to the same term by philosophers and historians. In Chapter 11, I will explain in more detail why I chose to characterize my view of mathematics by means of the expression "a *humanistic* discipline," instead of using terms such as *contextualized, socially constructed,* or *constructivist*—terms that have been used by other authors in the mathematics education literature to indicate at least some of the aspects of mathematics I am also trying to highlight.

Chapter 3

1. *Recursive* definitions may at first appear to contradict this rule, but on closer analysis one realizes that this is not the case, since an explicit definition of the beginning point is always provided as well as precise rules to construct any other instance of the concept from that point on.

2. I will use the terms *mathematical concept* or *concept* to indicate the "class (or set) of objects" we want to isolate and characterize by means of a definition; I may thus refer to figures such as *circle* and *polygon* or operations such as *multiplication* and *exponentiation* as "concepts."

3. In this text, I will use the term *metric* to refer to the definition of circle as "the set of all points (in a plane) at a given distance from a given point," (or an equivalent wording) to highlight the fact that this definition makes use of metric notions only, and as such it could easily be generalized to *any* metric space, not just the Euclidean plane.

Chapter 4

1. As I noted in Chapter 3, I am using the term *concept* to indicate the "class (or set) of objects" that a *definition* is trying to characterize and identify precisely; the term *instance of the concept* will be used to indicate an object that belongs to such a class and *noninstance of the concept* an object that does not belong to such a class.

2. In Figure 4–3f, the sum of the interior angles is obviously 2 × 180°, since the figure is composed of two triangles joining at a vertex; yet the figure has six sides; thus the formula stated in the theorem would suggest 4 × 180° as the value of the sum of its interior angles. In the case of figure 4–3d, the sum is obviously 4 × 360° = 8 × 180°, while the number of sides is eight.

Chapter 5

1. For a variety of logistical reasons, there was a break of about ten days between the previous activities with exponentiation and Episode 4.4. In the meantime, the students explored circles in taxicab geometry (see Episode 5), which probably had an impact on the critical way they approached the limitations in the extension of exponentiations presented here.

Chapter 6

1. To be precise, the points of the taxicircle form a square. I have chosen, however, to use the word *diamond* because this is how most students, including Katya and Mary, tend to describe the taxicircle.

2. Interestingly, mathematicians have chosen to maintain the customary geometric and intuitive meanings associated with *circle* and *sphere* and to use instead a new term—that of *ball* of radius r—for the generalized concept defined as "all the points at distance equal to or less than r from a given point in a metric space." But this choice has to do mainly with the *name* assigned to the mathematical concept rather than its *definition*, a distinction that may be worth some reflection, especially when discussing the "arbitrary" nature of mathematical definitions.

3. This definition is slightly ambiguous because of the use of the term "equidistant" instead of "at a given distance." This ambiguity, however, did not create any problem, since both the students and I attributed the same meaning to the two expressions.

Chapter 11

1. Scholars such as Stephen I. Brown, Philip Davis, Paul Ernest, Maxine Greene, Reuben Hersh, Stephen Lerman, and Alvin White among others have been using the term *humanistic mathematics* for several years; since the late 1980s, Alvin White has also organized a Humanistic Mathematics Network, including a growing number of mathematicians, mathematics teachers, and researchers in mathematics education interested in the aspects of mathematics highlighted here and in their implications for mathematics instruction.
2. The query "Who is a good mathematician you know?" was included in a questionnaire designed to access students' views and experiences about mathematics as well as about themselves as mathematicians, as part of a research project tentatively titled "Reading to Learn Mathematics for Critical Thinking" (Raffaella Borasi and Marjorie Siegel, principal investigators), currently in progress.

Chapter 12

1. I owe this pedagogical insight and some of the activities presented here to discussions with Judi Fonzi and Marjorie Siegel.
2. I thank Judi Fonzi for showing me, through her teaching, the importance of these reflective dialogues.

References

Atwell, Nancie. 1987. *In the middle: Writing, reading and learning with adolescents.* Upper Montclair, N.J.: Boynton/Cook.

Barnes, Douglas. 1985. *From communications to curriculum.* New York: Penguin Books.

Barnes, Douglas, and Denis Shemilt. 1974. Transmission and interpretation. *Educational Review* 26 (June).

Belenky, Mary Field, Blythe McVicker Clinchy, Nancy Rule Goldberger, and Jill Mattuck Tarule. 1986. *Women's ways of knowing.* New York: Basic Books.

Bergeron, Jacques C., Nicolas Herscovics, and Carolyn Kieran, eds. 1987. *Proceedings of the eleventh international PME conference,* July 19–25. P M E - X I, Montreal, Quebec: Psychology of Mathematics Education.

Beyer, Barry. 1984. Improving critical thinking skills—practical approaches. *Phi Delta Kappan* 65 (April):556–60.

Billstein, Rick, Shlomo Libeskind, and Johnny W. Lott. 1990. *A problem solving approach to mathematics for elementary school teachers.* 4th ed. Menlo Park, Calif.: Benjamin Cummings.

Bishop, Alan. 1988. *Mathematical enculturation.* Dordrecht, The Netherlands: Kluwer Academic Publishers.

Borasi, Raffaella. 1981. *Studio matematico e sperimentazione didattica sul concetto di distanza.* Master's thesis, University of Torino, Italy.

———. 1984. Some reflections on and criticisms of the principle of learning concepts by abstraction. *For the Learning of Mathematics* (Canada) 4 (3, November):14–18.

———. 1985. Errors in the enumeration of infinite sets. *FOCUS: On Learning Problems in Mathematics* 7 (3–4, Fall-Summer):77–90.

————. 1986a. On the educational uses of errors: Beyond diagnosis and remediation. Ph.D. diss., State University of New York at Buffalo.

————. 1986b. Algebraic explorations around the error: $16/64 = 1/4$. *Mathematics Teacher* (USA), 79 (4, April):246–248.

————. 1986c. On the nature of problems. *Educational studies in mathematics* 17 (2, May):125–41.

————. 1986d. Behind the scenes. *Mathematics Teaching* 117 (December): 38–39.

————. 1987. Exploring mathematics through the analysis of errors. *For the Learning of Mathematics* (Canada) 7 (3, November):1–8.

————. 1988a. Using errors as springboards to explore the nature of mathematical definitions: A teaching experiment. Preliminary report to the National Science Foundation (Grant # MDR-8651582). Copies available from the author or NSF.

————. 1988b. Towards a reconceptualization of the role of errors in education: The need for new metaphors. Paper presented at the annual meeting of the American Educational Research Association, New Orleans, Louisiana, April 4–8.

————. 1989a. Students' constructive uses of mathematical errors: A taxonomy. Paper presented at the annual meeting of the American Educational Research Association, San Francisco, March 27–31.

————. 1989b. Olympic medal counts: A glimpse into the humanistic aspects of mathematics. *The Arithmetic Teacher* (November):47–52.

————. 1990. The invisible hand operating in mathematics instruction: Students' conceptions and expectations. In *Teaching and learning mathematics in the 1990s*, ed. Thomas J. Cooney and Christian R. Hirsch, 174–82. 1990 Yearbook of the National Council of Teachers of Mathematics. Reston, Va.: National Council of Teachers of Mathematics.

————. 1991. Using errors as springboards for inquiry in mathematics instruction. Final report to the National Science Foundation (grant # MDR-8651582). Copies available from the author or NSF.

————. (in preparation). *Reconceiving mathematics education: A focus on errors.* Norwood, N.J.: Ablex.

Borasi, Raffaella, and Stephen I. Brown. (in preparation). *Empowering teachers as professionals: A case-study in mathematics education.*

Borasi, Raffaella, and Barbara J. Rose. 1989. Journal writing and mathematics instruction. *Educational Studies in Mathematics* (Netherlands) 20 (4, November): 347–65.

Borasi, Raffaella, John R. Sheedy, and Marjorie Siegel. 1990. The power of stories in learning mathematics. *Language Arts* 67 (4, February): 174–89.

Borasi, Raffaella, and Marjorie Siegel. 1989a. Reading to learn mathematics: A new synthesis of the traditional basics. Paper presented at the annual meeting of the American Educational Research Association, San Francisco, March 27–31.

————. 1989b. Reading to learn mathematics for critical thinking. Preliminary report to the National Science Foundation (Grant #MDR-8850548).

————. (in press). Reading to learn mathematics: New connections, new questions, new challenges. *For the Learning of Mathematics.*

Borman, Kathryn M., and Jane Reisman, eds. 1986. *Becoming a Worker*. Norwood, N.J.: Ablex.

Brown, Stephen I. 1969. Signed numbers: A "product" of misconceptions. *The Mathematics Teacher* 62 (3, March):183–95.

———. 1982. On humanistic alternatives in the practice of teacher education. *Journal of Research and Development in Education* 15 (4, Summer): 1–12.

———. 1984. The logic of problem generation: From morality and solving to de-posing and rebellion. *For the Learning of Mathematics* 4 (1, February): 12–13.

———. 1986. Liberal education and problem solving: Some curriculum fallacies. In *Proceedings of the Philosophy of Education Society*, ed. David Nyberg, 299–311. Normal , Ill.: Philosophy of Education Society.

———. (in preparation). Towards a pedagogy of confusion. In *Humanistic Mathematics*, ed. Alvin White.

Brown, Stephen I., and Thomas J. Cooney. 1988. Stalking the dualism between theory and practice. In *Second conference on systematic cooperation between theory and practice in mathematics education, Part I: Report*, ed. P. F. L. Verstappen, 21–40. Lochem, The Netherlands: National Institute for Curriculum Development.

Brown, Stephen I., and Marion I. Walter. 1970. What-If-Not? An elaboration and second illustration. *Mathematics Teaching* 51:9–17.

———. 1990. *The Art of Problem Posing*. 2nd ed. Hillsdale, N.J.: Lawrence Erlbaum.

Buerk, Dorothy. 1981. Changing the conception of mathematical knowledge in intellectually able, math-avoidant women. Ph.D. diss., State University of New York at Buffalo.

———. 1985. The voices of women making meaning in mathematics. *Journal of Education*, 167 (3):59–70.

Campione, Joseph C., Ann L. Brown, and Michael L. Connell. 1988. Metacognition: The importance of understanding what you are doing. In *The teaching and assessing of mathematical problem solving*, ed. Randall I. Charles and Edward A. Silver, 93–114. Reston, Va.: National Council of Teachers of Mathematics.

Carey, Robert, and Jerome Harste. 1985. Comprehension as context: Towards reconsideration of a transactional theory of reading. In *Understanding readers' understanding*, ed. Robert Tierney. Hillsdale, N.J.: Lawrence Erlbaum.

Charles, Randall I., and Edward A. Silver, eds. 1988. *The teaching and assessing of mathematical problem solving*. Reston, Va.: National Council of Teachers of Mathematics.

Connell, James P., and James G. Wellborn. (in press). Competence, autonomy, and relatedness: A motivational analysis of self-esteem processes. In *Minnesota symposium on child development*, vol. 22, ed. M. Gunnar and L. A. Sroufe. Hillsdale, N.J.: Lawrence Erlbaum.

Connelly, F. Michael, and D. Jean Clandinin. 1990. Stories of experience and narrative inquiry. *Educational Researcher* 19 (5, June-July): 2–14.

Connolly, Paul, and Teresa Vilardi, eds. 1989. *Writing to learn mathematics and science*. New York: Teachers College Press.

Cooney, Thomas J. 1985. A beginning teacher's view of problem solving. *Journal for Research in Mathematics Education* 16 (November):324–36.

Cornbleth, Catherine. 1983. Critical thinking and cognitive processes. In *Review of Research in Social Studies Education*, ed. William B. Stanley et al., 11–64. Washington, D.C.: National Council for the Social Studies.

Damarin, Suzanne. 1990. Teaching mathematics: A feminist perspective. In *Teaching and learning mathematics in the 1990s*, ed. Thomas J. Cooney and Christian R. Hirsch, 144–51. 1990 Yearbook of the National Council of Teachers of Mathematics. Reston, Va.: National Council of Teachers of Mathematics.

Davis, Robert B., Carolyn A. Maher and Nel Noddings, eds. 1990. *Constructivist views on the teaching and learning of mathematics*. Monograph no. 4 of the *Journal for Research in Mathematics Education*. Reston, Va.: National Council of Teachers of Mathematics.

Deci, Edward L., and Richard M. Ryan. 1985. *Intrinsic motivation and self-determination in human behavior*. New York: Plenum Press.

Dewey, John. 1933. *How we think*. Boston: D. C. Heath.

Eco, Umberto. 1979. *The role of the reader*. Bloomington: Indiana University Press.

Eisenhart, Margaret A. 1988. The ethnographic research tradition and mathematics education research. *Journal for Research in Mathematics Education* 19 (2):99–114.

Ennis, Robert. 1962. A concept of critical thinking. *Harvard Educational Review* 32 (February): 81–111.

Ernest, Paul. 1989. Social and political values. In *Mathematics Teaching*, ed. Paul Ernest, 197–202. New York: Falmer Press.

Fawcett, Harold P. 1938. *The nature of proof*. 1938 Yearbook of the National Council of Teachers of Mathematics. New York: Columbia University Teachers College Bureau of Publications.

Feinman-Nemser, Sharon, and Robert E. Loden. 1986. The cultures of teaching. In *Handbook of Research on Teaching*, ed. M. C. Wittrock. New York: Macmillan.

Fennema, Elizabeth, and Thomas P. Carpenter. 1981. Sex-related differences in mathematics: Results from national assessment. *The Mathematics Teacher* 74 (October):554–59.

Fennema, Elizabeth, and Penelope L. Peterson. 1985. Autonomous learning behavior: A possible explanation of gender-related differences in mathematics. In *Gender influences in classroom interaction*, ed. L. C. Wilkinson and C. B. Marrett. Orlando, Fla.: Academic Press.

Freire, Paulo. 1986. *Pedagogy of the oppressed*. New York: Continuum.

Gilligan, Carol. 1982. *In a different voice*. Cambridge, Mass.: Harvard University Press.

Ginsberg, Herbert. 1977. *Children's arithmetic*. New York: Van Nostrand.

Greeno, James G. 1988. For the study of mathematical epistemology. In *The teaching and assessing of mathematical problem solving*, ed. Randall I. Charles and Edward A. Silver, 23–31. Reston, Va.: National Council of Teachers of Mathematics.

Halmos, Paul R. 1981. Applied mathematics is bad mathematics. In *Mathematics tomorrow*, ed. Lynn Steen, 9–20. New York: Springer-Verlag.

Hanna, Gila, Erika Kundiger, and Christine Larouche. 1988. Mathematical achievement of grade 12 girls in fifteen countries. Paper presented at the Sixth International Congress on Mathematics Education (ICME-6), Budapest, Hungary, July 27–August 3.

Hanna, Gila, and Ian Winchester, eds. 1990. *Creativity, Thought and Mathematical Proof*. Special Issue of *Interchange* 21 (1).

Hofstadter, Douglas R. 1980. *Godel, Escher, Bach: An Eternal Golden Braid*. New York: Vintage Books.

Isaacson,Zelda. 1989. Of course you *could* be an engineer, dear, but wouldn't you *rather* be a nurse or a teacher or secretary? In *Mathematics teaching: The state of the art*, ed. Paul Ernest. New York: Falmer Press.

Isaacson, Zelda, Pat Rogers, and T. Dekker. 1986. Report on IOWME discussion group at PME 10. *IOWME* (International Organization of Women in Mathematics Education) *Newsletter* 2 (2):3–6.

Janvier, Claude ed. 1987. *Problems of representation in the teaching and learning of mathematics*. Hillsdale, N.J.: Erlbaum.

Kilpatrick, Jeremy. 1987a. What constructivism might be in mathematics education. *Proceedings of the Eleventh International Conference - PME-XI.*, ed. Jacques C. Bergeron, Nicolas Herscovics, and Carolyn Kieran, vol. 1, 3–27. Montreal, Quebec: Psychology of Mathematics Education, July 19–25.

———. 1987b. Problem formulating: Where do good problems come from? In *Cognitive science and mathematics education*, ed. Alan H. Schoenfeld, 123–47. Hillsdale, N.J.: Erlbaum.

Kline, Morris. 1980. *Mathematics: The loss of certainty*. New York: Oxford University Press.

———. 1985. *Mathematics and the search for knowledge*. New York: Oxford University Press.

Krause, Eugene. 1986. *Taxicab-geometry*. New York: Dover.

Krulik, Stephen, and Robert E. Reys, eds. 1980. *Problem solving in school mathematics*. 1980 Yearbook of the National Council of Teachers of Mathematics. Reston, Va.: National Council of Teachers of Mathematics.

Kuhn, Thomas. 1970. *The structure of scientific revolutions*. Chicago: The University of Chicago Press.

Lakatos, Imre. 1976. *Proofs and refutations*. Cambridge: Cambridge University Press.

———. 1978. *Mathematics, science and epistemology*. Cambridge: Cambridge University Press.

Lampert, Magdalene. 1986. Knowing, doing and teaching multiplication. *Cognition and Instruction* 3 (4):305–42.

———. 1990. When the problem is not the question and the solution is not the answer: Mathematics knowing and teaching. *American Educational Research Journal* 27 (Spring):29–63.

Lave, Jean. 1988. *Cognition in practice*. Cambridge: Cambridge University Press.

Lave, Jean, Michael Murtaugh, and Olivia de la Roche. 1984. The dialectic of arithmetic in grocery shopping. In *Everyday cognition: Its development in social contexts,* ed. Barbara Rogoff and Jean Lave. Cambridge, Mass.: Harvard University Press.

Lave, Jean, Steve Smith, and Michael Butler. 1988. Problem solving as everyday practice. In *The teaching and assessing of mathematical problem solving,* ed. Randall I. Charles and Edward A. Silver, 61–81. Reston, Va.: National Council of Teachers of Mathematics.

Lave, Jean, and Etienne Wenger. 1989. *Situated learning: Legitimate peripheral participation.* IRL report 89-0013. Palo Alto, Calif.: Institute for Research on Learning.

Lerman, Stephen. 1989. Constructivism, mathematics and mathematics education. *Educational Studies in Mathematics* 20 (2, May):211–23.

———. 1990a. A social view of mathematics: Implications for mathematics education. *Humanistic Mathematics Network Newsletter* 5 (May):26–28.

———. 1990b. What has mathematics got to do with values? *Humanistic Mathematics Network Newsletter* 5 (May):29–31.

Lincoln, Yvonne, and Egan Guba. 1985. *Naturalistic Inquiry.* Beverly Hills, Calif.: Sage Publications.

Maurer, Stephen B. 1987. New knowledge about errors and new views about learners: What they mean to educators and more educators would like to know. In *Cognitive science and mathematics education,* ed. Alan H. Schoenfeld, 165–87. Hillsdale, N.J.: Erlbaum.

McPeck, John. 1981. *Critical thinking and education.* New York: St. Martin's Press.

National Council of Teachers of Mathematics (NCTM). 1989a. *Curriculum and evaluation standards for school mathematics.* Reston, Va.: National Council of Teachers of Mathematics.

———. 1989b. *Professional standards for teaching mathematics (draft).* Reston, Va.: National Council of Teachers of Mathematics.

———. 1991. *Professional standards for teaching mathematics.* Reston, Va.: National Council of Teachers of Mathematics.

National Research Council (NRC). 1989. *Everybody counts: A report to the nation on the future of mathematics education.* Washington, D.C.: National Academic Press.

Neilsen, Allan R. 1989. *Critical thinking and reading.* Bloomington, Ind.: ERIC Clearinghouse on Reading and Communications Skills.

Oaks, Ann. 1987. The effect of the interaction of mathematical and affective constructs on college students in remedial mathematics. Ph.D. diss., University of Rochester, Rochester, N.Y.

Papy, Frederique. 1970–72. *Les Enfants et la Mathematique.* 5 vols. Brussels: Hachette.

Papy, Georges, and Frederique Papy. 1973. *Taximetrix.* Brussels: Hachette.

Pollak, Henry O. 1970. Applications of mathematics. In *Mathematics education,* ed. E. B. Begle, 311–34. Chicago: National Society for the Study of Education.

Polya, George. 1957. *How to solve it.* Princeton: Princeton University Press.

Poston, Tim. 1981. Purity in applications. In *Mathematics tomorrow,* ed. Lynn Steen, 9–20. New York: Springer-Verlag.

Resnick, Lauren B. 1988. Treating mathematics as an ill-structured discipline. In *The teaching and assessing of mathematical problem solving*, ed. Randall I. Charles and Edward A. Silver, 32–60. Reston, Va.: National Council of Teachers of Mathematics.

Rogoff, Barbara, and Jean Lave, eds. 1984. *Everyday cognition: Its development in social contexts*. Cambridge, Mass.: Harvard University Press.

Rose, Barbara J. 1988. Using expressive writing to support the learning of mathematics. Ph.D. diss., University of Rochester, Rochester, N.Y.

Rosen, Harold. 1984. *Stories and Meaning*. London: National Association for the Teaching of English.

Rosenblatt, Louise. 1979. *The reader, the text, the poem*. Carbondale, Ill.: Southern Illinois University Press.

Rowe, Deborah W., and Jerome Harste. 1986. Reading and writing in a system of knowing. In *The pursuit of literacy*, ed. M. Sampson, 126–44. Dubuque: Kendall Hunt.

Schoenfeld, Alan H. 1983. Beyond the purely cognitive: Beliefs systems, social cognitions and metacognitions as driving forces in intellectual performance. *Cognitive Science* 7: 329–63.

———. 1985. *Mathematical problem solving*. New York: Academic Press.

———, ed. 1987. *Cognitive science and mathematics education*. Hillsdale, N.J.: Erlbaum.

———. 1988. Problem solving in context(s). In *The teaching and assessing of mathematical problem solving*, ed. Randall I. Charles and Edward A. Silver, 82–92. Reston, Va.: National Council of Teachers of Mathematics.

———. 1989. Exploration of students' mathematical beliefs and behavior. *Journal for Research in Mathematics Education* 20 (4, July):338–55.

———. (in press). Reflections on doing and teaching mathematics. In *Mathematical thinking and problem solving*, ed. Alan H. Schoenfeld.

Siegel, Marjorie, Raffaella Borasi, and Constance Smith. 1989. A critical review of reading in mathematics instruction: The need for a new synthesis. In *Cognitive and social perspectives for literacy research and instruction*, ed. S. McCormick and J. Zutell, 269–77. Thirty-eighth Yearbook of the National Reading Conference. Chicago: National Reading Conference.

Siegel, Marjorie, and Robert F. Carey. 1989. *Critical thinking: A semiotic perspective*. Bloomington, Ind.: ERIC Clearinghouse on Reading and Communication Skills.

Silver, Edward A. 1985. Research on teaching mathematical problem solving: Some underrepresented themes and needed directions. In *Teaching and learning mathematical problem solving: Multiple research perspectives*, ed. E. A. Silver, 247–66. Hillsdale, N.J.: Erlbaum.

———. 1987. Foundations of cognitive theory and research for mathematics problem-solving. In *Cognitive science and mathematics education*, ed. Alan H. Schoenfeld, 33–60. Hillsdale, N.J.: Erlbaum.

Silver, Edward A., Jeremy Kilpatrick, and Beth Schlesinger. 1990. *Thinking through mathematics*. New York: College Entrance Examination Board.

Skinner, Ellen. (in press). Development and perceived control: A dynamic model of action in context. In: *Minnesota symposium on child development*, vol. 22, ed. M. Gunnar and L. A. Sroufe. Hillsdale, N.J.: Erlbaum.

Thompson, Alba. 1988. Learning to teach mathematical problem solving: Changes in teachers' conceptions and beliefs. In *The teaching and assessing of mathematical problem solving*, ed. Randall I. Charles and Edward A. Silver, 232–43. Reston, Va.: National Council of Teachers of Mathematics.

Van Maanen, John. 1988. *Tales of the field*. Chicago: University of Chicago Press.

Vygotsky, Lev S. 1962. *Thought and language*. Cambridge, Mass.: MIT Press.

Vygotsky, Lev S. 1978. *Mind in society*. Cambridge, Mass.: Harvard University Press.

Walter, Marion I., and Stephen I. Brown. 1969. "What-If-Not." *Mathematics Teaching* 46:38–45.

Wertsch, James V. *Vygotsky and the social formation of mind*. Cambridge, Mass.: Harvard University Press.

Wittgenstein, Ludwig. 1968. *Philosophical investigations*. Oxford: Blackwell.

Wood, David, Jerome S. Bruner, and Gail Ross. 1976. The role of tutoring in problem solving. *Journal of Child Psychology and Psychiatry* 17:89–100.